STRATEGIC
LEARNING
AND
KNOWLEDGE
MANAGEMENT

THE STRATEGIC MANAGEMENT SERIES

THE STRATEGIC MANAGEMENT SERIES

STRATEGIC LEARNING AND KNOWLEDGE MANAGEMENT

Edited by

RON SANCHEZ AND AIMÉ HEENE

JOHN WILEY & SONS

Chichester · New York · Brisbane · Toronto · Singapore

658.4
S8982

Other Wiley Editorial Offices

John Wiley & Sons, Inc., 605 Third Avenue,
New York, NY 10158-0012, USA

Jacaranda Wiley Ltd, 33 Park Road, Milton,
Queensland 4064, Australia

John Wiley & Sons (Canada) Ltd, 22 Worcester Road,
Rexdale, Ontario M9W 1L1, Canada

John Wiley & Sons (Asia) Pte Ltd, 2 Clementi Loop #02-01,
Jin Xing Distripark, Singapore 129809

Library of Congress Cataloging-in-Publication Data

Strategic learning and knowledge management / edited by Ron Sanchez
and Aimé Heene.
    p.   cm. — (The strategic management series)
    Includes bibliographical references and index.
    ISBN 0-471-96881-1 (cloth)
    1. Organizational change—Management.   2. Organizational learning—
Management.   3. Information resources management.   4. Strategic
alliances (Business)   I. Sanchez, Ron.   II. Heene, Aimé.
III. Series.
    HD58.8.S759   1997
658.4—dc20   96–27866
                                                           CIP

British Library Cataloguing in Publication Data

A catalogue record for this book is available from the British Library

ISBN 0-471-96881-1

Typeset in 10½/12pt Palatino by Dorwyn Ltd, Rowlands Castle, Hants
Printed and bound in Great Britain by Biddles Ltd, Guildford and King's Lynn
This book is printed on acid-free paper responsibly manufactured from sustainable
forestation, for which at least two trees are planted for each one used for paper production.

Contents

SECTION III:
STRATEGIC LEARNING BETWEEN ORGANIZATIONS

SECTION IV:
STRATEGIC KNOWLEDGE MANAGEMENT

Contributors

MAX BOISOT
Imperial College, The Management School, 53 Prince's Gate, Exhibition Road, London SW7 2PG.
Max Boisot is Professor of Strategic Management at ESADE in Barcelona and Senior Associate at the Judge Institute of Management Studies at the University of Cambridge. He holds an MSc in Management from MIT as well as a doctorate in technology transfer from the Imperial College of Science, Technology and Medicine, London University. From 1984 to 1989 he was dean and director of the first MBA program to be run in the People's Republic of China in Beijing. He is the author of *Information and Organizations* (1987, Harper Collins) and has recently published *Information Space: A Framework for Analyzing Learning in Organizations, Institutions, and Cultures* (1995, Routledge).

DAVID L. DEEDS
Department of General and Strategic Management, School of Business and Management, Temple University, Philadelphia PA 19122, USA.
David L. Deeds is Assistant Professor of Entrepreneurship and Strategy at Temple University. He received his PhD from the University of Washington in 1994. His current research interests include the development of high technology industries, strategic alliances, the interface between academic research and corporate research, and the process of making an initial public offering.

TOM ELFRING
Department of Strategic Management and Business, Rotterdam School of Management, Erasmus University Rotterdam, PO Box 1738, 3000 DR Rotterdam, The Netherlands.
Tom Elfring is Associate Professor of Strategy and Director of the PhD Program, Department of Strategy and Business Environment of the Rotterdam School of Management of the Erasmus University Rotterdam.

DOROTHY GRIFFITHS
Imperial College, The Management School, 53 Prince's Gate, Exhibition Road, London SW7 2PG.
Dorothy Griffiths is Senior Lecturer and Head of the Organizational Behaviour and Human Resource Management Section at The Management School, Imperial College, University of London. Within the Management School she teaches courses on National Innovation Policy and Technology Strategy and on Human Resource Management. Her research is focused on issues of corporate technology strategy. She has acted as a consultant to a number of large and small organizations.

KNUT HAANES
Norwegian School of Management, PO Box 580, 1301 Sandvika, Norway.
Knut Haanes is a doctoral fellow at the Norwegian School of Management. He has economics degrees from the Norwegian School of Economics and Business Administration and the Stockholm School of Economics, and has previously worked for the Norwegian Trade Council in Paris, Stockholm and Oslo. He has also headed a company, NorMan SA, in Fribourg, Switzerland, and been a research associate at IMD in Lausanne. His research topic is related to the mobilization of resources in firms and more generally on inter-firm collaboration.

RICHARD HALL
Durham University Business School, Mill Hill Lane, Durham DH1 3LB.
Richard Hall has an MA (Cantab.) in physics, and a PhD in business policy. His early industrial career was in operations management, both as a line manager and as a consultant. Thereafter he was, for 14 years, the chief executive of a company manufacturing consumer products. He is currently Professor of Operations and Procurement Strategy at Durham University Business School. His research interests are: the role of intangible resources in business success, the nature and characteristics of long-term surviving companies, and supply chain management.

AIMÉ HEENE
De Vlerick School voor Management, Bellevue 6, B 9050 Ledeberg, KB 448-0032521-27, Belgium.
Professor Doctor Aimé Heene holds a PhD in educational sciences and an MBA from De Vlerick School voor Management. He is an associate professor at the University of Gent, the vice-president of the Dutch–Flemish Academy for Management, a founding member and secretary of the Flemish Strategy Society, and a member of the advisory board of the European Foundation for Business Qualification. He is an Associate Director of Coopers & Lybrand Management Consulting and is a fellow of

the China–Europe Management Center at Fudan University (Shanghai) during the summer of 1996. Professor Heene served as a co-editor of several volumes on competence-based strategy theory: *Competence-Based Competition* (1995, Wiley; with Gary Hamel), *Dynamics of Competence-Based Competition* (1996, Elsevier; with Ron Sanchez and Howard Thomas).

RICHARD KLAVANS
Center for Research Planning, 2405 White Horse Road, Berwyn, PA 19312, USA.
Dick Klavans is President of the Center for Research Planning, a firm specializing in scientific and technical intelligence. He was also elected President of the Society of Competitive Intelligence Professionals in 1994. Dick received his PhD from the University of Pennsylvania in 1991. His publications are primarily in the field of science strategy.

JOHN W. LANG
The Judge Institute of Management Studies, University of Cambridge, Trumpington Street, Cambridge CB2 1AG.
John W. Lang is a researcher at the Judge Institute of Management Studies, and a member of Emmanuel College, University of Cambridge. He has studied and worked in the UK, USA, Germany and France, in staff and consultancy positions on behalf of multinational corporations. His current research interests are in the area of strategic alliances, innovation, and technology transfer, with particular reference to those alliances formed by small firms in high-tech environments such as telecommunications and semiconductor technologies.

BENTE R. LØWENDAHL
Norwegian School of Management, PO Box 580, 1301 Sandvika, Norway.
Bente R. Løwendahl is Associate Professor of Strategic Management at the Norwegian School of Management and has a PhD in Strategy from The Wharton School of the University of Pennsylvania, as well as a Siviløkonom-degree from The Norwegian School of Economics and Business Administration. She has published articles nationally and internationally on topics such as the strategic management of knowledge-intensive service firms, globalization of professional services, strategic management of competence and competent people, competitive advantage and core competence, strategic management in a post-modern economy, international project management, competence management in the Lillehammer Olympic Organizing Committee, and strategies for Norwegian defense industry companies. Her book *Strategic Management of Professional Service Firms* will be published later this year by Copenhagen Business School Press in cooperation with Blackwell.

VERONICA MOLES
Imperial College, The Management School, 53 Prince's Gate, Exhibition Road, London SW7 2PG.
Veronica Moles is a research associate at The Management School, Imperial College, University of London. Her current research focuses on the management of technology and builds on a background of research in the area of technological and organizational change.

HENK POST
Baan Business IT School, Baan Company NV, PO Box 250, 6710 BG Ede, The Netherlands.
Henk A. Post studied business administration at Erasmus University in Rotterdam. After his graduation in 1976, he was working in the fields of management journalism, management consultancy, and public relations. In 1991, he started his PhD study at Tilburg University, and at the same time became an assistant professor in international management. After finishing this study, he joined Baan Company in 1994. He is especially involved in strategic management, and business and IT research for this firm.

BERTRAND QUÉLIN
HEC School of Management, Strategic Management Department, F-78 351, Jouy-en-Josas, France.
Bertrand Quélin is Associate Professor of Strategic Management and Industrial Organization at HEC School of Management, Jouy-en-Josas, France. He has published a number of papers on transactions cost economics, competence-based competition, and economics of technological change. He has served as a consultant to several corporations and the European Commission at Brussels. Dr Quélin received his doctorate in economics from the University of Paris.

RON SANCHEZ
The Graduate School of Management, University of Western Australia, Medlands, WA 6907, Australia.
Ron Sanchez has degrees in psychology, comparative literature, architecture, engineering, and business administration. He received his PhD in technology strategy from MIT. He has taught strategic management and technology management, strategy, and policy courses at MIT, University of Illinois, Warwick Business School, and ESSEC. Prior to becoming a management researcher, he was a consultant in establishing international joint ventures for product and market development. He is now Associate Professor of Management in the Graduate School of Management at the University of Western Australia.

PETTERI SIVULA
Department of Strategic Management and Business Environment, Rotterdam School of Management, Erasmus University Rotterdam, PO Box 1738, 3000 DR Rotterdam, The Netherlands.
Petteri Sivula is Research Associate at Rotterdam School of Management, Erasmus University Rotterdam. His research and teaching centers on the strategic aspects of managing service firms. He is currently doing research for his PhD on the implications of client relationships for knowledge transfer and learning in a business service context. His research uses the resource-based theory of the firm and relationship marketing to study knowledge processes in client relationships. Petteri Sivula holds a MSocSc in economics from the University of Helsinki and a MSc in innovation and technology management from the University of Sussex (SPRU). The Academy of Finland and the Finnish Cultural Foundation have granted him scholarships for his PhD research.

FRANS A. J. VAN DEN BOSCH
Department of Strategic Management and Business Environment, Rotterdam School of Management, Erasmus University Rotterdam, PO Box 1738, 3000 DR Rotterdam, The Netherlands.
Frans A. J. van den Bosch is Professor of Management and Chairman of the Department of Strategy and Business Environment of the Rotterdam School of Management of the Erasmus University Rotterdam.

RUSSELL W. WRIGHT
University of Illinois, 165 Commerce West, 1206 South Sixth Street, Champaign, Illinois 61820, USA.
Russell W. Wright is Assistant Professor of Business Administration at the University of Illinois at Urbana-Champaign. He has taught courses in strategy, entrepreneurship, and technology innovation management. His research examines issues related to knowledge management in high technology organizations. He has conducted field research in the semiconductor, personal computer, and telecommunications industries across Japan, Taiwan, the US, and Europe. Prior to joining the University of Illinois, he was *professeur adjoint* at Groupe Essec in France. Before his academic career, he was an internal consultant at Shell Oil Company. He obtained his PhD in business administration from the University of Southern California and holds a Master of Organization Behavior and a BA in Economics from Brigham Young University.

Series Preface

The increasingly dynamic nature of competition has made the improvement of organizational learning and the development of more effective methods for managing knowledge central concerns of contemporary strategic management.

Strategic Learning and Knowledge Management draws on ongoing research into organizational competence to introduce several new approaches to the strategic management of learning and knowledge. Concepts from emerging theory in competence-based competition are used to investigate processes of strategic learning, examining both organizational contexts in which learning takes place and organizational dynamics for creating new knowledge. The search for competitive advantage, however, also challenges organizations to become more effective in using their existing knowledge to greatest strategic benefit. Accordingly, this volume also examines processes within firms that improve both the creation and application of new knowledge in competitive and cooperative interactions between organizations.

The volume is divided into four sections: section I provides an overview of the current competence perspective on strategic learning and knowledge management; section II explores strategic learning processes within organizations; section III examines strategic learning between organizations; and section IV investigates the strategic management of knowledge in competence-based competition.

Strategic Learning and Knowledge Management challenges many notions prevalent in current discussions of knowledge and learning, such as the strategic value of 'tacit knowledge' and the need to rely primarily on internal learning processes. Using case studies from American and European companies, the contributors introduce new approaches to managing strategically important knowledge in organizations.

Strategic Learning and Knowledge Management develops new theory and applications for the strategic management of 'learning organizations' and their knowledge assets. Extending the theoretical framework of competence-based strategic management to the analysis of learning and knowledge, the contributors explore strategically important learning processes within and between organizations. New concepts for categorizing strategically important knowledge are also introduced, as are new methods for effectively managing a firm's knowledge assets. The book investigates organizational learning and knowledge management in leading companies, examines learning and knowledge management in several industry contexts, including high-tech and more traditional industries, and explores the role of learning and knowledge management in strategic management.

Published in association with the Strategic Management Society, this volume provides a key resource of new ideas and issues being discussed by the Society, and aims to make them accessible to interested academics, consultants and practising managers.

Concepts of organizational learning and knowledge management addressed in this volume are of central importance in developing theory and practice for competence-based strategic management. Not surprisingly, the approach to understanding knowledge and learning presented in the volume both draws on and contributes to competence concepts developed in several recent edited volumes, beginning with *Competence-Based Competition* by Gary Hamel and Aimé Heene (Wiley 1994), *Dynamics of Competence-Based Competition* by Ron Sanchez, Aimé Heene, and Howard Thomas (Elsevier Pergamon 1996), and most recently *Competence-Based Strategic Management* by Aimé Heene and Ron Sanchez (Wiley 1996). Readers interested in understanding current thinking about the role of learning and knowledge in competence theory and practice development would no doubt find the Heene and Sanchez (1996) volume a useful companion to this book.

Editors' Preface

The increasingly dynamic nature of competition has made the improvement of organizational learning and the development of more effective methods for managing knowledge a central concern of contemporary strategic management. This volume draws on ongoing research into organizational competence to introduce several new approaches to the strategic management of learning and knowledge. Concepts from emerging theory in competence-based competition are used to investigate processes of strategic learning, examining both organizational contexts in which learning takes place and organizational dynamics for creating new knowledge. The search for competitive advantage, however, also challenges organizations to become more effective in leveraging their existing knowledge to greatest strategic benefit. Accordingly, this volume also examines processes within firms which enable more effective application of new knowledge, and it suggests new approaches to identifying and managing strategically important knowledge in competitive and cooperative interactions between organizations.

In Section 1, our introductory chapter to the volume gives an overview of the current competence perspective on learning and knowledge management.

Section 2 explores strategic learning processes within organizations. Bente Løwendahl and Knut Haanes use a competence framework to investigate firms as *activity systems* in which some measure of "incoherence, dilemma, and conflict" is important in maintaining learning processes. Richard Hall describes his studies of managers' decision making about intangible assets. Using concepts from complexity theory, he suggests that an organization's learning dynamics are limited by negative feedback "command-and-control" systems and require positive feedback to identify opportunities to create new intangible assets. Max Boisot, Dorothy Griffiths, and Veronica Moles study the way in which firms develop structures for their knowledge. They also suggest that firms face a *paradox of value* when using information efficiently and require actions that may also lead to loss of control of knowledge. Russell Wright discusses biases firms may develop in their learning processes. He suggests that some firms develop a "theorizing and codifying" bias in learning, while others develop a learning-by-doing bias that leads to "tangible knowledge integration".

Strategic learning between organizations is examined in Section 3. Dick Klavans and David Deeds study the biotechnology industry to identify different ways firms can go about learning in a knowledge-intensive competitive environment. Petteri Sivula, Frans van den Bosch, and Tom Elfring study knowledge transfer processes in the business service industry (e.g. consulting engineering services) to develop a model for better knowledge management through alliances within an industry. Bertrand Quélin discusses mechanisms which can improve the acquisition and integration of external knowledge and thereby improve a firm's ability to overcome path–dependency effects in learning.

The strategic management of a firm's knowledge is investigated in Section 4. Effective strategic management of a firm's knowledge assets requires recognition of the potential strategic value of each of the firm's different stocks of knowledge. Ron Sanchez proposes a classification of a firm's knowledge assets as *know-how, know-why*, and *know-what* and suggests strategies for managing each kind of knowledge asset in different competitive contexts. Henk Post explains the use of modularity by Baan Company, a rapidly growing Dutch software firm, and shows how modular product architectures can create knowledge structures that enable flexible reconfigurations of the firm's knowledge-intensive products. John Lang investigates the use of modular product architectures by ARM Ltd to structure its network of licensing relationships for the application of its knowledge-intensive RISC chip designs by global electronics firms.

Putting together this volume has been made a very pleasurable experience by the evident enthusiasm of the contributors for their research into organizational learning and knowledge. We have also appreciated the support of the Strategic Management Society and the encouragement from series editor Howard Thomas. The European Institute for Advanced Studies in Management also helped in organizing conferences on competence-based competition which encouraged the writing of the chapters.

Ron Sanchez would like to thank the University of Illinois at Urbana-Champaign and Ecole Supérieure des Sciences Economiques et Commerciales (ESSEC) for their institutional support. Aimé Heene expresses his appreciation to De Vlerick School voor Management for support of his work on organizational learning and knowledge.

RON SANCHEZ
Urbana, Illinois, and Cergy-Pontoise, France
and
AIMÉ HEENE
Gent, Belgium

Section I
Introduction

1

A Competence Perspective on Strategic Learning and Knowledge Management

RON SANCHEZ, AIMÉ HEENE

The growing prominence of accelerating change in the environments of organizations has brought processes for managing change within firms into the forefront of concerns in strategic management. As competition between firms increasingly takes on the character of a contest to identify, create, and leverage new competences (Hamel and Heene, 1994; Heene and Sanchez, 1996; Sanchez, Heene and Thomas, 1996a), effecting significant organizational change increasingly requires changing both the knowledge base within a firm and the way the firm uses its existing knowledge to compete more effectively. Consequently, improving a firm's strategic flexibility (Sanchez, 1993, 1995; Sanchez and Heene, 1996) to create new competences in response to environmental change is likely to require rethinking the ways a firm can create and acquire new knowledge and may require entirely new concepts for applying new knowledge to greatest strategic effect.

The topic of organizational learning and knowledge has received much recent attention from a number of perspectives, including economic and organization theory (Boisot, 1995), organization studies (Nonaka and Takeuchi, 1995), technological change (Durand, 1993), social

Strategic Learning and Knowledge Management.
Edited by Ron Sanchez and Aimé Heene.
Copyright © 1997 John Wiley & Sons Ltd.

systems (von Krogh and Vicari, 1993), cognition (Walsh, 1995), and international comparative studies (Hedlund and Nonaka, 1993), among others. In this discussion, we introduce a perspective on organizational learning and knowledge that is now being developed within the movement to build a theory of organizational competence and competence-based competition. A key interest of this perspective is understanding how better approaches to learning and knowledge utilization within organizations can improve the competence building and leveraging processes of firms. Thus, the emphasis in the competence perspective is on *strategic* forms of learning and knowledge management which can improve the performance of firms in competence-based competition.

We begin by proposing concepts of *strategic learning* and *strategic knowledge* based on ideas now being developed within the competence perspective. We suggest related definitions for strategic learning and strategically relevant knowledge. In so doing, we also suggest some important distinctions between forms of knowledge and processes of learning that occur in individuals and those that occur in organizations. We also discuss some fundamental ways in which knowledge assets differ from other kinds of strategic assets, and drawing on Boisot (1995) and Sanchez (1996a, in this volume), we suggest some implications of this conceptualization of strategic knowledge assets for strategy theory, research, and practice. Important aspects of the topics we discuss are developed more fully in the chapters in this volume, and we briefly review their contributions. We conclude by proposing an agenda for further research to improve our understanding of strategically significant learning and knowledge management processes.

STRATEGICALLY RELEVANT KNOWLEDGE AND LEARNING

What is meant by *knowledge*? What is *learning*? How are knowledge and learning interrelated conceptually and organizationally?

These fundamental questions have occupied researchers in cognitive studies for many years, but today are being approached from a variety of new perspectives. Our objective in this discussion is not to review these multiple initiatives to understand knowledge and learning, but rather to introduce a competence perspective on knowledge and learning to facilitate connecting the ongoing work in competence with work in other perspectives.

Knowledge is defined by Sanchez, Heene and Thomas (1996b: 9) as "the set of beliefs held by an *individual* about causal relationships among phenomena" (emphasis added). Causal relationships in this definition are cause-and-effect relationships between imaginable events or actions and likely consequences of those events or actions.[1] *Organizational knowledge* is then defined as the shared set of beliefs about causal relationships held by individuals within a group (Sanchez *et al.*, 1996b: 9). The intent of these definitions is threefold: First, to stipulate that strategically relevant knowledge is never certain, but rather only exists in the form of *beliefs*.[2] In other words, knowledge is not absolute or deterministic, but consists of more or less firmly held beliefs based on probabilistic assessments of possible causal relationships between phenomena. Second, to recognize that knowledge originates with and exists within individual humans, but that organizations may also have knowledge that may exist in various forms understood by more than one individual within an organization. We shall address below the potential strategic importance of individual and organizational forms of knowledge. Third, to refocus the concept of knowledge on conscious mental processes (beliefs) rather than lower-level neural processes at the level of sensory-motor coordination.[3]

Knowledge is fundamental to organizational *competence*, which Sanchez, Heene and Thomas define as an ability to sustain the coordinated deployment of assets and capabilities in a way that promises to help a firm to achieve its goals (1996b: 8). Having competence implies an organizational intention to achieve some desired result (goal) through specific actions. Since an intention to accomplish some goal through taking action(s) requires that individuals and groups within a firm have

---

[1] Knowledge therefore includes beliefs that some events or actions will have no significant consequences in a context of current interest. Human minds, like organizations, tend to merge beliefs about non-consequential events or actions into the background of consciousness and to focus limited cognitive processing capacities (Simon, 1957) on understanding and managing events and actions believed to be consequential in a context of current interest. Thus, the development of "cognitive blind spots" (van der Vorst, 1996) is inherent in creating and using knowledge in competitive environments, and managing the blind spots in firms therefore becomes an important aspect of managing strategic learning.

[2] We recognize that by defining knowledge as *beliefs* held by individuals or organizations rather than by some absolute standard of "certain knowledge", we are implying that different individuals or organizations might have specific instances of "knowledge" that are inconsistent or even contradictory. However, our interest is in understanding how knowledge and learning can improve the strategic management of organizations in a dynamically uncertain world. In this context, the important perspective is the *ex ante* perspective of managers in organizations who must make decisions under conditions of significant causal ambiguity. Thus, invoking a concept of certain knowledge would be inappropriate to this context. Indeed, the concept of causal ambiguity presumes that nothing can be "known" in a form other than belief based on assessments of probabilities (Lippman and Rumelt, 1982; Sanchez and Heene, 1996a).

[3] Here we allude to Polyani's (1962) famous skater who "knows" more than she can tell about how she skates. We suggest that whatever the skater cannot tell (albeit with some mental effort), she really does *not* "know", at least not within the concept of knowledge proposed by Sanchez, Heene and Thomas (1996b) and adopted by us here. We revisit Polyani's skater when we discuss the hazards of mapping knowledge concepts from one context of analysis directly onto another context.

some beliefs as to how a firm's capabilities and skills can be used to "cause" certain desired effects, knowledge and the application of knowledge through action are at the foundation of the concepts of skills, capabilities, and (ultimately) organizational competence. Sanchez, Heene and Thomas (1996b) make a further distinction between *skills*, which are defined as the "micro-level" knowledge-in-action of one or a few individuals, and *capabilities* of firms, which are defined as "macro-level" organizational knowledge-in-action expressed through "repeatable patterns of action in the use of assets" (1996b: 7). In this framework, *skill* may be seen as "a special form of *capability*, with the connotation of a rather specific capability useful in a specialized situation or related to the use of a specialized asset" (1996b: 7). For example, a firm may have a capability in efficient manufacturing that consists of a number of interrelated skills in routing flows of work-in-progress, maintaining machine settings, monitoring conformance to specifications, and other specific tasks involved in manufacturing.

Learning is a process which changes the state of knowledge of an individual or organization. A change in state of knowledge may take the form of the adoption of a new belief about new causal relationships, the modification of an existing belief, the abandonment of a previously held belief, or a change in the degree of confidence with which an individual or individuals within an organization hold a belief or set of beliefs.

Within the conception of the firm as an *open system* (Sanchez and Heene, 1996a) in which there are asset stocks and flows (Dierickx and Cool, 1989), knowledge is a stock of beliefs held by individuals or groups of individuals within an organization, and learning represents flows that lead to a change in the stocks of beliefs within the organization.

Knowledge stocks may vary not only by the "content" of knowledge an individual or organization has (i.e. by the causal relationship that is the object of belief), but also by the degree to which knowledge held by an individual or organization can be put to some use—*i.e.*, by the process capabilities of the organization in acting on its beliefs. Here we borrow the concept of *mastery* from education theory to suggest basic levels of action response which an acquired belief can facilitate. Education theory suggests that knowledge may be usefully characterized at four levels of "mastery": reproduction, explanation, application, and integration (Heene, 1993). As Sanchez (1996a, in this volume) notes,

> ... *reproduction* is like recall; an acquirer of articulated knowledge can only write it down, but is not able to impute a meaning to the articulated knowledge. *Explanation* indicates an understanding of the articulated knowledge in the sense that the acquirer can explain the knowledge in terms of some imputed meaning. *Application* implies an ability to apply some articulated knowledge correctly when asked to do so. *Integration* indicates attainment of mastery

of some knowledge in the sense that the acquirer understands the uses to which the knowledge can be applied and can selectively choose to apply that knowledge in situations where it is beneficial to do so.

These levels of knowledge mastery suggest that knowledge within an organization may exist at different levels of usefulness. In other words, an individual or organization may have varying abilities to apply different forms of knowledge to carry out actions that help a firm accomplish its goals. Thus, different levels of knowledge mastery within firms may lead to different competence levels across firms and subsequently to different competitive outcomes in competence-based competition.

Learning may therefore change not only what kind of knowledge a firm has, but also the level of mastery at which the firm knows and can act on what it knows. Increasing the level of mastery of individual and organizational knowledge-in-action both leads to and benefits from an increase in the degree of confidence with which an individual or individuals within an organization hold a belief or set of beliefs. As a firm develops different levels of mastery of organizational knowledge and different ways of using its organizational knowledge in different contexts, it will develop various artifacts and representations of its knowledge. At the most basic level, firms will develop or adopt language to express shared beliefs. Some language may be provided by established technical or professional vocabularies, but some words will be coined or used in idiosyncratic ways within firms as a languaging process (van Krogh, Roos and Slocum, 1994) begins to *articulate* and connect beliefs of individuals and create a framework for organizational knowledge. As knowledge is articulated by individuals and groups, the organization may try to codify this knowledge (Sanchez, 1996a, in this volume; Wright, 1996, in this volume). *Codification* employs various means in an attempt to provide a structure to knowledge—ranging from schema to make the subject of various knowledge recognizable within an organization, to various expressions (e.g. manuals, engineering drawings) of specific knowledge intended to make the substance of that knowledge comprehensible to various individuals in the organization. Codification schemes therefore become vital mechanisms for improving the *apprehensibility* of knowledge (Sanchez, 1996a, in this volume) and thus for transferring knowledge between groups within an organization and indeed between organizations.

A firm's processes for articulating, codifying, and transferring knowledge within the organization and to other organizations are important determinants of its ability to leverage its existing knowledge effectively—and thus of its ability to leverage its competences to greatest strategic effect. Similarly, a firm's processes for identifying, acquiring, codifying, and transferring new knowledge are central to its ability to build new organizational competences. Thus, strategically important organizational learning consists both of processes for creating new knowledge within individuals and groups within a firm (Nonaka and Takeuchi, 1995) and processes to leverage knowledge effectively within and across organizations (Sanchez, 1996a, 1996b; Sanchez and Mahoney, 1995).

INDIVIDUAL VERSUS ORGANIZATIONAL KNOWLEDGE AND LEARNING

Early work in cognition focused on studying knowledge and learning in individuals. With the increased recognition of the importance of organizational knowledge and learning to the effective performance of firms in dynamic environments, much attention is now being focused within the management literatures on the study of organizational forms of knowledge and learning. Not surprisingly, there has been a noticeable tendency in much of this research to use concepts of knowledge and learning developed in cognitive studies of individuals to represent knowledge and learning in organizations. We believe in many instances the simple mapping of knowledge and learning concepts from one context of analysis to another is theoretically unwarranted and has produced some misleading notions about organizational knowledge and learning processes.

We briefly revisit the example of Polyani's (1962) skater to make this point. Polyani uses the example of the skater (who can skate beautifully but who cannot explain how she manages to skate the way she does) to propose that "we know more than we can say" (1962). This example has been invoked by many writers to suggest that important knowledge within individuals and within organizations can be "tacit"—i.e. *incapable* of articulation. We believe that Polyani's use of the term "know" in his famous phrase is semantically unfortunate and, indeed, symptomatic of our need today for more carefully developed concepts and vocabulary for understanding knowledge. If our vocabulary is imprecise, the concepts we attempt to build with that vocabulary will be vague and of limited power to generate insights. We suggest that it is conceptually inadequate to use a single term like "knowing" to describe processes as different as what the skater does, what a manager or accountant does, and what a research and development organization does. We propose that there is no existent theoretical justification warranting extension of a concept of a skater's knowledge, that exists but cannot be articulated, to a manager engaged in work of a higher mental order or to the work of an organization. Similar problems of theoretical warrant exist for other concepts borrowed from studies of individual cognition and applied without adequate consideration to organizational knowledge and learning— or indeed to more complex contexts of individual knowledge and learning.

HOW KNOWLEDGE ASSETS DIFFER FROM OTHER KINDS OF ASSETS

Knowledge assets differ fundamentally from other kinds of economic assets. Boisot (1995: 11) identifies two strategically important idiosyncratic properties of knowledge as an economic asset: the value of information (as an expression of knowledge) to one party in a potential exchange can only be ascertained if the information is disclosed by the party holding the information, but disclosure transfers the information to the other party and thereby diminishes its value to the original holder. Both properties contribute to market failures in information exchange, and "it is the failure of markets on information grounds that gives rise in the real world to alternative institutional arrangements such as firms for the governance of [such] economic transactions" (1995: 18). Difficulties in appraising the value of knowledge and difficulties in obtaining the full potential value of acquired knowledge are discussed by Sanchez (1996a, in this volume), and these may also contribute to market failures in the exchange and use of knowledge in various forms.

We suggest that these market-failure-inducing properties of knowledge assets have significant strategic implications beyond those commonly recognized in the strategy literature to date. Thus far, a common view within the strategy literature has been to regard individual and organizational knowledge as an asset to be zealously guarded within a firm, lest it be revealed to competitors and its strategic value lost thereby. Much emphasis, for example, has been placed on creating "tacit" individual and organizational knowledge as strategic assets, on the premise that tacit knowledge would be more difficult for competitors to discover than articulated forms of knowledge. We suggest that this strategy for creating and managing knowledge assets overlooks some key concerns: not only will it be difficult for competitors to acquire and use knowledge that is tacit, but it will be difficult for other individuals and groups within a firm to access and use tacit knowledge. Not articulating and codifying knowledge limits its transferability within an organization and thus limits the benefits a firm might obtain if it could leverage its knowledge quickly and widely. Keeping knowledge in tacit forms may therefore incur high opportunity costs which must be weighed against the risk of diminished strategic value if codified knowledge were to be discovered and used by competitors.

Sanchez (1996, in this volume) has suggested that at least three categories of knowledge may exist within firms: know-how (practical knowledge), know-why (theoretical knowledge), and know-what (strategic knowledge). Recognition of the different strategic value of these kinds of knowledge assets in different competitive contexts may enable managers to codify and share some kinds of knowledge with suppliers and other firms to improve a firm's ability to benefit from leveraging its knowledge widely and quickly. At the same time, the most strategically valuable or sensitive kinds of knowledge may be protected to prevent their leakage beyond the firm. Such theoretical development of new concepts of organizational knowledge may lead to better concepts for managing knowledge strategically. Thus, there appears to be an especially promising and direct link between the potential for theory building in organizational knowledge and improved understanding of how knowledge assets can be managed to obtain greatest strategic benefit.

CONTRIBUTIONS OF CURRENT RESEARCH

The chapters in this volume explore various aspects of learning processes within organizations (Løwendahl and Haanes, 1996; Hall, 1996; Boisot, Griffiths and Moles, 1996; and Wright, 1996), learning processes across organizational boundaries (Klavans and Deeds, 1996; Sivula, van den Bosch and Elfring, 1996; Quélin, 1996), and the strategic management of knowledge within and across firm boundaries (Sanchez, 1996b; Post, 1996; Lang, 1996). We briefly review the contribution of each of the chapters to better strategic learning and knowledge management.

STRATEGIC LEARNING WITHIN ORGANIZATIONS

Using the concept of competence as a framework for studying organizational learning, Løwendahl and Haanes (1996) propose that the most useful unit of analysis for learning processes may be the various value-creating *activities* within a firm. Drawing on action theory and theories of collective action, they suggest that firms be viewed as *activity systems* in which learning takes place through participation in activities and in which "incoherence, dilemma, and conflict are seen to offer important avenues for learning". Applying this framework to a case study of Alcatel Telecom Norway, they suggest several characteristics of activities as units of analysis that show the dynamic, interconnected, and permeable nature of competence building and leveraging (Sanchez and Heene, 1996b).

The decision-making process of managers that determines what intangible assets a firm should develop is studied by Hall (1996). He reports a technique that managers have used to identify both current portfolios of intangible assets within their firms and the composition of future portfolios which could improve the competitive advantages of a firm. Hall introduces concepts from complexity theory to suggest ways in which organizational dynamics of learning can be improved within a firm. Extending the discussion of control loops within firms as open systems (Sanchez and Heene, 1996a), he suggests that negative feedback "command-and-control" processes in firms limit the ability of managers to identify strategically valuable new intangible resources, and he discusses ways to assure positive feedback that can help managers to identify opportunities to create valuable new intangible assets.

The way in which relevant knowledge becomes structured within and between firms is studied by Boisot, Griffiths and Moles (1996). Introducing a "culture space" as a conceptual tool, they develop an information-based interpretation of competence which clarifies ways in which the processing of information within firms governs the development and use of new competences. They also suggest a *paradox of value* that arises when using information in ways that increase the efficiency of a firm's use of a competence may also lead to loss of control of the competence.

The way in which learning processes may take on specific kinds of characteristics or *biases* within firms is discussed by Wright (1996). He suggests that the nature of the work firms perform will lead to systemic biases in the kinds of knowledge development systems firms adopt. His studies of firms in the semiconductor industry suggest that in that industry, some firms develop a "theorizing and codifying" form of learning bias, while others develop learning-by-doing systems that lead to "tangible knowledge integration". Each of these knowledge development systems leads to the development of specific kinds of knowledge and thus the creation of specific kinds of competences within firms.

STRATEGIC LEARNING BETWEEN ORGANIZATIONS

The building of new competences in the biotechnology industry is studied by Klavans and Deeds (1996) to gain further insights into different ways that firms can go about acquiring new knowledge. Their study assesses the impact of different organizational approaches to learning on the ability of a firm to create value in a knowledge-intensive competitive environment, using the value of initial public offerings of shares in biotechnology firms to evaluate different kinds of learning that may be used in building new competences: basic scientific discovery, technology development (conversion of scientific knowledge into products and processes), and absorptive capacity (the ability to recognize valuable information outside the firm, obtain it, and redeploy existing resources to use it effectively). Their study suggests that in the context of the biotechnology industry in the United States, both technology development and absorptive capacity modes of knowledge creation can be effective in creating new competences of significant strategic value.

Close interactions between business service firms and clients in knowledge-intensive industries (e.g. in consulting engineering services) may create many opportunities for service-providing firms to expand their knowledge bases and improve their competences. Sivula, van den Bosch and Elfring (1996) analyze knowledge transfer processes in service provider–client relationships to develop a model for better knowledge management of vertical alliances within an industry.

A firm's current knowledge creating capabilities constrain its ability to build competences, and thus a firm's potential for building new competences is path dependent. Quélin (1996) suggests that developing means for integrating external knowledge into the firm may open important new avenues for overcoming path dependency and allow more rapid acquisition of new competences through strategic alliances. He discusses mechanisms which can improve the acquisition and integration of external knowledge in three types of strategic alliances: alliances to access existing competences, alliances to combine complementary assets, and alliances to create new capabilities.

STRATEGIC KNOWLEDGE MANAGEMENT

Effective strategic management of a firm's knowledge assets requires recognition of the potential strategic value of each of the firm's different stocks of knowledge. Sanchez (1996) proposes a framework for analyzing a firm's knowledge assets that suggests several approaches to leveraging and controlling a firm's strategic knowledge assets. After a critical appraisal of the strategic value of "tacit" knowledge within organizations, he suggests that knowledge within firms has different *contents*—which are characterized as *know-how, know-why*, and *know-what*—that are used in different strategic *contexts*. He proposes a framework for developing knowledge management strategies based on analysis of the contents of a firm's knowledge and the context in which it will be used.

Modular product architectures may create an important framework for managing knowledge within a firm and within networks of firms

(Sanchez, 1995, 1996b; Sanchez and Mahoney, 1995). Post (1996) explains the use of modularity by Baan Company, a rapidly growing Dutch software firm, as an architecture for creating software applications programs for business. Explaining how the concept of modularity was developed through the strategic logic and management processes of Baan Company, Post shows how modular product architectures create knowledge structures that enable flexible expansion, modification, and redeployment of the firm's software capabilities and products. The flexibility derived from its modular knowledge architecture has become a strategic means for improving the competence leveraging and building of Baan Company.

Sanchez and Mahoney (1995) have argued that adopting modularity in product design as a knowledge management strategy may also enable the adoption of modular organization designs. Lang (1996) investigates the relationship between modular product design and modular organization structures through a study of ARM Ltd, a developer of RISC-chip technology that has used modular product design to improve its flexibility and adaptability in a highly dynamic product market. Using a modular product architecture to structure a network of licensing relationships, ARM Ltd has developed complementary capabilities in alliance management and technology transfer that give it considerable ability to build and leverage new competences.

CONCLUSION

We conclude by reiterating that organizational knowledge and learning cannot be understood adequately from a strategic perspective simply by projecting onto organizations concepts borrowed from studies of individual knowledge and learning. As the chapters in this volume suggest, however, new and strategically useful insights into organizational knowledge and learning may be developed by studying real organizations from a variety of competence-based perspectives. As more firms in industries with rapidly changing knowledge bases become interested in developing new processes for creating and leveraging knowledge, we suggest that there is both unique need and opportunity for researchers to develop more grounded and interactive theory-building relationships with organizations (Mahoney and Sanchez, 1996). We suggest that the potential gains from developing a more involved and interactive mode of research into strategic learning and knowledge management are significant, but that realizing those gains will challenge both strategy researchers and strategic managers to pursue new modes of learning about learning.

REFERENCES

Boisot, Max H. (1995). *The Information Space*, London: Routledge.

Boisot, Max H., Dorothy Griffiths and Veronica Moles (1996). "The dilemma of competence: Differentiation versus integration in the pursuit of learning", in Ron Sanchez and Aimé Heene, editors, *Strategic Learning and Knowledge Management*, Chichester: John Wiley & Sons.

Dierickx, Ingmar and Karel Cool (1989). "Asset stock accumulation and sustainability of competitive advantage", *Management Science*, **35**, pp. 1504–1511.

Durand, Thomas (1993). "The dynamics of cognitive technological maps", pp. 165–189, in Peter Lorange *et al.*, editors, *Implementing Strategic Processes: Change, Learning, and Co-operation*, Oxford: Blackwell.

Hall, Richard (1996). "Complex systems, complex learning, and competence building", in Ron Sanchez and Aimé Heene, editors, *Strategic Learning and Knowledge Management*, Chichester: John Wiley & Sons.

Hamel, Gary and Aimé Heene (1994). "Conclusions: Which theory of strategic management do we need for tomorrow?", pp. 315–320, in *Competence-Based Competition*, Gary Hamel and Aimé Heene, editors, New York: John Wiley.

Hedlund, Gunnar and Ikujiro Nonaka (1993). "Models of knowledge management in the West and Japan", pp. 117–144, in Peter Lorange *et al.*, editors, *Implementing Strategic Processes: Change, Learning, and Co-operation*, Oxford: Blackwell.

Heene, Aimé (1993). "Classifications of competence and their impact on defining, measuring, and developing 'core competence' ", paper presented at Second International Workshop on Competence-Based Competition, EIASM, Brussels, Belgium, November 1993.

Heene, Aimé and Ron Sanchez (1996). *Competence-Based Strategic Management*, Chichester: John Wiley & Sons.

Klavans, Dick and David L. Deeds (1996). "Competence building in biotechnology start-ups: The role of scientific discovery, technical development, and absorptive capacity", in Ron Sanchez and Aimé Heene, editors, *Strategic Learning and Knowledge Management*, Chichester: John Wiley & Sons.

Lang, John W. (1996). "Leveraging knowledge across firm boundaries: Achieving strategic flexibility through modularization and alliances", in Ron Sanchez and Aimé Heene, editors, *Strategic Learning and Knowledge Management*, Chichester: John Wiley & Sons.

Løwendahl, Bente and Knut Haanes (1996). "The unit of activity: A new way to understand competence building and leveraging", in Ron Sanchez and Aimé Heene, editors, *Strategic Learning and Knowledge Management*, Chichester: John Wiley & Sons.

Mahoney, Joseph T. and Ron Sanchez (1996). "Competence theory building: Reconnecting management theory and management practice", in Aimé Heene and Ron Sanchez, editors, *Competence-Based Strategic Management*, Chichester: John Wiley & Sons.

Nonaka, Ikujiro and Hirotaka Takeuchi (1995). *The Knowledge-Creating Company*, Oxford: Oxford University Press.

Polyani, M. (1962). *Personal Knowledge*, Chicago: University of Chicago Press.

Post, Henk A. (1996). "Modularity in product design, development, and organization: A case study of the Baan Company", in Ron Sanchez and Aimé Heene, editors, *Strategic Learning and Knowledge Management*, Chichester: John Wiley & Sons.

Quélin, Bertrand (1996). "Appropriability and the creation of new capabilities through strategic alliances", in Ron Sanchez and Aimé Heene, editors, *Strategic Learning and Knowledge Management*, Chichester: John Wiley & Sons.

Sanchez, Ron (1993). "Strategic flexibility, firm organization, and managerial work in dynamic markets: A strategic options perspective", *Advances in Strategic Management*, **9**, pp. 251–291.

Sanchez, Ron (1995). "Strategic flexibility in product competition", *Strategic Management Journal*, **16** (summer), pp. 135–159.

Sanchez, Ron (1996a). "Managing articulated knowledge in competence-based competition", in Ron Sanchez and Aimé Heene, editors, *Strategic Learning and Knowledge Management*, Chichester: John Wiley & Sons.

Sanchez, Ron (1996b). "Strategic product creation: Managing new interactions of technology, markets, and organizations", *European Management Journal*, **14**(2).

Sanchez, Ron and Aimé Heene (1996a). "A systems view of the firm in competence-based competition", in *Dynamics of Competence-Based Competition: Theory and Practice in the New Strategic Management*, Ron Sanchez, Aimé Heene and Howard Thomas, editors, Oxford: Elsevier.

Sanchez, Ron and Aimé Heene (1996b). "Competence-based strategic management: Concepts and issues for theory, research, and practice", in Aimé Heene and Ron Sanchez, editors, *Competence-Based Strategic Management*, Chichester: John Wiley & Sons.

Sanchez, Ron, Aimé Heene and Howard Thomas (1996a). *Dynamics of Competence-Based Competition: Theory and Practice in the New Strategic Management*, Ron Sanchez, Aimé Heene and Howard Thomas, editors, Oxford: Elsevier.

Sanchez, Ron, Aimé Heene and Howard Thomas (1996b). "Towards the theory and practice of competence-based competition", in *Dynamics of Competence-Based Competition: Theory and Practice in the New Strategic Management*, Ron Sanchez, Aimé Heene and Howard Thomas, editors, Oxford: Elsevier.

Sanchez, Ron and Joseph T. Mahoney (1995). "Modularity, flexibility, and knowledge management in product and organization design", University of Illinois Working Paper #95–0121, Champaign IL 61820.

Simon, Herbert (1957). *Models of Man*, New York: John Wiley & Sons.

Sivula, Petteri, Frans A.J. van den Bosch and Tom Elfring (1996). "Competence building by incorporating clients into the development of a business service firm's knowledge base", in Ron Sanchez and Aimé Heene, editors, *Strategic Learning and Knowledge Management*, Chichester: John Wiley & Sons.

van der Vorst, Roland (1996). "The blind spots of competence identification: A systems theoretic perspective", in Aimé Heene and Ron Sanchez, editors, *Competence-Based Strategic Management*, Chichester: John Wiley & Sons.

von Krogh, Georg, Johan Roos and Ken Slocum (1994). "An essay on corporate epistemology", *Strategic Management Journal*, **15** (Special Issue), pp. 53–71.

von Krogh, Georg and Salvatore Vicari (1993). "An autopoesis approach to experimental strategic learning", pp. 394–410, in Peter Lorange *et al.*, editors, *Implementing Strategic Processes: Change, Learning, and Co-operation*, Oxford: Blackwell.

Walsh, James P. (1995). "Managerial and organizational cognition: Notes from a trip down memory lane", *Organization Science*, **6**(3), pp. 280–321.

Wright, Russell W. (1996). "Tangible integration versus intellectual codification skills: A comparison of learning processes in developing logic and memory semiconductors", in Ron Sanchez and Aimé Heene, editors, *Strategic Learning and Knowledge Management*, Chichester: John Wiley & Sons.

Section II

Strategic Learning Within Organizations

Using the concept of competence as a framework for studying organizational learning, Løwendahl and Haanes propose that the most useful unit of analysis for learning processes may be the various value-creating *activities* within a firm. Drawing on action theory and theories of collective action, they suggest that firms be viewed as *activity systems* in which learning takes place through participation in activities and in which "incoherence, dilemma, and conflict are seen to offer important avenues for learning". Applying this framework to a case study of Alcatel Telecom Norway, they suggest several characteristics of activities as units of analysis that show the dynamic, interconnected, and permeable nature of competence building and leveraging.

The decision-making process of managers that determines what intangible assets a firm should develop is studied by Hall. He reports a technique that managers have used to identify both current portfolios of intangible assets within their firms and the composition of future portfolios which could improve the competitive advantages of a firm. Hall introduces concepts from complexity theory to suggest ways in which organizational dynamics of learning can be improved within a firm. Extending the discussion of control loops within firms as open systems, he suggests that negative feedback "command-and-control" processes in firms limit the ability of managers to identify strategically valuable new intangible resources, and he discusses ways to assure positive feedback that can help managers to identify opportunities to create valuable new intangible assets.

The way in which relevant knowledge becomes structured within and between firms is studied by Boisot, Griffiths, and Moles. Introducing a "culture space" as a conceptual tool, they develop an information-based interpretation of competence which sheds new light on ways in which the processing of information within firms governs the development and use of new competences. They also suggest a *paradox of value* that arises when using information in ways that increase the efficiency of a firm's use of a competence may also lead to loss of control of the competence.

The way in which learning processes may take on specific kinds of characteristics or *biases* within firms is discussed by Wright. He suggests that the nature of the work firms perform will lead to systemic biases in the kinds of knowledge development systems firms adopt. His studies of firms in the semiconductor industry suggest that in that industry, some firms develop a "theorizing and codifying" form of learning bias, while others develop learning-by-doing systems that lead to "tangible knowledge integration". Each of these knowledge development systems leads to the development of specific kinds of knowledge and thus the creation of specific kinds of competences within firms.

2

The Unit of Activity: A New Way to Understand Competence Building and Leveraging

BENTE R. LØWENDAHL, KNUT HAANES

Despite its popularity, the resource-based perspective and its recent "sibling" the theory of competence-based competition face a number of challenges which still need to be resolved in research as well as in practice. Competence cannot be allocated like traditional productive resources, as it is both embedded in mobile individuals and highly fluid in terms of both quantity and quality. Competence cannot be measured independent of its application, and is in particular linked to motivation and collective values. We suggest that a shift in focus from the firm or its resources to the value-creating activities to which competences and resources are applied may help us counter these challenges. Six observations on "competence in action" are presented and illustrated by a case study of the reorganization of the marketing and sales division of Alcatel Telecom Norway, and a number of implications are discussed.

INTRODUCTION

One of the main topics of strategic management is the explanation and improvement of value creation in firms. After a long period with

Strategic Learning and Knowledge Management.
Edited by Ron Sanchez and Aimé Heene.
Copyright © 1997 John Wiley & Sons Ltd.

substantial emphasis on industry characteristics, firm positioning, generic strategies, and corporate financial (including portfolio) management, the last decade has seen a return to the analysis of intra-firm factors contributing to such value creation. The award of the *Strategic Management Journal*'s "Best Paper Prize" for 1994 to Birger Wernerfelt for his 1984 article describing a resource-based perspective of the firm, highlights the impact of this stream of research on our strategic management thinking today. However, despite its many strengths, an application of the perspective to the analysis of firm value creation also introduces several challenges.

In our chapter we start by linking the resource-based perspective to the theory of competence-based competition and draw attention to some of the strengths and future challenges of both. Second, we outline the rationale behind the concept of the unit of activity, which builds on a number of traditions, including activity theory and theories of collective action, and explain why an activity framework may improve our understanding of competence in organizations. Third, the framework—incorporating insights from the expanded theory of competence-based competition—is applied to the case of Alcatel Telecom Norway. Finally, implications for practice and further research are discussed, based on the findings of the case study.

THE THEORETICAL FOUNDATIONS

The theory of competence-based competition introduced by Hamel and Heene (1994) and Sanchez, Heene and Thomas (1996) provides an important deepening and extension of the resource-based perspective (e.g. Barney, 1986, 1991; Rumelt, 1984; Penrose, 1959; Wernerfelt, 1984). Among the strengths of the competence-based perspective is its emphasis on an open, holistic and systemic view of the organization (Sanchez, Heene and Thomas, 1996), its focus on the dynamics of competence building and leveraging (Sanchez and Heene, 1996), and its extension of the concept of core competence (Prahalad and Hamel, 1990) from the intra-firm to the competitive and industry levels. In building on, rather than replacing, the resource-based perspective, the theory of competence-based competition carries with it the three main strengths of the resource-based perspective, by emphasizing:

- the dynamics of value creation and the role of managers in that process, building on Penrose's seminal work on firm growth (1959);
- the heterogeneity of firms, seen as a result both of initial resource endowments and of managerial decisions about which products, markets, and critical resources to create and leverage;

- firm resources as a bundle of intangibles as well as tangibles, with particular emphasis on the long-underestimated intangibles such as client loyalty, stakeholder relations, recognized brands, reputation, and capabilities.

In highlighting the role of competence, the theory of competence-based competition emphasizes what we consider to be the most important aspects of the management of firm resources, in particular learning both at the individual and the collective levels. However, in our view, the theory of competence-based competition is also faced with some of the same challenges as the resource-based perspective, including the following.

First, the notion of a firm's competence needs to be challenged for two reasons: (a) individual capabilities, which constitute a key component of the firm's total competence base (Nordhaug, 1993), are not owned by the firm, but rather hired from individuals on a contractual basis. One excellent and recent example may be the controversy described in the press concerning the acquisition of the advertising firm Saatchi & Saatchi, and the ownership of the Saatchi name, the reputation, and the client relations. Could Maurice Saatchi himself be prevented from carrying a large part of these invisible assets (Itami, 1987) with him upon leaving the firm? Clearly not, as neither seller nor buyer controls the image and expectations for future services which the clients of the firm hold after the acquisition. It is their opinion of the expected value added from the firm versus Mr Saatchi which determines their loyalty. Moreover, (b) firm value creation depends on both intra-firm and extra-firm resources and competences, a fact which is highlighted in both the increasing literature on joint ventures and alliances, and the research on national or regional clusters (Porter, 1990), where firms are cross-fertilized from each others' competences as a result of interactions facilitated by geographical proximity. Both of these factors speak to the challenge of identifying meaningful firm boundaries, and the fact that ownership of resources is not all that is involved in the creation and appropriation of value from the use of resources.

Second, the literature on competence has so far showed only limited interest in the motivational characteristics of human resources which are the sources of competences. As pointed out by Itami (1987), human resources can be divided into two categories: one is the labor part, where one hour of labor input to a given process yields a relatively fixed and easily measured yield in terms of output, costs or potential revenues. The other is the problem solving or competence part, where—in the extreme—individuals are not substitutable and hours are highly heterogeneous. A five-person team may, in one hour, generate a tremendous breakthrough with income potential similar to that of thousands of labor hours in normal operations, but may also spend weeks together without generating anything but conflict. A number of factors affect the value of an hour's input of competence, including but not limited to team composition, interpersonal "chemistry", personal health, motivation, culture, physical and structural context. This fact complicates the discussion of the competence and capabilities even further, and highlights the importance of recognizing that competence in this sense is "a beast of a different kind" from labor and tangible resources. The value of Mr Jones' capabilities when motivated, for example, can hardly be compared to its value when he only goes by the rules and performs what is in his job description.

Third, the value of a resource or a competence is extremely hard to measure. One of the main problems in operationalization of intangible resources in empirical testing of the resource-based perspective is the challenge of the flexibility of a competence, and the impossibility of measuring its value in isolation from the task to be solved or the market which is to buy its product or solution. For competence-based services in particular, this challenge is substantial. Similarly, the less routine-based the operations of the firm, the harder it is to estimate the value of the competence in future applications. As Penrose (1959) pointed out: one key feature of firms is that their managers are not bound by the products and services delivered in previous periods, and hence they are also free to choose alternative applications of the resources in order to access alternative markets where the value of the resources is more appreciated.

The shift in focus at this stage of theory development from an emphasis on competences and resources that the firm *has* to the competences and resources that the firm *utilizes* appears helpful, as suggested by the systemic and dynamic view of competence-leveraging and competence-building activities (Sanchez and Heene, 1996). Accompanying this shift in emphasis is the observation substantiated in field studies, that only a relatively small portion of the firm's competence is actually used at any given point in time. The combination of tasks to be accomplished and an organization structure cementing bundles of tasks into fixed positions, limits individuals and their chances of utilizing their capabilities fully. Hence, there is a surprising slack in the competence of most organizations, and an increased emphasis on possible ways of mobilizing this competence might improve value creation substantially. This would, however, require both a different mindset of most managers as well as employees, and a different type of organization structure allowing for a more efficient and flexible competence configuration (Nordhaug, 1993; and Løwendahl and Nordhaug, 1994).

TOWARDS A FOCUS ON ACTIVITIES

We therefore suggest a shift from the firm as the focal unit of analysis (e.g. Barney, 1986, 1991; Conner, 1991; Itami, 1987; Rumelt, 1984; Penrose, 1959; Wernerfelt, 1984). In order to analyze activities as the source of competences, we have proposed a framework where the "unit of activity" is the central concept. This framework is not, in our opinion, an alternative to the theory of competence-based competition, but rather an extension and partial application of it, albeit with a different primary focus. For the purpose of explaining and improving firm value creation, we suggest that it may be fruitful to emphasize "resources in action" (paraphrasing Thompson, 1967), rather than resources *per se*. And we also suggest that an emphasis on value creation as the result of resource leveraging and resource building needs to focus on the actual activities resulting in value creation, rather than limiting the focus to whatever goes on within some elusive and hard to define firm boundaries (Sanchez and Heene, 1996).

The theoretical foundation of the activity framework is primarily threefold: (1) the current attention to activities of business firms in strategic management, (2) activity theory, as originally developed by the Russian scholar Vytgosky, and (3) theories of collective action.

In strategic management, the focus on activities has primarily been occupied with understanding firm activities, as opposed to seeing firms as activity systems. Van de Ven and Poole (1990) saw action as impossible without authority, shared rules and information, arguing that coordinated action requires common goals. Spender (1993) argued that collective tacit knowledge is built through activities, and that this process is socially constructed (Berger and Luckmann, 1966). Activities might in turn evolve into routines (Nelson and Winter, 1982) through the emergence of collective skill building. The value chain (Porter, 1985) conceptualized the operations of the firm as a chain of activities (see also Porter, 1991), from input to output. Subsequent criticism has pointed out that the value chain might be well suited for industrial firms engaged in the transformation of physical goods, but that it might be less suited for service firms (Normann and Ramirez, 1993) and also for firms in networks (Stabell and Fjeldstad, 1995). Løwendahl (1994) introduced the "firm as a collection of projects", also with a focus on how firms actually work more and more through the coordination of project-driven activities rather than through hierarchical directives and controls.

In activity-theory (Blackler, 1993; Engestrom, 1987) individuals and collectives—as well as cognition and action—are analyzed without making a distinction between individuals (who have control of and are free to choose their actions) and organizations (which impose boundaries on the individuals belonging to the organization) (see Poole and Van de Ven, 1989). Activities are seen to be the appropriate way to understand organizations because participants both think and act collectively. Learning in organizations takes place through participation in activities, consisting of interactions, tools, rules and labor. Incoherence, dilemma and conflict are seen to offer important avenues for learning. The theory provides an intellectual framework for studying the development of organizational structures and their reproduction. "Activity theory examines the nature of practical activities, their social origins, and the nature of the 'activity systems' within which people collaborate" (Blackler, 1993: 863).

Smelser (1963) suggests that there are four main components of collective action: (1) values—a purpose leading to behavior, (2) norms—rules governing the pursuit of goals, (3) motivation—reasons for participating and organizing, and (4) situational facilities—the knowledge, tools and skills that can be mobilized. The defining driver of collective action is seen to be the kinds of underlying beliefs, i.e. action is seen to be driven by shared ideas. A study by Snow, Zurcher and Ekland-Olson (1980) extends this, finding that the underlying ideas ("why be active") cannot be understood without looking at the process through which this happens ("how to become active"), where social links are the key for mobilization of action. Thus, people will mobilize and act based on the values or the objectives, but this cannot be understood without studying their social connections. In fact, both conditions must be present—(a) values, and (b) social networks; both formal and informal (Gould, 1991).

From these theories on activities it is clear that a framework for understanding business activities must jointly address network and value characteristics. Furthermore, it must be able to identify both emergent and formalized activities, inside and across the "boundaries" of a given firm.

IMPLICATIONS OF THE UNIT OF ACTIVITY FRAMEWORK

In previous studies we analyzed organization, competence utilization, and value creation in organizations as different as the project organization for the Lillehammer Winter Olympics (Løwendahl and Nordhaug, 1994), the Dynal biotech joint venture (Haanes and Lorange, 1995) and Fiat Auto in post-Communist Poland (Haanes and Lorange, 1995a, 1995b). Through an iterative multiple case logic, the present sketch of a theoretical approach has emerged, but we would like to emphasize that this theory development still bears all the characteristics of a snap-shot of an ongoing work-in-progress, and we do by no means intend this to be a complete and testable framework. We do, however, suggest that the observations give interesting insights and suggestions for the continuation of this work, and hope that these insights may lead to a new and fruitful theoretical framework in the future. The concept of the unit of activity consists of some fundamental observations about how contemporary organizations are changing:

1. People increasingly belong to several activities simultaneously.
2. Organizations consist of many—dynamic and less dynamic—units of activity.
3. Units of activity will appear and disappear over time.
4. Relevant units of activity exist inside, between and outside of the organization.
5. Management is only a part-time role in units of activities.
6. The changing role of customer relations often calls for joint activities.

The unit of activity cannot be understood simply in terms of formal structure, but rather must be seen as an entity where learning, innovation and work take place. Thus, the unit of activity might not be defined only in terms of ownership, but also in terms of managerial grasp and a joint understanding of an idea or a task. A unit of activity may emerge formally or informally, may have more than one participant, and may have implicit or stated objectives. It can be distinguished from other units of activity by common expectations and an understanding of—and practice towards—the shared objectives. The building of tacit knowledge (Polanyi, 1966) in groups or organizations is a defining characteristic of a unit of activity. The size of the unit is scalable due to the possibility of extensive activities which again consist of sub-activities. Furthermore, the unit of activity should be distinguished from a project, because whereas units of activity include both espoused and actual practice, a project tends to be initiated formally. This discussion is in line with the framework presented in the notions of competence-based competition and "core competence" (Prahalad and Hamel, 1990), e.g. Hamel (1994: 12) stating that: "A core competence is not an inanimate thing, it is an activity, a messy accumulation of learning." By use of the activity framework we may better understand the "triggers" of activity creation such as the network and the development of shared values in the case study.

THE CASE OF ALCATEL TELECOM NORWAY

After developing the above six observations on "competences in action", we wanted to look into the implications of these observations in an atypical but fortuitous situation, namely that of a newly reorganized division where management tried to view value creation as a set of activities and to organize the division entirely according to the ongoing activities. The case chosen, Alcatel Telecom Norway, was expected to fit well with all the observations presented above, and hence was not designed to test these. Rather, what we wanted to look into were the organizational and individual *implications* of taking the unusual approach of designing the organization structure according to an activity-based logic. We would like to highlight at this stage that this case study was *not* designed as action research or as a quasi-experiment. The managers of Alcatel Telecom Norway planned their reorganization long before we came in contact, and hence the reorganization was not influenced by our theoretical efforts. On the other hand, when our framework was presented to them, they became very interested and invited us to do the study. As a result, we have met with an unusual openness to discuss different aspects and challenges of this "experiment". After initial discussions with top management of the marketing section it was decided that we would focus specifically on the organizational change taking place. A qualitative study was undertaken in the period from April 1995 to August 1995. We interviewed employees at various levels in the section, including the three top managers, all key project leaders and multiple project members. (The actual field-work was undertaken by the second author.) This involved more than twenty in-depth interviews. All interviews lasted for more than one hour, some as long as three hours. Several of the interviewees were contacted after the interviews to clear up uncertainties and were confronted with the documentation after the interview. Some people were also interviewed several times. Direct observations of meetings and administrative procedures took place, and a range of internal and public documents pertinent to Alcatel Telecom Norway and more specifically the marketing section were reviewed. In addition, several industry observers were interviewed to better understand the dynamics of the telecom industry, since these had an impact on the case studied.

To address some major shortcomings of process research on organizations (Pettigrew, 1987; Nutt and Backoff, 1993), namely that it tends to ignore the historical, contextual and processual issues involved, a brief description of the telecom industry and the main activities of Alcatel Telecom Norway are introduced before we discuss implications of the case results for our observations.

THE TELECOM INDUSTRY

The notions of competence groups—groups that engage in similar competence-building and/or competence-leveraging activities at a given point in time (Gorman, Thomas and Sanchez, 1996)—and competence alliances seem well suited for a clarification of many of the changes taking place in the telecom industry. The central idea, namely that an industry can be seen in a competence-building and competence-leveraging perspective (Sanchez, Heene and Thomas, 1996), might for instance help us better analyze the alliances and competitive interactions taking place in the industry.

In the 1980s the telecom industry started experiencing a set of important external stimuli (Gorman, Thomas and Sanchez, 1996), such as some major technological developments (i.e. optic fibre, digitization, new software), deregulation, liberalization and changing consumer demands. This led to two parallel developments in the industry: first, a "convergence" of the telecom industry with other industries—such as computer software and hardware, consumer electronics and media. Second, the new technological possibilities led to an expansion of the main activities taking place in the telecom industry. Having consisted mainly of equipment manufacturing and telecom operations, it expanded into information and service provision. This implied a new set of competences needed to capitalize on new possibilities opened up by improved technology and liberalized markets. As seen by an Alcatel Telecom Norway manager:

> The industry is important, and telecommunication has been very technical. The manager has traditionally had a weak role. But this has changed—slowly— because of the drive towards the market.

For the telecom operators, the "convergence" of telecoms with other industries led to significant changes in the strategic group composition of the industry. The drive for new capabilities for product innovation (see Sanchez, 1995), such as access to software, infrastructure, film libraries, clients or operating licenses, led to strategic group cooperation, strategic alliances and takeovers. So, whereas the telecom operators previously had built barriers in their home markets, the uncertainty of the new industry structure fostered new types of cooperation. The cooperative activity— both within strategic groups and between firms—seemed to be driven by two ambitions: (1) to become global, and (2) to leverage and build competences. Hence, one category of alliances was clearly aimed at achieving global presence, whereas the other was to achieve competence leveraging and building for the future (Gorman, Thomas and Sanchez, 1996).

The equipment suppliers—such as Alcatel Telecom—were affected by (and partly caused) these changes in several ways: first, new companies entered telecom operations, increasing the number of potential customers. Second, operators became more international, making new kinds of investments in infrastructure in countries that traditionally had poor coverage and service. Third, competition forced the operators to implement a totally new purchasing strategy. Before, when they sold to monopoly operators, the role of the equipment manufacturers had been to develop technologically advanced equipment from specifications. Thus the telecom operators had often financed the manufacturers' research activities. But as the operators became more cost conscious, they no longer cared to finance development of new equipment that (due to liberalization) could be used by their competitors. Consequently, a more market-oriented strategy was required from the manufacturers.

Nevertheless, the telecom equipment manufacturers faced interesting prospects. Factors such as the expansion and modernization of existing networks and the construction of new networks to obtain multimedia capabilities were propelling the equipment industry. Furthermore, the high complexity of digital equipment required large investments in research and development which again led to concentration. The barriers to entry in classical equipment, such as switching, transmission, subscriber units, mobile phones and wireless infrastructure, were getting higher. Simultaneously, telecom technology became increasingly homogeneous. Hence, competition among suppliers was largely a question of differentiation based on compatible technology. Due to the networked nature of telecom operations there was a need for compatible technology, so competitive uniqueness was speed, service and advanced applications rather than unique products. In short, the importance of developing technologically compatible technologies, the high entry barriers and the fast growing market made the telecom equipment manufacturers become a strategic group in terms of competence building and leveraging. They had a collective interest in maintaining high barriers to entry. Consequently, viewing industries through competence theory opens up for a different perspective (Gorman, Thomas and Sanchez, 1996: 91, emphasis in original):

> Competence theory suggests possibilities for joining economic and cognitive perspectives through the concept of *competence groups*. By recognizing that firm strategies consist of both competence building and competence leveraging, which in turn are influenced by both current resource endowments and managerial cognitions, researchers may be better able to discover dynamic patterns of competitive interactions that provide a more systemic and holistic view of competitive interactions at any point in time.

It was clear that many of the challenges faced by Alcatel Telecom Norway were to adapt its internal competence leveraging and development to this new industrial theater with new opportunities and threats and new industrial constellations.

ALCATEL TELECOM NORWAY

STK—a Norwegian company then owned by ITT—was chosen in 1983 to be the developer and supplier of the digital network in Norway. This was labelled "contract of the century" as Norway became a pioneer country for the digital "System 12". This meant an intensive research and installation activity until 1989. In the meantime, in 1987, STK became part of the Alcatel group as a result of the merger between ITT and GEC. In the following years Alcatel STK made some export attempts in order to reduce its dependence on one client (i.e. the national operator Telenor). However, when Alcatel STK in 1990 no longer could prevent Ericsson from re-entering the Norwegian market, a major restructuring was launched and staff was reduced substantially. This led to radical changes in the Telecom division (from 1991 Alcatel Telecom Norway), and accentuated the need for increased sales abroad. Although some contracts were won in the early 1990s, such as in Latvia and China, a transformation of the whole sales and marketing section was called for. In 1994, a new head of marketing was recruited and exports and domestic sales were put together. Also, large changes were taking place in the Norwegian telecom sector, where Telenor became managed as a private business. A corporate manager saw the changes going on in Alcatel Telecom Norway's environment in terms of the general transformation of the market:

> We are forced to change since our customers change. Traditionally sales had been from engineer to engineer, making things increasingly complex technologically. We had forgotten how to make money on all this.

In the marketing and sales section dramatic change was needed in order to strengthen marketing to deal with the increasingly differentiated and integrated projects both domestically and abroad. It was seen as necessary to better assign responsibility and to better leverage competences. Furthermore, there was a need for more cross-functional work, team building and innovation. To address these issues the new manager wanted a less hierarchical structure with fewer boundaries internally and to other parts of the company and customers. He also saw a need to reduce formality in the system: "We have to accept chaos but try to manage it", adding about the intentions behind the new structure:

> We wanted more out of the existing resources, and to be more competition-oriented. We also needed to understand more what the market requires. In fact, we need to develop our ability to learn.

Therefore, a more activity-oriented structure was introduced. Every activity was made into a "project" with one person responsible, to be defined by deadlines, activities and specification of the needed resources, including people.

ANALYSIS OF FINDINGS

Below, the main observations from the field study of the "activity structure" are linked to the activity framework.

1. People increasingly belong to several activities simultaneously. One aim with the new structure was to allocate people according to their capabilities and to assign responsibility. Each employee was to participate as member of several projects with responsibility for some. Prior to the organizational changes people were relatively free to spend time where they saw it as appropriate; now it increasingly became a reflection of the defined project specifications. So, the roles gradually changed to more differentiated activities through cross-functional teams, projects, etc. A key observation about the project focus was that each employee had several defined activities simultaneously, e.g. belonging to development projects, teaching at training courses and undertaking staff tasks. The project structure represented an effort to deal with the challenge of allocating resources, and as such it seemed to help in optimizing resource deployment. However, the multitude of roles posed a dilemma. As seen by a project manager:

> In Alcatel it is "survival of the fittest". The first one to get a contract and show initiative gets responsibility. This is very complex with global operations. We all fight for getting attention on our products.

Clearly, the recognition and formalization of a set of activities imposed a need for a more holistic understanding in the whole organization: it was important that every project member saw the link to other activities and to the strategy of the company. But the search for common ground seemed to suffer as a result of a clearer focus on each specific project. The incentives for helping out and feeding off possibilities to others were low. As seen by another project manager, who was concerned about the new mentality:

> People only think about their own projects. We are losing our team-spirit. This must come back. We have to pull this thing together. And we have to see the whole, so that I get the feedback that what I'm doing might be good by itself, but not for the whole.

Furthermore, the new structure seemed to have one crucial managerial implication. The contributions of each individual became more visible because each person was exposed to defined projects. This meant that management had to start dealing with individuals, as opposed to the prior focus on the organization. In the words of one of the top managers:

> The new way of working gets the individual contribution out in the open. This is good for the ones who have always been contributors, but less so for the others. Some don't take the responsibilities offered to them, and consequently get less freedom. Our new structure requires excellent people.

2. Organizations consist of many—dynamic and less dynamic—units of activity. The pattern of activity took different forms: some activities were cancelled because they were not creating value, others were spun off. One stated aim of the new structure was to encourage the emergence of new activities through more cooperation across prior boundaries. Innovation was seen as the core process. But, in fact, one major problem with the project structure turned out to be the trade-off between spending time on allocated projects and creating slack allowing people to create and innovate. The problem was widely acknowledged, as noted by one project manager:

> What you need to have in a project structure is many times more activities than we need: a critical mass. There must be a balance between slack and efficiency so that we can create new initiatives.

This was dealt with by giving some people time to "be creative", but it turned out to be difficult for several reasons: first, the requirements of project definitions implied a loss of flexibility. Second, it was clearly impossible to plan for contingencies, spin-offs, up-coming problems, etc. The formality surrounding projects could lead to a situation where the most defined—not the most interesting—projects were chosen. On the individual level one could see that the creative people were turned off by the formality of getting a new project off the ground. To a certain extent the project definition ran a danger of trying to "plan the unplannable". In short, there seemed to be a trade-off between doing what was planned and following new possibilities. Also, several people mentioned that whereas new projects had "just emerged" in the old system, they had to be planned for by giving more freedom in the new structure. Some employees complained that new initiatives came *in spite* of the new incentives:

> In a project organization one has to define the objectives very clearly. But that is not possible. It is impossible to set milestones, because we are selling total solutions. We have to improve, to do what seems most promising here and now because changes happen so fast.

3. Units of activity will appear and disappear over time. It was clear that some activities disappeared over time and that others emerged. The projects developed over time and ideally they should shift from people with one capability to another as needed. This turned out to be more difficult, however, since some held onto pet projects. Each project, having an entrepreneurial and an administrative aspect, seemed to be over-emphasizing the latter, especially in the dialogue with top management, where there was a focus on optimization and efficient management. This was most likely linked to the prior culture, where routines and implementation were key and where innovation often came from the customer contacts. The follow-up of each project was more based on overseeing the management of the resources than seeing possibilities and creating new competences. This was, however, more an effect of the way the new structure was run than a direct effect of the structure.

4. Relevant units of activity exist inside, between and outside of the organization. Many of the relevant value-creating activities were taking place outside of the boundaries of the market division—both in-firm and entirely outside of Alcatel; mainly through cooperative efforts with customers and suppliers. Such cooperation came about for several reasons, namely the need for more integrated solutions, more complex tasks to solve, and the need for investments that were too large for Alcatel Telecom Norway to handle alone. One area where improvement was sought was in the cooperation with the technical department. The intention had been to create a freer structure, so that it would be natural to set up teams of people as this was needed. A more open attitude towards working across boundaries was seen, as noted by a project member:

> There are several sides to this. I think that for many the will has always been there. But there were no linking mechanisms. People did not dare or know how to work across the boundaries. Often it was "this is not my table", or "this is not your table".

The problem with this turned out to be that it was difficult to get people to work together on pre-project efforts. The cross-functional cooperation was shifted to formal projects, leading to less informal assistance and cooperation, which—in turn—had been one of the keys for innovation in the old structure. Thus, innovation needed to be addressed differently in the new structure. As pointed out by a project manager regarding the internal workings of the sales and marketing division:

> The team spirit has suffered a lot. We used to be more linked, now it is less the case. Everybody is more in his own box. But, I think a lot of people work as they always have. You only draw in somebody when it is really needed.

5. Management is only a part-time role. Even the top managers of the new organizational structure were initially to be participants in many activities, with responsibility for some of these. This had been true before the restructuring, but the changes were meant to reduce "red tape" so that the management team could participate in client-focused projects. Management initially tried to combine, not separate, managerial and operational activities as much as possible. Decisions were pushed towards the problem, so that each manager would have time to provide expertise and knowledge. The outcome of the changes were, however, somewhat contradictory. First, it turned out that the management team got more tasks as a result of having to manage the new operations and to deal with the routines from the prior structure. Thus, they gradually retreated from projects. So, whereas the managers previously could give inputs to projects on an *ad-hoc* basis, they became preoccupied with managing projects formally (defining budgets, identifying participants and solving conflicts) and addressing individual issues. It was widely acknowledged that they used less time actually being a resource in projects than before. Consequently, the ambition of also having "their own" project responsibilities was soon dismissed as a result of the work flow created through project supervision. As people realized that the management team was not to participate in projects—which was announced prior to the restructuring—some disappointment was voiced. One of the top managers acknowledged this, arguing that the new organization required a more stable set of shared ideas than before:

> We need to make people realize that we need a better foundation. A metaphor can be taken from modern jazz, where there seems to be a chaos, but where there are shared values and a common underlying understanding and structure.

The restructuring, which implied a whole new philosophy of operations where managers were to be activity drivers like the other project managers, early on met a lot of resistance, partly due to the fact that some of the employees wanted management to perform the "classic" management tasks. As seen by one of the managers: "Some people still want the manager to be the boss. But today the management should only be facilitators—a professional discussion partner."

6. The changing role of customer relations often calls for joint activities. As fewer and fewer of the complex products commercialized by Alcatel Telecom Norway, such as transmission systems, switches and wireless installations, could be conceptualized in isolation from the suppliers and customers, a substantial cooperative effort was required. Hence, as products and services became more complex, integrated and long term, these relations became more interlinked. Addressing this issue was another main objective of the project organization: people were to perceive fewer boundaries towards their clients. Thus, cross-organizational projects, teams and groups were created to provide a vehicle for activities that required close relations. The new organizational structure facilitated such efforts by giving each employee more direct responsibility. As seen by one of the project leaders who worked closely with the main domestic customer: "We are becoming cooperative partners with our customers. Therefore we are doing this in a different way. Now it is more a joint effort." In such relations the value creation for the customer and the client could often not be separated. But the clear assigning of tasks and responsibilities seemed to have the unforeseen effect of hindering innovation through the reduction of slack:

> The project organization is too objectives-oriented and it kills creativity, too mechanical, so creativity is only connected to reaching the pre-set goal, not to identifying new possibilities.

Finally, there were some issues connected to the way the organizational changes were implemented. Among some employees, there seemed to be an opinion that it was rather top-down, in contradiction to the aims of the new structure itself: "Management had not studied enough what change really implies. They started drawing, made the ideal picture, and then we had to adapt to that, rather than adapting the structure to the people." This was how some employees saw it. One employee also noted that it seemed as if management were the only ones not affected by the new structure, thus sending a signal of indifference. This might have represented a barrier to efficient implementation:

> It requires top management commitment. That they show us that it is important. This is a classical problem, though. In all my years I have heard the phrase "management must this and management must that". They have to set the direction.

DISCUSSION

Our initial observations in terms of theoretical framework seem to hold. Activities are possible to identify, and the cost benefits of competences in action may be measured. However, there is a need to develop the framework further in terms of defining and operationalizing activities, which might be done by undertaking longitudinal studies and cross-case comparisons. Furthermore, organizing in the extreme form of activities is not necessarily an improvement over the traditional organization, and it turned out that the reorganization to an activity structure did not really address the issues at hand. Problems with organization structure were not at the core of what needed to be "fixed". Hence, the original problems did not require this solution. It seemed to be a paradox that organizing by activities improved competence leveraging—in the labor sense of the human resources—but that creativity was not enhanced, and that solutions became local. The structural response was highly efficient, but not so good at motivating, leading to problems with creating a team spirit and the building of collective competences. Thus, we found the new structure to be less suitable for competence building.

In fact, there seems to be an implicit assumption in most strategic management literature that to address the managerial issues raised by competence and knowledge intensity there is a need to transform firms' structures. This might be a reflection of the in-built notion that structure must follow strategy (Chandler, 1962). Consequently, strategic changes stemming from people as the source of competitive advantage seem to require structural changes. We will argue that this might be partially wrong because structure and strategy are linked so closely to shared ideas, challenges, vision, professional relations and capabilities. The challenge of building and leveraging competences is one of mentality and strategic vision, rather than merely structures. As noted by one employee: "I still miss a more systematic craze."

IMPLICATIONS FOR RESEARCH AND PRACTICE

So what does competence building and leveraging imply? Based on the case study we will argue that one fruitful place to start is to look at the competences addressable by the organization, to understand how they are disposed to be mobilized to leverage and build resources together. The theory of competence-based competition divides between firm-specific and firm-addressable resources (Sanchez, Heene and Thomas, 1996). To get a grip on how to do this we will draw attention to Andrews' (1971) observation that a company's strategy should encompass what the firm (1) might do, (2) can do, (3) wants to do, and (4) should do. In seeing competence systems as sets of activities—the crux of the activity framework—we emphasize the last two because they are often ignored (suggesting the fallacy of a competence-driven organization where people leave easily): "Strategy is a human construction; it must in the long run be responsive to human needs. It must ultimately inspire commitment. It must stir an organization to successful striving against competition. People have to have their hearts in it" (Andrews, 1971: 63).

Hence, creating an organization that facilitates both competence leveraging and competence building is difficult; here we need to search for new solutions. In such a search managers need to be careful because motivation and creativity are among the factors that suffer first thus destroying both the building and leveraging of competence.

In our view, these observations have a number of further implications. The emphasis on competence implies a shift in emphasis from the efficient leveraging of fixed assets to the support and development of an effective climate where competence and resources are expanded and new solutions developed. The critical factor may no longer be human resource productivity in the sense of maximum output per hour, but rather competence building through a creative search for new solutions and applications. Formal organization structures may hamper such a development, and new structures with an extreme emphasis on competence leveraging may actually prevent the organization from building and enhancing competence. If motivation and creativity suffer, so do both competence leveraging—as the quantity of competence applied shrinks—and competence building—as there is no room for the search for new solutions and applications. The emphasis on goal orientation and strategic direction may be more important than ever, but they need to be manifested in terms of shared values and commitment rather than formal structures. We seem to need organizations which enhance flexibility and individual responsiveness, rather than restrict it through rules, routines, or project milestones. In this respect, we are still searching for solutions, both as managers and as researchers. At present, we cannot offer any ready models, but rather suggest a direction for our future search for solutions; namely, that we start by investigating activities and what the firm does, rather than focusing on future competences and all that it could potentially do. After all, it is the "competences in action" that lead to value creation!

REFERENCES

Andrews, K. (1971). *The Concept of Corporate Strategy*, Homewood, IL: Dow-Jones-Irwin.

Barney, J. (1986). "Types of competition and the theory of strategy", *Academy of Management Review*, **11**, pp. 123–141.

Barney, J. (1991). "Firm resources and sustained competitive advantage", *Journal of Management*, pp. 99–120.

Berger, P. and T. Luckmann (1966). *The Social Construction of Reality*, Garden City, NY: Doubleday.

Blackler, F. (1993). "Knowledge and the theory of organizations: organizations as activity systems and the reframing of management", *Journal of Management Studies*, **30**, pp. 863–884.

Chandler, A. D. (1962). *Strategy and Structure: Chapter in the History of the American Enterprise*, Cambridge, MA: The MIT Press.

Conner, K. E. (1991). "A historical comparison of resource-based theory and five schools of thought within industrial economics: Do we have a new theory of the firm?", *Journal of Management*, **17**(1), pp. 121–154.

Engestrom, Y. (1987). *Learning by Expanding: An Activity Theoretical Approach to Developmental Research*, Helsinki: Orienta-Konsultit.

Gorman, P., H. Thomas and R. Sanchez (1996). "Industry dynamics in competence-based competition", in *Dynamics of Competence-Based Competition: Theory and Practice in the New Strategic Management*, R. Sanchez, A. Heene and H Thomas, editors, Oxford: Elsevier.

Gould, R. E. (1991). "Multiple networks and mobilization in the Paris Commune, 1871", *Journal of Sociology*, **56**, pp. 716–729.

Hamel, G. (1994). "The concept of core competence", in *Competence-Based Competition*, G. Hamel and A. Heene, editors, Chichester: John Wiley and Sons.

Hamel, G. and A. Heene (eds) (1994). *Competence-Based Competition*, Chichester: John Wiley and Sons.

Haanes, K. and P. Lorange (1995). "The Dynal Biotech joint venture", IMD case study. GM 593.

Haanes, K. and P. Lorange (1995a). "Transformation of Fiat Auto Poland (A): Background and setting", IMD case study, GM 594.

Haanes, K. and P. Lorange (1995b). "Transformation of Fiat Auto Poland (B): Managing the change process", IMD case study, GM 595.

Itami, H. (with T. Roehl) (1987). *Mobilizing Invisible Assets*, Cambridge, MA: Harvard University Press.

Løwendahl, B. R. (1992). "Global strategies for professional service firms", unpublished doctoral thesis, University of Pennsylvania, the Wharton School.

Løwendahl, B. (1994). "Organizing the XVII Olympic Winter Games", *Proceedings*, The IRNOP Conference on Temporary Organizations & Project Management, Lycksele, Lappland, Finland.

Løwendahl, B. and O. Nordhaug (eds) (1994). *OL 1994: Inspirasjonskilde for framtidens næringsliv?*, Tano. Norway.

Nelson, R. and S. Winter (1982). *An Evolutionary Theory of Organizational Change*, Cambridge, MA: Harvard University Press.

Nordhaug, O. (1993). *Human Capital in Organizations: Competence, Training and Learning*, Oslo, Norway: Scandinavian University Press.

Normann, R. and R. Ramirez (1993). "From value chain to value constellation: Designing interactive strategy", *Harvard Business Review*, July–August, pp. 65–77.

Nutt, P. C. and R. W. Backoff (1993). "Transforming public organizations with strategic management and strategic leadership", *Journal of Management*, **19**(2), pp. 299–347.

Penrose, E. (1959). *The Theory of the Growth of the Firm*, London: Basil Blackwell.

Pettigrew, A. (1987). "Context and action in the transformation of the firm", *Journal of Management Studies*, **24**(6), pp. 649–670.

Polanyi, M. (1966). *Tacit Dimension*, New York: Doubleday.

Poole, M. S. and A. H. Van de Ven (1989). "Using paradox to build management and organization theory", *Academy of Management Review*, **14**(4), pp. 562–579.

Porter, M. E. (1985). *Competitive Advantage*, New York: Free Press.

Porter, M. E. (1990). *The Competitive Advantage of Nations*, New York: Free Press.

Porter, M. E. (1991). "Toward a dynamic theory of strategy", *Strategic Management Journal*, **12**, pp. 95–117.

Prahalad, C. K. and G. Hamel (1990). "The core competence of the corporation", *Harvard Business Review*, **68**(3), pp. 79–91.

Rumelt, R. (1984). "Towards a strategic theory of the firm", pp. 556–570, in *Competitive Strategic Management*, R.B. Lamb, editor, Englewood Cliffs, NJ: Prentice-Hall.

Sanchez, R. (1995). "Strategic flexibility in product competition", *Strategic Management Journal*, **16** (Special Issue), summer, pp. 135–159.

Sanchez, R. and A. Heene (1996). "A systems view of the firm in competence-based competition", in *Dynamics of Competence-Based Competition: Theory and Practice in the New Strategic Management*, R. Sanchez, A. Heene and H. Thomas, editors. Oxford: Elsevier.

Sanchez, R., A. Heene and H. Thomas (eds) (1996). *Dynamics of Competence-Based Competition: Theory and Practice in the New Strategic Management*, Oxford: Elsevier.

Smelser, N. (1963). *Theory of Collective Behavior*, New York: The Free Press.

Snow, D. A., L. A. Zurcher and S. Ekland-Olson (1980). "Social networks and social movements: A microstructural approach to differential recruitment", *American Sociological Review*, **45**, pp. 787–801.

Spender, J. C. (1993). "Competitive advantage from tacit knowledge? Unpacking the concept and its strategic implications", *Academy of Management Best Paper Proceedings*, pp. 37–41.

Stabell, C. and Ø. Fjeldstad (1995). "On value-chains and other value configurations", *Working paper series*, Norwegian School of Management.

Thompson, J. D. (1967). *Organizations in Action*, New York: McGraw-Hill.

Van de Ven, A. and M. S. Poole (1990). "Paradoxical requirements for a theory of organizational change", in *Paradox and Transformation: Toward a Theory of Change in Organization and Management*, R. E. Quinn and K. S. Cameron, editors, Ballinger.

Wernerfelt, B. (1984). "A resource-based view of the firm", *Strategic Management Journal*, **5**, pp. 171–180.

3

Complex Systems, Complex Learning, and Competence Building

RICHARD HALL

INTRODUCTION

This chapter is concerned with intangible assets, in particular with knowledge, organizational learning, and management style. The chapter summarizes the author's ongoing work regarding the portfolios of intangible assets which CEOs hold to be important, and a new approach to the management of know-how is proposed. In considering these issues the impact of complexity theory on our understanding of organizational dynamics is acknowledged. The advocates of the application of complexity theory to organizational dynamics suggest that the flexibility which is required to survive in turbulent environments will only be achieved if positive feedback is not suppressed; they suggest that a traditional *command and control* style of management, which strives for predictability and stability by means of strong negative feedback, will not be conducive to long-term survival. This proposition has been tested by means of a study of long-term surviving British companies.

Sanchez, Heene and Thomas (1996) point out that a critical dimension of managerial cognition is the decision regarding the kinds of resources a firm should develop, or access, in order to build and leverage competencies. Strategic logic is concerned with developing a rationale

Strategic Learning and Knowledge Management.
Edited by Ron Sanchez and Aimé Heene.
Copyright © 1997 John Wiley & Sons Ltd.

with respect to the assets which will be useful to the firm; these assets will be intangible as well as tangible. This chapter reports the author's ongoing work with respect to a technique which enables practitioners to analyse their company's important intangible assets and to develop the portfolio of intangible assets which may produce future competitive advantage. Employee know-how is usually identified as a company's most important intangible asset, and it is suggested that a deeper understanding of the issues concerning the management of know-how may be obtained from the concepts contained in Boisot's (1995) Social Learning Cycle model. Organizational learning is closely related to management style, and it is appropriate in this context to consider the impact which complexity theory has on our understanding of organizational dynamics. Finally, the results of some initial research designed to test the types of management style which complexity theory suggests is required for long-term survival are reported.

INTANGIBLE ASSETS

The Just in Time (JIT) and Business Process Reengineering (BPR) initiatives which have gained currency in recent years emphasize the need to focus attention on those primary activities which add value for the customer. One systems view of the firm suggests that, in addition to the customer value chain, there are two resource feedback loops which are also value chains. This model is illustrated in Figure 3.1.

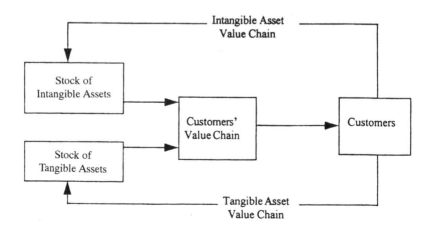

FIGURE 3.1   The Three Value Chains

All management functions and procedures should be able to justify their existence by virtue of their adding-value role in one or more of these value chains. The process mapping procedures incorporated in BPR provide management with the ability to analyse the *customer value chain*. The accountancy profession provides management with the taxonomies and functions to audit the *tangible asset value chain* and to audit the stocks of tangible assets, but the procedures for auditing the *intangible asset value chain* are much less developed. If one considers the market capitalization of a publicly quoted company it is often the case that the market value exceeds the balance sheet net worth by a factor of three or four; i.e. between two-thirds and three-quarters of the value of the firm, as represented by the value of the shares traded, may be due to *off balance sheet* items—or intangible assets. A key feature of fiduciary control concerns the management of the company's portfolio of tangible assets—it is necessary to achieve an appropriate mix of current and fixed assets, of cash and near cash, etc. In a similar fashion executives need to manage their company's portfolio of intangible assets by ascertaining the relative contribution which each makes, or will make, to business success and in the light of this analysis they then need to formulate strategies with respect to the protection, leverage and enhancement of the key intangible assets. Hall (1994) has identified different types of intangible asset and has categorized them as shown in Table 3.1.

TABLE 3.1   Intangible Assets Placed in Four Categories

Regulatory assets: those with property rights	*Positional assets: those without property rights*
Patents, trademarks, copyright, registered designs, trade secrets, assignable contracts, licences, proprietary operating systems.	Reputation of company and products, value chain configuration, distribution network, unique access to raw materials, organizational networks, installed operating systems, e.g. MRP, EPOS, etc., databases.
Functional assets: individual or team skills	*Cultural assets: the characteristics of the organization*
Employee know-how, Distributor know-how, Supplier know-how, *and* groupings of the above.	Perception of high quality standards The organization's ability to: • manage change • innovate • work as teams • respond to challenge. Tradition of customer service, etc.

If the following questions can be answered unambiguously then each intangible asset can be placed unambiguously in a category.

"Is the intangible asset a possession, something which one *has*, like a patent, or a reputation?" If "Yes":

"Does it possess property rights?"
- If "Yes" it is a *Regulatory Resource*.
- If "No" it is a *Positional Resource*.

"Is the intangible asset a possession, something which one *has*, like a patent, or a reputation?" If "No":

It must be a talent—a *"doing"* capability.
- If it is the talent of an individual, or a functional team, then it is a *Functional Resource*.
- If the talent is concerned with the shared values and attitudes of the organization as a whole then it is a *Cultural Resource*.

No theoretical rationale is offered here to justify describing this framework as a taxonomy. Further, the unambiguous placement of intangible assets into these categories may only be possible for a specific organization at a point in time, and even then some degree of judgement may be required; for example, opinions may differ as to whether a certain database enjoys property rights.

However, advantages have been experienced in using this framework with practitioners, including the realization that a major source of competitive advantage may be something other than a skill or a talent; very often it is identified as a positional asset such as reputation or a distribution network. Such assets are the results of previous endeavour, usually over a long period of time, and as such can constitute entry barriers by virtue of the long time it would take a new entrant to achieve the positional asset. Of course, the total source of a competitive advantage may be a grouping of intangible assets drawn from the different resource categories. For example, the capability which produces competitive advantage for a manufacturer may comprise:

- A *Regulatory Resource* comprising licences.
- A *Positional Resource* comprising a certain configuration of the supply chain.
- A *Functional Resource* comprising the know-how of employees and suppliers.
- A *Cultural Resource* which contributes to the organization's learning ability.

A competitor of this manufacturer may try to emulate this capability but may only be able to recognize, or replicate, one or two of the intangible assets and thus fail to match the total capability. The analysis suggested by this categorization therefore facilitates the realization that a capability may have several types of constituent parts. This echoes Prahalad and Hamel (1990) who assert that a core competence will be difficult for a competitor to imitate if it is a complex harmonization of individual technologies and production skills.

A Technique for Analysing the Role of Intangible Assets in Business Success

A technique for analysing the role which intangible assets play in business success has been devised and is currently being validated. The technique codifies the tacit knowledge which senior managers have of their organizations thus enabling it to be communicated throughout their organization *and* to suppliers who enjoy a partnership status (cf. Sanchez 1996).

The structure of the technique will be presented in this section together with a summary of some of the results achieved to date. The technique initially analyses the nature of the current sales advantage—why do current customers buy the products? It then goes on to identify the intangible assets which produce the key product and/or delivery system attributes.

The Nature of the Current Sales Advantage

Any company making sales has a sales advantage *in the eyes of the customers who are buying from it.* The nature of this advantage may be defined in terms of product and/or delivery system attributes. Examples are given in Table 3.2.

The essence of the sales advantage can usually be captured with five or six attributes. Sometimes CEOs will know this as a result of market research, sometimes it will be necessary to carry out market research. Having defined the nature of the sales advantage currently enjoyed in terms of product and/or delivery system attributes, the chief executives who have used the technique have found little difficulty in identifying the intangible assets which they believe are responsible for the attributes. A summary of some results obtained to date is given in Table 3.3.

The following observations are appropriate

- It is usually the case that the *Regulatory Resource* contains fewer intangible assets than do the other three resource categories. Assets which

TABLE 3.2 Typical Product Delivery System Attributes Which Define Sales Advantage

---

Image What is the image of your product range? Is it important?

Price Is a low price a key buying criterion?

Value for money Is the achievement of a certain ratio of specification/price crucial?

User friendliness Is it important for the product to be user friendly?

Availability Is product range availability crucial?

Rapid response to enquiry Is it important to produce designs, quotations, etc., very quickly?

Quick response to customer demand Will sales be lost to the competition if they respond more quickly than you?

Achievement of advised delivery Is it important to stick to advised delivery dates?

Width of product range Is it important to offer a wide range of products and/or services to your customers?

New product to market time Is it important to minimize the product development time?

Quality—the product's fitness for purpose Does the product, or service, deliver exactly the benefits which the customers want?

Quality—the consistent achievement of defined specification Is constant conformation to specification vital?

Safety Is *safety in use* a major concern?

Regulatory requirements Does meeting regulatory requirements earlier/better than the competition give you an edge?

Provision of advanced specification or specialist service Are you the only people able to do what you do, and is this important to the customers?

Aesthetic attributes Is the appearance of the product, or the perception of the service, important?

Degree of innovation Is it important for the product or service to represent "state of the art"?

Ability to vary product specification Is it important for you to produce product or service modifications easily and quickly?

Ability to vary product volume Is it important for you to be able to increase, or decrease, production volume easily?

Customer service Is the quality of the overall service which customers receive a key to winning business?

Provision of after sales service Is the supply of spares, advice, etc., a key aspect of winning business?

etc.

---

enjoy property rights are usually not viewed as representing a key source of lasting advantage.

- *Reputation* is always identified as an important asset in the *Positional Resource* category, with *networks* being the next most frequently mentioned asset. It is appropriate to suggest that companies should strive to make employees the custodians and promoters of their employer's reputation—if employees do not hold the company in high regard why should anyone else? When employees hold their employer in high regard then it is probably also the case that the

TABLE 3.3 The Key Intangible Assets Related to the Key Product/Delivery System Attributes—Summary of Five Analyses

| Company | | Intangible assets | | | |
Company	Regulatory resources	Positional resources	Functional resources	Cultural resources
Manufacturing (Co. 11)	Patents. Trademarks.	Reputation. Supply chain configuration. Customer knowledge database.	Supply chain know-how. Product development expertise. Design for innovation know-how.	Organization's ability to: • manage change. • innovate. Perception of high quality standards. Tradition of customer service.
Services (Co. 12)	Contracts.	Reputation. Networks.	Sales and marketing know-how.	Organization's ability to: • manage change • innovate. Tradition of customer service. Team working; Perception of high quality.
Services (Co. 13)		Reputation. Networks.	Technological know-how. Project management. Sales and marketing. IT skills.	Perception of high quality. Enthusiasm. Tradition of customer service. Team working. Organization's ability to: • manage change • innovate.
Chemicals (Co. 14)	Contracts. Licences. Patents.	Reputation. Unique access to raw materials.	Technological know-how.	Organization's ability to: • manage change • innovate.
Transport (Co. 15)		Reputation. Location. Installed planning system. Networks.	Asset utilization. Technical/safety know-how. Training skills. Planning know-how.	Tradition of customer service.

company possesses a core ideology which employees can relate to—a situation reported by 92% of the long-term surviving companies surveyed.

- The key intangible assets identified under the *Functional Resource* category vary with the sector but are usually in either the Sales and Marketing and/or the Operations areas. This is not surprising as these functions are responsible for identifying what the customer wants and for the adding value process which results in the required benefit being delivered.

- The *Cultural Resource* category usually has a rich content and issues regarding the organization's ability to: *learn, manage change, manage innovation, perceive high quality standards* and to *possess a tradition of customer service* are the intangible assets which typically are identified; these are also the characteristics espoused by many of the CEOs of the long-lived companies which were surveyed.

The detailed results of the five analyses which are summarized in Table 3.3 are given in Appendix I.

DEVELOPING INTANGIBLE ASSETS

Having identified the key intangible assets which are producing current sales advantage, management needs to determine the degree to which it is possible to protect, sustain, leverage and enhance them:

With respect to protection	• Do all concerned recognize value of this intangible asset to the company? • Can the asset be protected by law?
With respect to sustainability	• How durable is the asset, will it decline with time? • How easily and quickly can others imitate the asset? —Can others easily "buy" the asset? —Can others easily "grow" the asset?
With respect to enhancement	• Is the "stock" of this asset increasing? • How can one ensure that the "stock" of this asset *continues* to increase?
With respect to leverage	• Is the best use being made of this asset? • How else could it be used?

It is then necessary to ascertain the gap (Sanchez and Heene, 1996) which exists between this portfolio and the portfolio which is needed to achieve competitive advantage. In order to establish whether the company has, or can achieve, a sustainable competitive advantage, as opposed to a sales advantage, it is necessary to carry out comparative analysis with respect to the competition. This analysis tries to determine the product/delivery system attributes which will win sales from the customers who comprise the desired market segment; it will then be possible to identify the *portfolio of intangible assets* which is needed to produce these attributes. The strategic task thereafter is to determine whether the protection, enhancement and leverage strategies identified earlier will adequately close the gap which has been identified; if not further analysis and planning will be necessary.

In the research carried out to date all analyses have listed *employee know-how* as one of the most important assets, indeed it is usually the case that there are many different categories of employee know-how which are identified as being major sources of competitive advantage. In considering the management of know-how it is appropriate to identify not only the *types* of knowledge, i.e. subject areas, which constitute competence but also the *nature* of the knowledge. This issue will be explored in the next section.

THE MANAGEMENT OF KNOW-HOW

Boisot (1995) has proposed a dynamic model of knowledge acquisition which allows a deeper understanding of the nature and management of know-how. He describes his model as "The Social Learning Cycle". The basic features of the model as presented at the Third International Workshop on Competence Based Competition (Ghent, Nov. 1995) are shown in Figure 3.2.

Boisot describes the characteristics of regions A, B, C and D as follows:

- *Region A* This *Personal Knowledge*, which is uncodified and undiffused, is held by individuals or small groups of people. It is described by other authors (Polanyi, 1948; Nonaka, 1994; Badaracco, 1991) as *Tacit*, or *Embedded, Knowledge*. This knowledge is characterized by causal ambiguity, it is acquired by observation and experience, e.g. the training of a Buddhist novice.
- *Region B* This *Proprietary (Explicit) Knowledge* is codified but undiffused. The codification, which has been produced in order to reduce its uniqueness and specificity also renders it liable to diffusion; it can leak away.

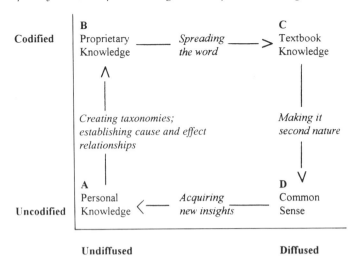

FIGURE 3.2   The Social Learning Cycle (Boisot, 1995)
Printed with kind permission of Elsevier Science

- *Region C*   This *Textbook Knowledge* is codified and diffused. It is the public knowledge which is the stuff of education.
- *Region D*   This skill (*Common Sense*) is diffused and uncodified, i.e. tacit. It is *Textbook Knowledge* become second nature, e.g. fluency in a language.

Boisot suggests that knowledge acquisition normally proceeds in an iterative cycle from "A" to "B" to "C" to "D" and back to "A". More limited cycles may be experienced when, for example, a profession limits the diffusion of its proprietary knowledge; the cycle is then restricted to regions "A" and "B".

Boisot's (1995) Learning Cycle model complements the technique for analysing intangible resources. The complementary nature of the two approaches may be illustrated as follows:

- A company's "stock" of *Personal*, or *Tacit, Knowledge* is related not only to its *Functional Capability* but also to its *Positional Capability* as this "stock" takes time to accumulate, it is difficult to communicate, and it cannot be bought.
- A company's "stock" of *Proprietary Knowledge* is closely related to its *Regulatory Capability* when that knowledge is protected by means of patents, copyright or trade secrets.
- A company's ability to diffuse internally its *Proprietary Knowledge* is closely related to its *Functional Capability*, i.e. its conventional learning capability.

● The translation of a company's *Textbook Knowledge* into *Skills* and then into new *Personal Knowledge* is closely related to its *Cultural Capability* ("The way we do things around here").

Given the close relationship between organizational learning and the issues of management style and corporate culture it is appropriate to acknowledge the impact which complexity theory has on our understanding of organizational dynamics.

A SYSTEMIC VIEW OF THE FIRM

The concept of the firm as a system is not new (Forrester, 1961; Sanchez and Heene, 1996); however there has been considerable interest recently in the application of complexity theory to organizational dynamics. Complexity theory is concerned with non-linear dynamic systems. In a linear system there is a straight line relationship between the independent and the dependent variables—10% more output results in 10% more bonus. In a non-linear system change is either accelerating due to positive feedback, or decelerating due to negative feedback. Many natural ecosystems possess both positive and negative feedback. When positive feedback is dominant, explosive population growth may result. When negative feedback dominates, stabilization results. When a small group of rats is introduced into a farmyard, positive feedback resulting in explosive growth will occur; at some point, however, the system begins to experience negative feedback as food becomes scarce and overcrowding occurs, eventually a state of bounded instability comes about when a degree of balance has been achieved. When circumstances change the potential for population explosion or implosion may occur. Complexity theory tells us that in some systems the potential for such catastrophic change may not only be as a result of external factors but may also be due to the characteristics of the system itself. Levy (1994) points out that:

> . . . chaotic systems do not reach a stable equilibrium; indeed, they can never pass through the same exact state more than once. If they did, they would cycle endlessly through the same path because they are driven by deterministic relationships. The implication is that industries do not "settle down" and any apparent stability, for example in pricing or investment patterns, is likely to be short lived.

Non-linear dynamic systems, with both positive and negative feedback, are both predictable and unpredictable—like the weather. We know that summer follows spring and that the average temperature in the summer is likely to be "x" degrees but we have little idea what the weather will be four days hence. The weather system is susceptible to what has become known as the *butterfly effect*. The metaphor of a butterfly taking flight in the Amazon causing a hurricane in Texas is used to suggest that in complex systems small, even minute, changes in inputs can cause huge changes in outcomes. The implication is clear—in complex dynamic systems it is not possible to establish cause and effect. It is not possible to determine which butterfly causes which hurricane! If apparently stable systems can experience spontaneous catastrophic change *and* if it is not possible to establish all cause and effect relationships then the future is unknowable. Stacey (1993) explains that if a firm is to innovate and change, it *must* operate in a state of bounded instability—somewhere between the explosive growth conditions when positive feedback dominates and ossification when negative feedback dominates. He goes on to claim that:

> . . . if a firm is operating in the border area between stability and instability, as it must if it is to innovate, then any decision-making process that involves forecasting, envisioning future states . . . will be ineffective. . . . We can apply the conventional wisdom on strategic management only if we do not want an organisation to innovate, or if we accept that it will die.

The characteristics of a state of bounded instability are influenced by a factor known as "the attractor". Covey (1994) suggests that discovering an attractor in an organization can show the commonality of purpose that is shared by individual members of the organization. He gives the example of a crowded ski slope where apparent chaos reigns as the different skiers all choose different routes to the bottom. While the skiing activity looks random, in fact the skiers do not collide and they all achieve their objectives of arriving at the bottom of the run—an attractor is at work. If a command and control system was introduced in order to guide each individual skier it would probably not work—the ski slope manager must give up control in order to achieve it! Covey (1994) suggests that in today's business environment managers may have to give up a degree of direct control of their organization in order to manage it.

The critical issue is what to control and what to let go. There *is* a role for a ski slope manager who will need to control the number of skiers allowed onto the run, etc. As those who have managed an empowerment initiative have learnt, the key to success is the achievement of a contract, be it implicit or explicit, with respect to who owns what.

By nature and training, managers are inclined to strive for stability and predictability. Typically they will do this by the operation of negative feedback. Negative feedback will counteract variances from a plan in the same way that a thermostat counteracts variances from the desired room temperature. Too much negative feedback in a human organization, however, will damp out the lead indicators of required change. The need to balance negative with positive feedback so that the genuine lead indicators of change are not damped out is "... the high tolerance to people and ideas, both from inside as well as outside the company ..." which de Geus (1995) observes in long-lived companies.

COMPLEX LEARNING

To have meaning and to be successful, an organization needs a sense of identity and purpose—a mindset, a dominant logic, a culture. This is often both its greatest strength and its greatest weakness. For reasons of self-esteem, possibly even sanity, we justify our past behaviour by looking for information which justifies it. Francis Bacon (1620) wrote:

> The human understanding when it has once adopted an opinion draws all things else to support and agree with it. And though there be a great number and weight of instances to be found on the other side, yet it either neglects and despises, or else by some distinction sets aside and rejects, in order that by this great and pernicious predetermination the authority of its former conclusion may remain inviolate.

We all have objectives and these objectives give our mental faculties the criteria by which information, or stimuli, is accepted. Tice (1980) explains that we all possess a reticular activating system which *filters in* stimuli which constitute a pay value, or a threat, and *filters out* those which do not. For example, a mother may sleep through the sounds of city night life but in all likelihood will wake when her baby in the next room cries—the city noises are not relevant to her, but the baby's cries are.

Prahalad and Bettis (1986) suggest that managers process organizational events through pre-existing knowledge systems, or schemas. They define schemas as beliefs, theories and propositions that have developed over time based on the manager's personal experiences. Our schemas are a product not only of our past experience but also of our objectives, because it is our objectives which influence the selection of the information which we accumulate.

It is counter-intuitive to be constantly on the look out for evidence which contradicts our beliefs; and yet that is what Karl Popper (1959) exhorts us to do in the pursuit of rigorous science. Popper suggested that the merit of a scientific theory is related to its ability to withstand our efforts to refute it—we test the assertion that all swans are white by looking, not for more and more white swans, but for one black one. In consequence, rational beings should search for information which refutes already held views, because it is only by virtue of the repeated triumph of theory through lack of contradictory evidence that the theory survives.

How do we feel about this approach if, for *theory*, we substitute *strategy*? In the received wisdom, strategy used to be about *fit*—the *fit* of resources with the environment; recently it has been conceptualized as being more about *vision*—the *vision* of the capabilities required to meet the opportunities to be created. The visionary leader is unlikely to welcome the constant testing of his vision by a *Popperian* disciple; such a disciple might find his behaviour was severely career limiting! On the contrary, everyday experience suggests that our preferred behaviour is closer to that described by Bacon, than to that suggested by Popper's logic—we do not enjoy *rocking the boat* or proclaiming that *the Emperor has no clothes* as such activities may destroy the cohesion of the group. However, notwithstanding our preference for accepting evidence which supports our current mindset and rejecting evidence which does not, we *are* capable of recognizing the need for fundamental change and practising what Argyris and Schon (1978) describe as double loop learning:

> Double loop learning occurs when error is detected and corrected in ways that involve the modifications of an organisation's underlying norms, policies and objectives.

Double loop learning is more fundamental than single loop learning. Argyris and Schon (1978) explain that single loop learning is similar to a simple feedback system, such as a thermostat; whereas double loop learning involves questioning whether one should begin measuring, say, humidity instead of temperature. They suggest that a double loop learning process will involve conflict between the groups who retain the *temperature mindset* and those who recognize the need for a *humidity mindset*. Change is more likely to occur if the humidity mindset group includes the senior management team because they control the resources which can be used to implement change, but it must frequently be the case that it is the junior (young) management team which possesses the double loop learning capability and not the senior (old) management team.

Senge (1990) describes two types of organizational learning: *adaptive*, or reactive, learning is about responding to the environment, while *generative* learning is about anticipating the future environment. Batchelor, Donnely and Morris (1995) relate adaptive learning to anxiety avoidance routines and generative learning to rewarding routines. The relationship between learning styles and management styles may be represented in terms of a spectrum as shown in Figure 3.3.

Management Style	*High Tolerance*		*Command and control*
Learning Style	*Generative*		*Adaptive*

FIGURE 3.3   Management Styles and Learning Styles

Stacey (1993) describes the extremes of the spectrum of management styles in terms of *Ordinary Management* and *Extraordinary Management*.

Ordinary Management
Ordinary Management is practised when most of the managers in an organisation share the same mental models or paradigm. Cognitive feedback loops then operate in a negative feedback manner so that shared mental models are not questioned. . . . Ordinary Management is about rational processes to secure harmony, fit, or convergence to a configuration, and it proceeds in an incremental manner.

Extraordinary Management
Extraordinary Management involves questioning and shattering paradigms, and then creating new ones. It is a process which depends critically upon contradiction and tension. . . . Extraordinary management, then, is the use of intuitive, political, group learning modes of decision making and self organising forms of control in open-ended change situations. It is the form of management that managers must use if they are to change strategic direction and innovate.

It would seem from this argument that, where change is required, confrontation and conflict are not only inevitable, they are desirable. The organization which is flexible and adaptive to the extent that it is able automatically to revise accepted norms is viewed as possessing the ultimate competitive capability; and yet when does this adaptability become inconsistency of purpose? Organizations need to *lock on* to objectives, and yet be able to *lock off* when the objectives become inappropriate—a key aspect of strategic management, or strategic leadership, is striking the right balance between consistency and inconsistency of purpose. Judgement is required in order to avoid initiating change too soon on the basis of weak evidence and to avoid leaving it too late for effective corrective action. This issue can be expressed alternatively in terms of the balance between positive and negative feedback. When negative feedback predominates, little change is tolerated; when positive feedback is not suppressed, change is encouraged. The traditional command and control style of management, with predominantly negative feedback, runs the risk of damping out the lead indicators of required change by suppressing positive feedback. Too much negative feedback results in ossification, too much positive feedback results in explosive change. The key is an appropriate balance.

Access to a population of long-term surviving British companies made it possible for the following proposition to be tested:

> *A command and control style of management, involving predominantly negative feedback, will not be conducive to long-term survival.*

The results of the survey of long-term surviving British companies is reported in the next section.

THE CHARACTERISTICS OF LONG-TERM SURVIVORS

The traditional measures of success are usually assumed to be profitability and growth—it is assumed that the attainment of these objectives will result in survival; however, some authors suggest that giving primacy to these objectives may diminish a company's chances of survival.

Meyer and Zucker (1989) have identified a paradoxical state of affairs:

> Whereas mortality tends to decline with age for broad classes of organisations—old organisations are *less* likely to die than are young ones—what little evidence there is suggests that performance does not improve correspondingly with age.

In other words, if a company is 100 years old it has a better chance of surviving to 101 than a 40-year-old company has of surviving to 41! de Geus (1995) suggests that prioritizing economic returns may not be conducive to long-term survival. He observes that companies which have survived for many years have the characteristics of ecosystems:

> Economic Companies strive for efficiency: going for maximum results with minimum resources. The minimisation of resources is easier with a management style based on strong internal controls. Management policies of low tolerance and strong hierarchical controls reduce the openness to the outside world and require a degree of influence over that world. Long term living systems survive through policies of high tolerance to people and ideas, both from inside as well from outside the company. They are better suited to life in a world which they do not control.

and he concludes that the "economic company" may be hard wired for a short life expectancy.

Much of the research into business success has been concerned with identifying the characteristics of companies which are currently successful—the *cross-sectional* perspective (Porter, 1991). Comparatively little work has been done to identify the nature and characteristics of companies which have survived for many years—the *longitudinal* perspective. This section reports a survey which has been carried out on 57 independent British companies which started trading prior to 1800. A list of 214 independent British companies which started trading prior to 1800 was obtained from Trends Business Research Ltd. Two questionnaire surveys were carried out.

THE STAGE ONE SURVEY

The first survey was addressed to the CEOs of the 214 members of the population, to which 57 replied. Details of the 57 respondents are shown in Table 3.4.

Caulkin (1995) has identified five major characteristics of long-lived companies. These assertions were tested in the survey and the results are shown in Table 3.5.

TABLE 3.4   Distribution of Old Companies Over Sectors and Current Sales Levels

Sector	No. in sample	Current sales	No. in sample
Services	2	0–£10m	32
Construction	6	£10–£50m	17
Manufacturing	24	£50m–£100m	3
Transport	2	>£100m	5
Trading	18		
Finance	5		
Total	57		57

TABLE 3.5   The Response to Caulkin's Five Assertions

	Tend to agree %
1. Profit is not necessarily the primary objective	61
2. The company has had a core ideology which employees can relate to	92
3. CEOs usually come from within the company	81
4. CEOs facilitate rather than direct	73
5. The company has been a "living" organization which can adapt and learn	94

These responses were further analysed by publicly quoted and private companies but there was no significant difference in the responses. The high percentages *tending to agree* provide broadly supporting evidence for the findings reported in the literature on corporate longevity.

THE STAGE TWO SURVEY

The Stage Two questionnaire was carried out in order to probe more specifically the issue of management style. The Stage Two survey approached the 57 Stage One respondents; 24 replied. From the three management styles shown below respondents were asked to choose the one which best summarized the style which had been practised over the life of the company.

- *Command and Control* style of management is practised when most of the managers in the organization share the same mental models; it is about rational processes aimed at securing stability and predictability—about being in control. (The "Ordinary Management" described by Stacey (1993).)
- *Evolutionary* style of management involving a high tolerance to people and ideas, both from inside as well as outside the company—people can assert that "The emperor has no clothes". (The "High Tolerance" style described by de Geus (1995).)
- *Revolutionary* style of management involving questioning and occasionally shattering mental models in order to create new ones, it is often a political process which may involve conflict and tension. (The "Extraordinary Management" described by Stacey (1993).)

The responses are summarized in Table 3.6.

TABLE 3.6   Summary of Management Styles Most Frequently Practised

Style of management	Percentage choosing
Command and control only	41
Evolutionary only	45
Revolutionary only	nil
All at different times	14
Total	100

Approximately 95% of the respondents were equally split between espousing "Command and Control" and "Evolutionary" styles of management. This discussion has suggested that companies which have had to adapt to changing circumstances over such a long period of time would be likely to espouse the "Evolutionary", or the "Revolutionary" style and that few would choose the "Command and Control" style. While the majority did choose the "Evolutionary" style, it is interesting that a significant number did choose the "Command and Control" style and very few chose the "Revolutionary" style of management. Further research is planned to explain these results.

CONCLUSION

The research into the portfolio of intangible assets which CEOs hold to be important suggests that they are: reputation, aspects of organizational culture and know-how. The following observations are appropriate:

- *Reputation* is an important intangible asset in the *Positional Resource Category*. It is a mental construct applicable to insiders as well as outsiders. In the case of insiders the high regard in which they hold their organization will be associated with the core ideology which they relate to. This regard, this pride, this esprit de corps will be evident to outsiders and it will enhance the reputation of the organization in their eyes.
- *Aspects of Organizational Culture*: a perception of high quality standards, high levels of customer service, together with an organizational ability to manage change and to manage innovation, were nearly always identified as important aspects of culture.
- *Know-how*: the effective management of know-how requires the recognition of the fact that know-how has two dimensions. The first dimension is to do with the nature of the know-how—design, production engineering, etc. The second dimension is to do with the composition of the know-how in terms of tacit knowledge, explicit knowledge, and skills (cf. Sanchez, 1996).

The literature which has been surveyed in this chapter suggests that the styles of organizational learning and management which will enhance the chances of survival in turbulent environments are generative and tolerant. The literature does not suggest that long-term surviving companies will have practised a command and control style of management. Half of the old companies surveyed *do* claim to have practised a command and control style of management. The validity of this finding may be questioned on a variety of issues, not the least of which is the ability of the current generation of managers accurately to assess the management style which had been practised in their companies over a period in excess of 200 years, although the respondents were offered the option of not answering this question if they thought it inappropriate to do so. It can also be argued that the Stage Two respondents reporting a command and control style are somewhat at odds with the 94% of the Stage One respondents reporting that their company has been a living organization which can adapt and learn. Clearly more work is needed to obtain a better understanding of this issue, and further research is planned with a much larger number of British companies which started trading in the nineteenth century.

Notwithstanding these concerns, the question regarding the balance of positive with negative feedback is valid and fundamental. More work is necessary with respect to the degree to which complex non-linear dynamic systems with suppressed positive feedback can be effective over long periods of time while operating in turbulent environments. A degree of order *is* necessary in human affairs, but the question is "How best to achieve it?" Order may be achieved in complex non-linear dynamic systems either by the operation of a strange attractor, such as a moral code, or by the suppression of positive feedback, or both. What it would be interesting to understand better is the extent to which fundamental innovations, even paradigm shifts, are possible when negative feedback dominates.

REFERENCES

Argyris, C. and D. A. Schon, (1978). *Organisational Learning: A Theory of Action Perspective*, Reading, MA: Addison-Wesley Publishing Company Inc.

Bacon, F. (1620). *The New Organon and Related Writing*.

Badaracco, J. L. (1991). *The Knowledge Link*, Boston, MA: Harvard Business School Press.

Batchelor, J., T. Donnely and D. Morris (1995). "Learning networks within supply chains", a paper presented at the 4th International Purchasing and Supply Education and Research Association Conference, Birmingham, April 1995.

Boisot, M. (1995). "Is your firm a creative destroyer? Competitive learning and knowledge flows in the technological strategies of firms", *Research Policy*, **24**, Amsterdam, Elsevier Science BV, pp. 489–506. Figure 3.2 printed with the kind permission of Elsevier Science - NL, Sara Burgerhartstraat 25, 1055 KV Amsterdam, The Netherlands.

Caulkin, S. (1995). "The pursuit of immortality", *Management Today*, May 1995, pp. 36–40, Management Publications Ltd.

Covey, S. R. (1994). "The strange attractor", *Executive Excellence*, August 1994, pp. 5–6.

de Geus (1995). "Organisational principles of long term corporate survivors", Proceedings of Santa Fe Institute Conference on Complexity and Strategy, London, May 15–17, 1995.

Forrester, J. W. (1961). *Industrial Dynamics*, Portland, Oregon: Productivity Press.

Hall, R. (1994). "A framework for identifying the intangible sources of sustainable competitive advantage", pp. 140–169, in *Competence-Based Competition*, Gary Hamel and Aimé Heene, editors, Chichester: John Wiley & Sons.

Levy, D. (1994). "Chaos theory and strategy: Theory, application, and managerial implications", *Strategic Management Journal*, Vol. 15 (Special Issue), pp. 167–178.

Meyer, M. W. and L. G. Zucker (1989). *Permanently Failing Organisations*, London: Sage Publications.

Nonaka, I. (1994). "A dynamic theory of organisational knowledge creation", *Organisation Science*, Vol. 5, No. 1, pp. 14–37.

Polanyi, M. (1948). *Personal Knowledge: Towards a Post-Critical Philosophy*, Chicago: University of Chicago Press.

Popper, K. (1959). *The Logic of Scientific Discovery*, Hutchison.

Porter, M. E. (1991) "Towards a dynamic theory of strategy", *Strategic Management Journal*, Vol. 12, pp. 95–117.

Prahalad, C. K. and R. A. Bettis (1986). "The dominant logic: A new linkage between diversity and performance", *Strategic Management Journal*, Vol. 7, pp. 485–501.

Prahalad, C. K. and G. Hamel (1990). "The core competence of the corporation", *Harvard Business Review*, May–June 1990.

Sanchez, Ron (1996). "Managing articulated knowledge in competence-based competition," in R. Sanchez and A. Heene, editors, *Strategic Learning and Knowledge Management*, Chichester: John Wiley & Sons.

Sanchez, Ron, and Aimé Heene (1996). "A systems view of the firm in competence-based competition," in R. Sanchez, A. Heene, and H. Thomas, editors, *Dynamics of Competence-based Competition: Theory and Practice in the New Strategic Management*, Oxford: Elsevier Pergamon.

Sanchez, R., A. Heene and H. Thomas (1996) *Dynamics of Competence-Based Competition: Theory and Practice in the New Strategic Management*, Oxford: Elsevier.

Senge, P. M. (1990). "The leader's new work: building learning organisations", *Sloan Management Review*, Fall, pp. 7–23.

Stacey, R. D. (1993). *Strategic Management and Organisational Dynamics*, Pitman Publishing.

Tice, L. (1980). *New Age Thinking*. Seattle: The Pacific Institute.

Trends Business Research Ltd., St Thomas St Business Centre, St Thomas St, Newcastle upon Tyne, UK, NE1 4LE.

APPENDIX I

THE KEY INTANGIBLE ASSETS RELATED TO THE KEY PRODUCT/DELIVERY SYSTEM ATTRIBUTES

Company No. 11—Manufacturing consumer products

Product/delivery system attributes →	%	Regulatory	Positional	Functional	Cultural
Availability	30		rorecasting and planning systems.	Supply chain know-how. Forecasting and planning know-how.	Organization's ability to manage change.
Image/brand	19	Patents. Registered trademarks.	Company reputation. Product reputation.		Perceptions of high quality standards.
Value for £	18		Configuration of supply chain.	Product development expertise.	Organization's ability to manage change.
Customer service	15		Systems for customer service.		Tradition of customer service.
Innovation	11	Patents.	Customer knowledge database.	Design for innovation know-how.	Organization's ability to innovate.
Width of range	$\frac{7}{100}$		Configuration of supply chain.	All above know-how. Sell in skills.	
Key intangible assets →		Patents. Trademarks.	Reputation. Supply chain configuration. Customer knowledge database.	Supply chain know-how. Product development expertise. Design for innovation know-how.	Organization's ability to: • manage change • innovate. Perception of high quality standards. Tradition of customer service.

61

Company No. 12—Services

Key product attributes	%	Intangible assets			
		Regulatory resources	Positional resources	Functional resources	Cultural resources
Customer service	30	Contracts.	Reputation.	Sales and marketing know-how.	Organization's ability to manage change. Tradition of customer service.
Value for money	20			Sales and marketing know-how.	Perception of quality. Tradition of customer service.
Width of product range	20		Networks.	Sales and marketing know-how.	Organization's ability to innovate. Team working.
Products fitness for purpose	20		Reputation.	Sales and marketing know-how. Suppliers' know-how.	
Ability to vary specifications	$\frac{10}{100}$			Understanding customer needs.	Tradition of customer service.
The key intangible assets →		Contracts.	Reputation, Networks.	Sales and marketing know-how.	Organization's ability to: • manage change • innovate. Tradition of customer service. Team working. Perception of quality.

Company No. 13—Services

Key product attributes	%	Intangible assets			
		Regulatory resources	Positional resources	Functional resources	Cultural resources
Provision of advanced spec.	20		Reputation.	Technological know-how.	Perception of high quality standards.
Degree of innovation	20		Networks with universities.	Client management.	Organization's ability to innovate. Enthusiasm.
Achievement of advised delivery	20		Networks.	Project management.	Tradition of customer service.
Availablity	15		Networks.	Sales and marketing skills.	Team working. Organization's ability to manage change
Rapid response to enquiry	15			IT skills.	Enthusiasm. Traditions of customer service
Working with customers on a "win–win" basis	$\frac{10}{100}$			Technological know-how.	Perceptions of high quality standards. Team working.
The key intangible assets	→		Reputation. Networks.	Technological know-how. Project management. Sales and marketing. IT skills.	Perceptions of high quality. Enthusiasm. Tradition of customer service. Team working. Organization's ability to manage change, innovate.

Company No. 14—Chemicals

	Intangible assets			
	Regulatory resources	Positional resources	Functional resources	Cultural resources
Key product attributes →				
Quality	Contracts. Licences.	Reputation. Unique access to raw materials.	Technological know-how.	Organization's ability to: ● change ● innovate.
Technical back-up	Patents.		Technological know-how.	Organization's ability to: ● change ● innovate.
The key intangible assets →	Contracts. Licences. Patents.	Reputation Unique access to raw materials.	Technological know-how.	Organization's ability to: ● change ● innovate.

Company No. 15—Transport

Key product attributes →	Intangible assets			
	Regulatory resources	Positional resources	Functional resources	Cultural resources
Customer service		Reputation. Installed planning system.	Planning know-how.	Tradition of customer service.
Price		Location.	Ability to operate with minimum overheads. Asset utilization skills.	
Safety			Technical/safety know-how. Training skills.	
Complying with regulations		Networks with trade associations.	Training skills.	
Quick response to customer demand		Installed planning system.	Planning know-how.	
The key intangible assets →		Reputation. Location. Installed planning system. Networks.	Ability to operate with minimum overheads. Asset utilization. Technical/safety know-how. Training skills. Planning know-how.	Tradition of customer service.

4

The Dilemma of Competence: Differentiation versus Integration in the Pursuit of Learning

MAX BOISOT, DOROTHY GRIFFITHS, VERONICA MOLES

Since the publication of Prahalad and Hamel's *Harvard Business Review* article "The core competence of the corporation" (1990), the concept of core competence has attracted a great deal of attention (Hamel and Heene, 1994; Sanchez, Heene and Thomas, 1996). It remains, however, more discussed than understood. The paper, using the Culture Space or C-Space (Boisot, 1986, 1987, 1994) as a conceptual tool, offers an information-based interpretation of the term. The C-space allows a unified representation of a firm's organizational, cultural, and technological processes, taking them to be—each in its own way—expressions of the way that socially relevant knowledge gets structured within and between firms. The evolution of a core competence over time is modelled in the C-Space, and drawing on the authors' current research in a large British firm, a *paradox of value*—whereby the more efficiently value is extracted from a competence the more rapidly the latter escapes the firm's control—will be identified and discussed. The paper concludes by discussing how firms might deal with

---

Strategic Learning and Knowledge Management.
Edited by Ron Sanchez and Aimé Heene.
Copyright © 1997 John Wiley & Sons Ltd.

the paradox of value and by discussing the implication of these for the management of technological and knowledge assets.

1 INTRODUCTION

In an increasing number of markets, particularly those characterized by global competition, being second ranked is no longer an option (Porter, 1985). Unless a firm can position itself among the best-in-class it had best not try to compete at all. Yet to achieve outstanding performance a firm has first to know what it is good at doing and second to understand how to stay good at doing it. In short, the firm has to know what its *core competences* are. The term, first popularized by Prahalad and Hamel in a *Harvard Business Review* article (Prahalad and Hamel, 1990), heralds a revival of what has come to be known as the resource-based view of the firm (Wernerfelt, 1984), a perspective that goes back to the work of Selznick (1957), and that was eclipsed for nearly three decades by the so-called positioning view of the firm—the assumption that corporate strategy is a response to an external correlation of forces objectively given (Ansoff, 1965; Porter, 1980). Yet, as Prahalad and Hamel themselves have pointed out (1990, 1994), the two perspectives are in fact complementary: a firm's strategic environment can be shaped by a judicious deployment of its internal resources and vice versa.

As used by Prahalad and Hamel, the term "core competence" refers to an organizationally embedded knowledge asset that can deliver differential value through a functionality that a customer is willing to pay for and that competitors find hard or impossible to imitate. The emphasis in this definition, on the securing of a differential competitive advantage, justifies the adjectival use of the term "core" to describe the competence that achieves this. This emphasis is complemented by a more generic use of the term "competence" by Sanchez, Heene and Thomas (1996) in which coordination and goal identification and attainment are also emphasized. In what follows we try to develop insights into the notion of "core" competence.

If we take the meaning of the term "value" developed by Walras (1926), a core competence must achieve both *utility* and *scarcity*, that is to say, it must deliver something that is experienced by a user as being simultaneously useful and difficult to acquire from alternative sources. Many theoreticians and practitioners find it convenient to think of such a competence as a system of interrelated technologies—these may or may not be proprietary—which are integrated organizationally in ways that are specific to a firm and that deliver a tangible customer benefit (Sanchez, Heene and Thomas, 1996).

Unlike physical assets which depreciate in value over time as they are used up, core competences, being based on knowledge assets, appreciate with repeated use as a result of a learning process. To the extent that such knowledge is tacit, it cannot easily be bought (or, for that matter, sold); it must therefore accumulate within the organization in which it will be exploited (Dierickx and Cool, 1989). The organization need not be a firm as such. In certain cases it can incorporate suppliers and customers within its boundaries. It is by no means clear, however, that just because continuous practice in the use of a competence delivers ever more re-fined performance, it necessarily enhances perceived customer benefits proportionately. Quite plausibly, and as is demonstrably the case with the technologies that it incorporates (Foster, 1987), a competence will be subject to increasing returns up to some given level of performance and to decreasing returns thereafter. Furthermore, as a core competence deepens with use, it can also come to acquire a certain inertia within an organization and, over time, become a trap that effectively blocks subse-quent adaptation to new opportunities or competitive threats (Utterback, 1994; March, 1991; Leonard-Barton, 1992).

In sum, a core competence is something of a double-edged sword: neglect it and you forgo an important source of competitive advantage; hold on to it for too long and you incur a strategic opportunity cost. Understanding how a competence evolves over time as a firm-specific knowledge asset, and knowing up to what point to invest in it and when to let go of it—Sanchez, Heene and Thomas (1996) frame the issue in terms of competence building and competence leveraging—thus both become an important part of managing competences. This dynamic aspect of com-petence management is only just now receiving the attention it deserves.

In this chapter, we briefly explore the issue by means of a conceptual framework—the Culture Space or C-Space—developed by Boisot (1986, 1994) to analyse knowledge flows within and between organizations. The framework takes it as a basic premise that the way that knowledge is structured and shared between data processing agents is a cultural phe-nomenon (Boisot, 1982, 1983, 1986; Nonaka and Takeuchi, 1995). In the next section we briefly outline the framework and use it to identify a paradox of value that firms encounter when seeking to exploit their knowledge assets. In Section 3, we apply the framework to an analysis of how the paradox of value affects the evolution of core competences. In Section 4, we present and discuss a short case that illustrates the paradox of value at work. A conclusion follows in Section 5.

2 THE C-SPACE

The C-Space relates the extent to which knowledge can be diffused to its degree of codification (see Figure 4.1). Codification describes how far an item of knowledge can be articulated and compressed into codes. Some knowledge may remain tacit or unarticulated; some can be presented in image or iconic form; some can be reduced to text; some can even be quantified. Tacit or uncodified knowledge can usually only be transmitted slowly in face-to-face situations and often only to a limited audience under conditions of trust and shared experiences (region A in Figure 4.1). Codified knowledge, by contrast, can be transmitted much more rapidly and impersonally to large audiences. It is the kind of knowledge which can be standardized and from which uncertainty and ambiguity have been largely expunged thus allowing its unproblematic transmission over large distances to total strangers (region C in Figure 4.1). The transmission of knowledge, which is intentional, facilitates its diffusion, which may or may not be intentional.

The need to communicate clearly and quickly to large audiences across space and time creates a pressure to codify what might otherwise remain tacit knowledge (Sanchez, 1996, in this volume). Yet the act of codification leaves behind some tacit knowledge with the transmitter who always knows more than she can ever say (Polanyi, 1958). An act of communication is therefore always, in some fundamental sense, incomplete (Boisot, 1995). In spite of the data losses incurred by the process, new knowledge emerges from a cyclical flow of information in the C-space. Figure 4.2 describes such flows as a Social Learning Cycle (SLC) that can be subdivided into four distinct phases: (1) scanning; (2) problem-solving; (3) diffusion; (4) absorption. The characteristics of each phase are given in Table 4.1.

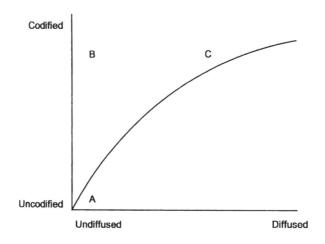

FIGURE 4.1   The C-Space

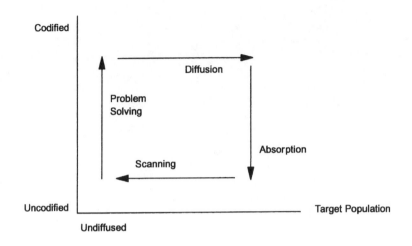

FIGURE 4.2   The Social Learning Cycle

TABLE 4.1   The Four Phases of a Social Learning Cycle Description

---

1. *Scanning*
Identifying threats and opportunities in generally available but often fuzzy data—
i.e. weak signals. Scanning patterns such data into unique or idiosyncratic insights
that then become the possession of individuals or small groups. Scanning may be
very rapid when the data is well codified and abstract and very slow and random
when the data is uncodified and context specific.

2. *Problem Solving*
The process of giving structure and coherence to such insights—i.e. codifying them.
In this phase they are given a definite shape and much of the uncertainty initially
associated with them is eliminated. Problem solving initiated in the uncodified
region of the I-Space is often both risky and conflict laden.

3. *Diffusion*
Sharing the newly created insights with a target population. The diffusion of well-
codified and abstract data to a large population will be technically less problematic
than that of data which is uncodified and context specific. Only a sharing of context
by sender and receiver can speed up the diffusion of uncodified data; the
probability of achieving a shared context is inversely proportional to population
size.

4. *Absorption*
Applying the new codified insights to different situations in a "learning-by-doing"
or a "learning-by-using" fashion. Over time, such codified insights come to acquire
a penumbra of uncodified knowledge which helps to guide their application in
particular circumstances. Where newly acquired uncodified knowledge clashes
with already extant implicit models, a new round of scanning activity may be
initiated in order to eliminate the discrepancy.

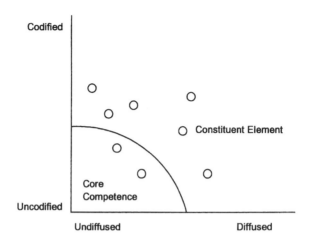

FIGURE 4.3   A Core Competence and its Constituent Elements in the C-Space

A competence can be represented in the C-Space as an interrelated set of processes or technologies that are systematically managed and integrated in such a way as to yield a higher level of performance than competitors might achieve with the same means (Sanchez and Heene, 1996). Arguably, and as has already been hinted at, insofar as tacit knowledge and organizational processes are involved, a core competence would appear in the C-Space as less codified and diffused than its constituent elements (Figure 4.3).

In the C-Space the tacit components of a core competence, being uncodified and hard to diffuse, will be grouped together in the region labelled A in Figure 4.1. Maximum value, however, can only be achieved in region B, the one in which the utility of the knowledge underpinning the competence has been maximized through a process of debugging, testing, and standardization, and in which, being as yet undiffused, such knowledge retains a maximum scarcity. The tacit components of a core competence can then be thought of as constituting a launching pad located in region A for the delivery of useful information embedded in goods and services into region B. As these rise towards B, however, they encounter a *paradox of value* since information goods located in region B, being much more codified than those in region A, are subject to strong diffusion pressures. For a start, information goods, when articulated, are as likely to be embedded in documents or in physical objects as in the heads of individuals. Documents, though, can be read and physical objects reverse engineered. Second, those institutional devices designed to act as barriers to diffusion—patents, copyrights, etc.—often turn out to act as a stimulus to it. Patents, for example, by demonstrating technical feasibility, reduce search costs and invite circumvention. Finally, when knowledge is radically new, much of it must of necessity be diffused in order to reduce the perceived risk of adopting the goods that incorporate it. Region B, then, is the least stable region of the C-Space and for that reason it is one that is costly to occupy for any length of time. The issue thus becomes one of costs versus benefits: given the costs of residing in region B, does one gain more by hoarding the knowledge embedded in the goods or services reaching B from A or by sharing it with potential adopters (Boisot, 1995)?

The answer to the question will partly depend on the population that one is diffusing one's knowledge to. Figure 4.1 leaves the issue open so that in each case one must specify what is the diffusion population. If one chose to place all the firm's employees along the horizontal scale in the diagram, for example, then the preferred strategy might well be one of sharing knowledge. If, however, all the firms in an industry were to be placed along the scale, then hoarding one's knowledge may seem the better bet. It is thus quite conceivable that one would wish to share one's knowledge with respect to one diffusion population yet to hoard it with respect to another (cf. Sanchez, 1996, in this volume).

3   CORE COMPETENCE AND THE PARADOX OF VALUE

The paradox of value that we have just described is unique to information goods. It arises because, in contrast to physical goods, information goods are virtually costless to reproduce. Put more graphically, it is possible to photocopy the chemical formula for benzene, but not to photocopy an oil field. The proposition of this chapter is that core competences themselves, like the technologies and the products that they spawn, tend over time to follow the trajectory from A to B in the C-Space. Therefore they also confront the paradox of value. How so?

The ownership of knowledge at point A is highly ambiguous. Being tacit, such knowledge is located in individual heads and is either the personal possession of single employees or the collective possession of teams (Alchian and Demsetz, 1972). Either the individual or the team can walk out of the door thus depriving an employer of an important cognitive resource. Instinctively, therefore, firms attempt to have such knowledge codified and embedded into documents or explicit procedures in order to forestall opportunistic behaviour by their employees. It is, in effect, only through some form of codification that a firm can credibly take possession of such knowledge.

Yet, once codified, the knowledge embedded in a core competence loses much of its earlier flexibility. The reason for this is that all acts of codification involve a selection among alternative possibilities, and thus it is in the nature of codification to eliminate options. The choice of alternative *a*, for example, implies the rejection of alternatives *b, c, d, . . . z*. Proficiency attained along selected performance dimensions is thus paid for by the neglect of others so that by degrees a competence acquires a certain inertia. The result is a bias in the firm's way of adapting to new situations (cf. Wright 1996, in this volume). At the same time the very process of codifying the constituent elements of a core competence makes them more diffusion prone, thus eroding the scarcity value of the competence for a firm. The competence, if acquired by others, then gradually becomes an industry recipe (Spender, 1989) if what is codified is embedded in organizational routines, or a technology if what is codified is embedded in physical processes. Either way, the firm, out of sheer force of habit—and the learning-by-doing associated with the absorption of codes will further reinforce such habits—finds itself holding on to what may well have become depreciating knowledge assets while believing that, as the result of its increasing organizational or technological mastery, the assets are appreciating.

We believe that the above describes a pervasive dynamic. Organizations are designed to reduce uncertainty. They achieve uncertainty reduction by making their operations more predictable and by moving them up the C-Space. Informal ways of doing things, over time, get formalized, and habits gradually give way to explicit rules and routines. Family firms and high tech start-ups may originate as small, highly personalized, fief-like organizations in region A of the C-Space, but as they grow in size, internal coordination needs and external competitive pressures inevitably push them towards the more impersonal bureaucratic style characteristic of region B. Formalization offers considerable advantages to the growing firm, for, as the Aston studies of the 1960s showed, it holds the key to the effective decentralization of an ever larger volume of transactions—i.e. the codification of transactionally relevant information facilitates its diffusion to a larger population of organizational players (Pugh *et al.*, 1969). With further growth, more decentralization becomes necessary so that, beyond a certain size, organizations switch to a multidivisional format and introduce internal markets for the governance of critical transactions (Chandler, 1962). Where decentralization is attempted without first codifying organizational procedures, its reach is more modest. Typically, and in the absence of constant efforts at socialization (an important caveat), a limited number of players end up sharing transactionally relevant knowledge—and the power that goes with it—in what we might call a clan form of governance (Ouchi, 1980).

The technologies that firms deploy, being information goods, are subject to the same logic of uncertainty reduction as the organizations that operate them, and, we argue, so are the firm's core competences. Our hypothesis is that *the organizational quest for uncertainty reduction, in the long run, is destructive of core competence because the paradox of value will ensure that any gain in utility achieved by codification is paid for with a value-eroding loss of scarcity.* In most cases, however, the codification imperative is probably too strong for a firm to resist so that a move up the C-Space sooner or later becomes inevitable. This is so even if the learning-by-doing associated with the absorption phase of the SLC appears to bring one once more down the Space. For the most part, learning-by-doing is an unconscious internalization of *existing* codes that further entrenches them in the upper reaches of the SLC. It is only when "doing" encounters anomalies beyond the capacities of currently used codes that "learning" becomes habit- and code-breaking. If learning is to occur sooner, then the core competence has to be replaced, and this must occur in region A through the action of the SLC. If it is to be later, then the SLC itself has to be slowed down in its trajectory up the C-Space from A to B. Either way, the appropriate orientation for managing a core competence—as distinct from a technology or a simple organizational procedure—is not so much uncertainty *reduction* as uncertainty *absorption.* Far from always trying to escape from the lower region of the C-Space, a strategy of uncertainty absorption explicitly requires a firm to develop some organizational capacity in that region. Such capacity has a value, a cognitive and an institutional component.

The Value Component calls for the fostering of a culture of trust based on a socialization to shared values rather than one based on distrust and external controls. In the uncodified region of the C-Space, incomplete, asymmetrical, and ambiguous information greatly increases the cost of monitoring while increasing the scope for opportunistic behaviour (Williamson, 1985). The lower the degree of congruence between the goals of the firm and those of employees, the greater the likelihood that one of the contracting parties will engage in opportunistic behaviour. Achieving goal congruence is a matter of selection, motivation, and socialization.

The Cognitive Component requires organizational actors explicitly to recognize the difference between risk and uncertainty in the firm's processes and to view the latter as much as a source of opportunities as of threats (Sanchez, 1993). In contrast to risk, uncertainty cannot easily be quantified, for the runderlying probability distributions are often either flat or unknown (Granger Morgan and Henrion, 1990; Knight, 1965). If, however, the range over which such distributions might occur is known and they are either symmetrical or positively weighted with respect to favourable and unfavourable outcomes, then uncertainty can be given a more positive valuation than it tends to be accorded by decision makers (Tversky and Kahneman, 1974): as option theory has demonstrated, at the very least, it can be tolerated—i.e. absorbed—rather than fled (Dixit and Pindyck, 1994; Sanchez, 1993).

The Institutional Component is a source of delicate problems. The tacit knowledge associated with the lower regions of the C-Space and with core competences, poses difficult issues of property rights. Firms routinely claim ownership of their employees' tacit knowledge when they feel that they have contributed to its creation. Yet ownership is not possession, and possession—ownership claims made by the firm notwithstanding—may well remain with an employee when she or he leaves the firm. The firm can deal with the issue in one of two ways: it can either seek to extract tacit knowledge from the employee prior to departure while asking for a commitment to secrecy thereafter, or it can create incentives for the employee to stay. The first course will inevitably lead to some form of codification of the employee's tacit knowledge and hence to an upward move away from the lower region of the C-Space; the second course will lead to a redistribution of bargaining power between the firm and its more knowledgeable employees.

Operating in the lower regions of the C-Space is not free of problems, especially for large firms. If formalizing organizational procedures facilitates decentralization and more effective managerial coordination in the large firm, then keeping them informal makes decentralization and firm-wide coordination that much more difficult. Breaking a firm up into smaller units in which face-to-face relationships can be maintained—the approach adopted by some technology-driven firms like Hewlett-Packard and ABB—helps to bring about intra-unit integration but often at the expense of inter-unit coordination.

Hamel and Prahalad (1994), framing the issue in terms of core competences, see a need to strike a balance between the claims of differentiation—an SBU's need for focus and operational autonomy—and those of integration—the centre's responsibility in fostering corporate-wide competences. Yet research that we are currently conducting in a large British firm—Courtaulds Plc—suggests that "striking a balance" between the centrifugal claims of SBUs and the centripetal claims of the head office is a particularly difficult trick to pull off. It seems to involve something other than merely finding a stable midpoint up the codification scale that the parties are prepared to live with (Boisot *et al.*, 1995). In the next section we address the issue by presenting and discussing a brief case study of Courtaulds' earlier development of viscose and its more recent development of a new cellulosic fibre (NCF).

4 CASE STUDY: NEW CELLULOSIC FIBRES AT COURTAULDS

Courtaulds had been a considerable manufacturer of crepe throughout the greater part of the nineteenth century. As the market for crepe declined, the firm turned to the manufacture of artificial silk by the viscose process. Viscose found a wide range of applications and enjoyed a dramatic expansion from the 1920s onwards. As a result Courtaulds was gradually transformed from a textile to a chemical firm. But with the expiry of patents and the worldwide disseminating of the basic technologies associated with viscose, Courtaulds' sales began to flatten out in the 1940s.

Many of Courtaulds' products have been developed by the firm only after the initial inventions that underpin them have been made elsewhere. In the absence of basic chemical research, technical achievements are brought about by the close alignment of the company's research policy with the demands both of the textile markets and of the firm's production processes; this allows continuous practical advances which combine quality and product improvements with lower costs. It also allows repositioning in new but similar markets. Yet, in the case of viscose, by 1950 the firm was lagging behind the US and Europe in its technical development. It had become increasingly apparent that viscose textile yarn, which had made Courtaulds big money in the past, had had its day and that in the near future a replacement would be needed. In the early 1970s, accordingly, Courtaulds began searching for a safer and more environmentally friendly technology based on cellulose to replace the viscose process.

In the 1970s, Research and Technology (R and T) at Courtaulds was organized along university lines and characterized by a certain informality. Funding was not as narrowly controlled as it has become since and there was sometimes enough in the budget to indulge in a bit of exploratory research. In the 1980s, on his retirement, the firm recruited Akzo's technical director. With his help, pilot plant work was undertaken the objectives of which were to develop fibre spinning and solvent recovery operations. It was fibre spinning technology and cellulose technology expertise that led to the development of Courtaulds' New Cellulosic Fibre (NCF), the world's first commercial solvent spun fibre. The NCF was quickly recognized as a potentially valuable new product in its own right and, in 1983, in order to develop and commercialize it, it was set up as a new and independent business within Courtaulds. In the course of the NCF's development, it gradually became clear that the firm was not only dealing with a complicant process technology that could replace the viscose process, but with a new product technology offering new product properties. In a paper to the board, David Giachardi, the board member responsible for R and T, also mentioned that in addition to its novel properties, the NCF offered a strong potential for cost savings. There was a clear feeling that the NCF might turn out to be a radically new fibre for which there would be a strong demand.

The ability to create a NCF was based on an underlying firm-specific competence in spinning technologies. It was this competence that allowed the firm to recognize the new material for what it was. Courtaulds has been involved in three types of spinning: liquid spinning, melt spinning, and air-gap spinning. It was because Courtaulds had mastered a *repertoire* of spinning processes that it was in a position to devise the kind of spinning required by the NCF. Interestingly, many of the technologies finally developed for the NCF production processes were originally drawn from *failed* experiments and development projects carried out within the firm for other purposes. They were thus present and available in the organization's memory and in its technology repertoire.

The research is not yet sufficiently advanced to yield unambiguous evidence that the firm's development skills in fibres meets all the criteria for possession of a competence that could be classified as "core". It does, however, offer promising leads. Both with viscose in the early years of the century and then later, with the NCF, we see the company trying to identify and explore the range of fibre properties on offer while at the same time securing efficiency gains from scaling up and standardizing the relevant process technologies. It is clear that a healthy tension exists inside the firm between the need to explore new value-adding fibre properties and the need to exploit economies of scale in order to reduce costs. March (1991) distinguishes between exploratory and exploitative forms of learning, two processes that have some overlap with what, in an organizational context, Sanchez, Heene and Thomas (1996) refer to as competence building and competence leveraging. March claims that balancing them out constitutes a key organizational skill. Attempts to achieve such a balancing out is visible in the product development process at Courtaulds. Exploratory learning is located in the lower regions of the C-Space; it corresponds to the *absorption* and *scanning* phases of an SLC. Exploitative learning, by contrast, amounts to a move up and across the C-Space towards the right; it corresponds to the *problem-solving* and *diffusion* phases of an SLC. Whether these two forms of learning impose incompatible performance requirements or complementary ones depends on what the firm is trying to achieve. If time to market is the predominant consideration, for example, then exploratory learning may well be sacrificed to the needs of rapid exploitation. If, however, identifying markets and understanding their specific product needs before expanding into them is important, then exploitative learning can often create the necessary organizational slack within which exploration can occur. In this second case, exploration and exploitation will work in tandem.

From this second perspective it can be hypothesized that a core competence in fibre development requires an ongoing ability to strike a balance in the SLC between investments respectively oriented towards absorption and scanning (exploratory learning) on the one hand, and problem-solving and diffusion (exploitative learning) on the other. Too much emphasis on exploration and nothing solid is ever created that a firm can durably build on, but too much emphasis on exploitation and the core competence quickly reduces to well-codified chemical engineering processes—i.e. it becomes itself a technology. In balancing out the competing claims of exploration and exploitation, one is in effect involved in managing what Hampden-Turner (1990) calls a *dilemma*—seemingly incompatible choices that have to be reconciled. Dilemmas are further discussed in the concluding section.

Is this balancing trick, when applied to fibres, likely to be specific to Courtaulds—a critical requirement if it is to be accepted as a *core* competence—or might it be imitated by others? Again, the evidence is still inconclusive. At the turn of the century, following a successful development process, the firm went on to achieve market dominance in viscose. Yet by the fourth decade of the century, its competitive position had become severely eroded. The scope for developing new properties— i.e. for exploratory learning—was then exhausted, and efficiency gains from exploitation were rapidly transformed into a common possession of the industry leaders. Such a development is certainly consistent with the idea that as segments of the firm's knowledge base moves up the C-Space towards greater codification, so they tend to diffuse more rapidly to the rest of the industry. In the case of the NCF, however, Courtaulds only faces one major competitor at present. If this competitor perceives the NCF essentially as an environmentally friendly substitute for viscose, one could argue that Courtaulds may be the only one currently undertaking the kind of exploratory learning required to expand the fibre's envelope of value-adding properties. Such exploration, as already indicated, can deliver to the firm a secure lead over potential competitors in the early years of the product's life cycle.

Finally, does the ability to balance exploration and exploitation confer some irresistible functionality on the product that a customer is willing to pay for? Here the answer must be an unambiguous *yes*, but with a novel twist. For what we are dealing with in the exploratory process is an ability to generate *a whole range* of functionalities that will appeal to a variety of market segments. In effect, the skill, once more, is one of balancing out, of *tuning* fibre properties to yield a *configuration* of performance possibilities rather than of pursuing outstanding performance along a single dimension. As a core competence, the ability to achieve such "tunability" of product properties appears to be less single minded than those typically discussed in the competence literature. (For an exception, see Sanchez 1995.) In effect, it argues for a broader definition of core competence than is often on offer.

In sum, although a claim to the possession of a core competence in the development of fibres is not as yet strongly supported by the data, such a claim is not refuted by the data either. Hopefully, the research currently underway will help to settle the matter.

What would be the organizational implications for Courtaulds of having such a core competence? Core competences are the product of organizational constructs (Bijker, Hughes and Pinch, 1987; Latour and Woolgar, 1986). Variously located groups in a firm will attempt to define and represent them in different ways. They are not simply given but rather emerge as the outcome of a political process of negotiation between internal interest groups. In the balancing-out process mentioned above, exploratory and exploitative learning will each be championed by different constituencies within a firm according to their respective interests. One hypothesis that we are exploring is that organizational actors located at the centre and responsible for longer-term research and technology at Courtaulds will favour more time and effort being devoted to uncodified scanning and exploration in the lower regions of the C-Space, whereas organizational actors in the businesses and responsible for products and markets will favour the gains in efficiency and time savings associated with moving up the Space towards more codified performance targets. Give either group too strong (or too weak) an organizational voice, and the balancing act which we believe to be the key to the preservation and deepening of the competence will be lost. Managing a core competence, therefore, as Prahalad and Hamel have pointed out (1994), may well require a measure of recentralization with respect to the highly decentralized SBU model that is currently popular in many firms and that certainly has been used in Courtaulds in recent years. Lord Kearton, the firm's CEO in the 1950s, had been a centralist; yet Arthur Knight, his successor, initiated a decentralization process that was later taken further by Sir Christopher Hogg. The issue that emerges from our study is whether in such a regime the type of core competence discernible in the case can be maintained.

5   CONCLUSION

Weber (1978) distinguished between formal and substantive rationality. The first draws its legitimacy from the procedures followed in pursuing rational deliberations, the second from the outcomes actually achieved. Charles Hampden-Turner, in his book *Charting the Corporate Mind* (1990), points out that formal rationality cannot deal with a conflict between different values. Yet different values are precisely what SBUs and the corporate centre invoke as the one seeks to move towards ever greater differentiation and autonomy and the other towards ever greater integration. Hampden-Turner suggests that in such a situation one is dealing not with a binary choice but with a *dilemma*—two seemingly opposed propositions converging simultaneously on a decision maker (see Section 4). Dilemmas are not managed in the same way as binary choices. As Hampden-Turner puts it, "Value creation lies in the capacity of acknowledging those dilemmas which arise from competing and contrasting claims and of combining both horns of the dilemmas in a resolution which enhances all values in contention" (p. 10). But, he goes on to point out, "Confronting dilemmas is both dangerous and potentially rewarding. Opposing values 'crucify' the psyche and threaten to disintegrate both leader and organization. Yet to resolve these same tensions enables the organization to create wealth and outperform competitors. If you duck the dilemma you also miss the resolution. There is no cheap grace" (p. 14).

The implication of the foregoing is that, pulled as they are between regions A and B in the C-Space, core competences—at least where the development of fibres is concerned—have to be managed as dilemmas. The challenge is not so much to strike a balance between the competing claims of the two regions as to reconcile them in a creative synthesis. To simplify somewhat, we might say that if SBUs represent the claims of an already well-codified present, of current operations, and of quarterly profit and loss statements, then the building of core competences represent the claims of an uncodified future, of operations not yet imagined, and of the next generation's profit and loss statements.

Managing a dilemma takes us beyond the disjunctive logic that requires us to choose between A or B and moves us towards the conjunctive logic of choosing A and B—i.e., of having one's cake and eating it too. Translated into organization processes it suggests a superimposition of different managerial styles and organization structures, some responding to current operational needs, others to future development possibilities. Traditionally, the respective claims of the present and of the future have been the responsibility of different units within an organization—i.e., the sales department and the SBU might look after the present, for example, whereas central Research and Development and corporate headquarters might look after the future—an arrangement that mightily favoured the differentiation agenda. It may be, however, that such claims can only successfully be managed as dilemmas when their reconciliation has become the direct responsibility of each and every unit within a firm. If so, the successful management of core competences requires that the firm as a whole operate at a lower level of codification in the C-Space than is favoured by current management practice. This poses a cultural challenge of a high order.

Given the increasingly turbulent environment in which firms are called upon to operate, a number of authors have stressed the need for them to manage chaos, uncertainty, and emergent phenomena (Peters, 1992; Mintzberg and Walters, 1985; Schön, 1971). Yet firms typically approach the task with organizational models and cultures drawn from the upper reaches of the C-Space, regions in which transactions are well codified and controllable and where uncertainty can be kept to a minimum. The result is a fundamental mismatch between the institutional orientation of firms with respect to issues such as intellectual property rights and employment on the one hand, and their new task requirements on the other. As one of the authors has argued elsewhere, they are, in effect, approaching the new information economy with the institutional tools of the energy economy (Boisot, 1995). In this chapter we have stressed the need to come to terms with the lower regions of the C-Space, approaching them not as territory to be avoided but as a potential source of competitive advantage in their own right. We have argued that, viewed from this perspective on strategic knowledge assets, a core competence is an emergent product of the C-Space's lower regions which over time is driven towards its upper regions where it encounters the paradox of value. We view the upward move as inevitable, the product of a firm's own internal organizational dynamic working in tandem with external competitive forces. Managing a core competence can thus be interpreted as managing its trajectory in the C-Space in response to the conflicting forces that pit the upward move against the paradox of value. Insofar as this involves reconciling the divergent cultural claims of the upper and lower regions of the Space, we see this as being equivalent to managing a dilemma.

ACKNOWLEDGEMENTS

The case draws heavily on the three-volume history of the firm by D. C. Coleman (1969, 1980), on information given by Dr Hilda Coulsey and Dr Terry Lemmon, both of Courtaulds plc, and on Boisot *et al.* (1995).

REFERENCES

Alchian, A. and H. Demsetz (1972). "Production, information costs, and economic organization", *The American Economic Review*, **62**, pp. 777–795.
Ansoff, I. (1968). *Corporate Strategy*, Middlesex: Penguin Books.

Bijker, W. E., T. P. Hughes and T. Pinch (eds) (1987). *The Social Construction of Technological Systems: New Directions in the Sociology and History of Technology*, Cambridge, MA: The MIT Press.

Boisot, M. (1982). "The codification and diffusion of knowledge in the transactional strategy of firms", *Keio Economic Studies*, Vol. XIX, No. 1.

Boisot, M. (1983). "Convergence revisited: The codification and diffusion of knowledge in a British and a Japanese firm", *Journal of Management Studies*, Vol. 20, No. 2, April.

Boisot, M. (1986). "Markets and hierarchies in cultural perspective", *Organization Studies*, Vol. 7, Issue 2, pp. 135–158.

Boisot, M. (1994). *Information and Organization: The Manager as Anthropologist*, London: Harper and Collins.

Boisot, M. (1995a). *Information Space: A Framework for Learning in Organizations, Institutions and Culture*, London: Routledge.

Boisot, M. (1995b). "Is your firm a creative destroyer? Competitive learning and knowledge flows in the technological strategies of firms", *Research Policy*, **24**, pp. 589–606.

Boisot, M., T. Lemmon, D. Griffiths, V. Moles (1995). "Spinning a good yarn: The Identification of core competencies at Courtaulds", *International Journal of Technology Management*, Volume II, no. 3/4, pp. 425–440.

Chandler, A. (1962). *Strategy and Structure: Chapters in the History of the American Industrial Enterprise*, Cambridge, MA: MIT Press.

Coleman, D. C. (1969). *Courtaulds: An Economic and Social History—Vol. I. The Nineteenth Century, Silk and Crepe*, Oxford: Clarendon Press.

Coleman, D. C. (1969). *Courtaulds: An Economic and Social History—Vol. II. Rayon*, Oxford: The Clarendon Press.

Coleman, D. C. (1980). *Courtaulds: An Economic and Social History—Vol. III. Crisis and Change, 1940–1965*, Oxford: The Clarendon Press.

Dierickx, I. and K. Cool (1989). "Asset stock accumulation and sustainability of competitive advantage", *Management Science*, 35(12), pp. 1504–1514.

Dixit, A. and R. Pindyck (1994). *Investment Under Uncertainty*, Princeton, New Jersey: Princeton University Press.

Foster, R. N. (1987). *Innovation: The Attacker's Advantage*, London: Pan Books.

Granger Morgan, M. and M. Henrion (1990). *Uncertainty: A Guide to Dealing with Uncertainty in Quantitative Risk and Policy Analysis*, Cambridge: Cambridge University Press.

Hamel, G. and A. Heene (eds) (1994), *Competence-Based Competition*, Chichester: John Wiley and Sons.

Hampden-Turner, C. (1990). *Charting the Corporate Mind*, Oxford: Basil Blackwell.

Knight, F. (1965). *Risk, Uncertainty, and Profit*, New York: Harper and Row.

Latour, B. and S. Woolgar (1986). *Laboratory Life: The Construction of Scientific Facts*, Princeton, New Jersey: Princeton University Press.

Leonard-Barton, D. (1992). "Core capabilities and core rigidities: A paradox in managing new product development", *Strategic Management Journal*, Vol. 13, pp. 111–125.

March, J. G. (1991). "Exploration and exploitation in organizational learning", *Organization Science*, Vol. 2, No. 1, February.

Mintzberg, H. and J. Waters (1985). "Of strategies, deliberate and emergent", *Strategic Management Journal*, July–September.

Nonaka, I. and H. Takeuchi (1995). *The Knowledge Creating Company: How Japanese Companies Create the Dynamics of Innovation*, New York: Oxford University Press.

Ouchi, W. (1980). "Markets, bureaucracies, and clans", *Administrative Science Quarterly*, Vol. 25, No. 1, March, pp. 129–141.

Peters, T. (1992). *Liberation Management*, New York: Alfred A. Knopf.
Polanyi, M. (1958). *Personal Knowledge: Towards a Post-Critical Philosophy*, London: Routledge and Kegan Paul.
Porter, M. (1980). *Competitive Strategy: Techniques for Analyzing Industries and Competitors*, New York: Free Press.
Porter, M. (1985). *The Competitive Advantage: Creating and Sustaining Superior Performance*, New York: Free Press.
Prahalad, G. K. and G. Hamel (1970). "The core competence of the corporation", *Harvard Business Review*, **68**(3), pp. 79–91.
Prahalad, G. K. and G. Hamel (1994). *Competing for the Future*. Boston, MA: Harvard Business School Press.
Pugh, D., D. Hickson, C. Hinings and C. Turner (1969). "The context of organization structures", *Administrative Science Quarterly*, Vol. 14, No. 1, pp. 91–114.
Roussel, P., K. Saad and T. Erikson (1991). *Third Generation R and D: Managing the Links to Corporate Strategy*, Boston, MA: Harvard Business School Press.
Sanchez, R. (1993). "Strategic flexibility, firm organization, and managerial work in dynamic markets: a strategic options perspective", *Advances in Strategic Management*, **9**, pp. 251–291.
Sanchez, Ron (1995). "Strategic flexibility in product competition," *Strategic Management Journal*, **16** (Summer), pp. 135–159.
Sanchez, Ron (1996). "Managing articulated knowledge in competence-based competition," in R. Sanchez and A. Heene, editors, *Strategic Learning and Knowledge Management*, Chichester: John Wiley & Sons.
Sanchez, R. and A. Heene (1996). "A systems view of the firm in competence-based competition", in Sanchez, R., A. Heene and H. Thomas, editors, *Dynamics of Competence-Based Competition: Theory and Practice in the New Strategic Management*, London: Elsevier.
Sanchez, R., A. Heene and H. Thomas (eds) (1996). *Dynamics of Competence-Based Competition: Theory and Practice in the New Strategic Management*, London: Elsevier.
Sanchez, R., A. Heene and H. Thomas (1996). "Towards the theory and practice of competence-based competition", in Sanchez, R., A. Heene and H. Thomas, editors, *Dynamics of Competence-Based Competition: Theory and Practice in the New Strategic Management*, London: Elsevier.
Schön, D. (1971). *Beyond the Stable State*, New York: Random House.
Selznick, P. (1957). *Leadership in Administration: A Sociological Interpretation*, New York: Harper and Row.
Spender, J. C. (1989). *Industry Recipes*, Oxford: Basil Blackwell.
Tversky, A. and D. Kahneman (1974). "Judgement under uncertainty: Heuristic and biases", *Science*, **185**, pp. 1124–1131.
Utterback, J. M. (1994). *Mastering the Dynamics of Innovation*, Boston, MA: Harvard Business School Press.
Walras, L. (1926). *Elements of Pure Economics or the Theory of Social Wealth*, Philadelphia: Orion Editions, p. 65.
Weber, M. (1978). *Economy and Society*, Roth, G. and C. Wittich, editors, Berkeley: University of California Press.
Wernerfelt, B. (1984). "A resource-based view of the firm", *Strategic Management Journal*, **5**, pp. 171–180.
Williamson, O. E. (1985). *The Economic Institutions of Capitalism: Firms, Markets, Relational Contracting*, New York: Free Press.
Wright, Russell (1996). "Tangible integration versus intellectual codification skills: A comparison of learning processes in developing logic and memory semiconductors," in R. Sanchez and A. Heene, editors, *Strategic Learning and Knowledge Management*, Chichester: John Wiley & Sons.

5

Tangible Integration versus Intellectual Codification Skills: A Comparison of Learning Processes in Developing Logic and Memory Semiconductors

RUSSELL W. WRIGHT

INTRODUCTION

This chapter is concerned with the development and use of knowledge within organizations. The chapter argues that organizations are likely to be systematically biased in their knowledge development systems, and that variations in the organizational capabilities of firms are often caused by differences in their knowledge development systems. In essence, different knowledge development systems create different sets of organizational capabilities which result in different types of competences. The type of knowledge development processes a company puts into place

Strategic Learning and Knowledge Management.
Edited by Ron Sanchez and Aimé Heene.
Copyright © 1997 John Wiley & Sons Ltd.

and the resulting knowledge-based competences that emerge there from, enable and constrain organizations over time.

New product development (NPD) is a strategically important competence that, due to the complexity of new product development processes in most industries, is fundamentally a multidisciplinary process (Mc-Cann and Galbraith, 1981; Wind, 1981). Increased global competition and rapid technological change, along with increased use of flexible production processes and modularized designs, have made effective integration and accumulation of knowledge across functional specialties (e.g. product engineering, process engineering, marketing, sales, industrial design, manufacturing, etc.) critical for successfully creating new products (Sanchez, 1995; Souder, 1987; Urban and Hauser, 1993; Page, 1993; Griffin and Hauser, 1994).

This chapter argues that distinctive competences in new product development result from asymmetrical processes for developing knowledge and capabilities across firms. Differences in firms' cumulative capabilities are sources of sustainable advantage to the extent that they are difficult or impossible to imitate. Whether intended or unintended, therefore, the type of knowledge development system that a firm has adopted over time affects the type and scope of its competences.

The first section of this chapter introduces a general framework for identifying and analyzing the systematic biases in knowledge development processes that may exist across firms. The second section briefly discusses important stages in new product development processes. The third section examines ways in which biases in knowledge development processes can influence the development of organizational competences within the new product development stages. The final section discusses the semiconductor industry and differences among knowledge development processes in firms that produce DRAMs, SRAMs, EPROMs, and logic integrated circuits (ICs). A concluding section suggests implications of this research for strategy theory and practice.

KNOWLEDGE DEVELOPMENT

FROM AWARENESS TO IMPLEMENTATION

Knowledge is a set of beliefs that includes interpretations of data (Sanchez and Heene, 1996) to create information and practical understanding or "know-how" (Sanchez, 1996a, 1996b). Different types of organization have their own (more or less) distinctive learning processes that create and use different types of knowledge. Knowledge may be created through at least two paths: knowledge may be developed through an explicit process of theorizing and codification. This process draws on a theoretical level of understanding which Sanchez (1996a, in this volume) has characterized as "know-why" and which underlies Boisot, Griffiths and Moles' (1996, in this volume) notion of knowledge codification. A new idea in an engineer's head will become progressively more refined and defined as she or he conceptualizes, analyzes, and eventually puts it on paper. New patent applications, which are often submitted without a physical prototype ever being developed, may be expressions of this know-why mode of knowledge development. As engineers create more designs, develop more patent submissions based on the original concept, and begin drawing up product specifications, this form of new knowledge becomes increasingly codified and explicit.

New knowledge may also be expressed in various material or physical states without going through significant explicit theoretical development or codification. Many production technologies, for example, have evolved through a process of "hands-on" trial and error with little or no benefit from explicit theorizing or scientific explanations of phenomena. This form of learning seemed to be evident when the chemical industry began replacing batch production of pigments with computerized process controls (Buchanan and Bessant, 1985). Firms created new process know-how even though their understanding of the basic science of pigment chemistry was weak, with neither chemical reaction rates nor potential side effects well understood. Other examples of important technical systems in which much of the existing knowledge base is built up empirically at the know-how level of understanding include the smelting of aluminum from bauxite and the bonding of metal parts in aircraft. New technologies based on empirical development of knowledge often create problems for process operators at first, but continued "learning-by-doing" enables the technology to become better understood. As learning proceeds surprises recede, and a reliable body of "know-how" emerges.

A number of familiar tools and devices seem to have evolved in this empirical mode of learning, which I will hereafter refer to as a *tangible integration* process, including such elaborate contraptions as weaving machines and early airplane wings. In these cases, the creation of important knowledge was not separated from the development and implementation of the machine or product itself. Attempts to formalize know-how and to abstract and codify an underlying theoretical level of knowledge came later. Weaving and glass blowing were once processes requiring the know-how and skills of experienced craftspeople. Eventually, however, engineers like Gutemberg and Jacquard were ingenious enough to build machines that at first imitated and then progressively improved on the skills of craftworkers.

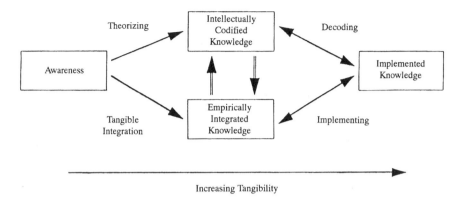

Increasing Tangibility

FIGURE 5.1   From Awareness to Implementation

KNOWLEDGE DEVELOPMENT BIASES

Both individuals and organizations may have characteristic biases in the ways they process information, create new understanding, and apply knowledge. The "information style" of an individual or organization is a behavior pattern in information search, development, and use. Many studies on the information styles of researchers and engineers try to identify the information needs of individuals, the most appropriate sources and means of information transfer, and the relationship between the kind and amount of information transferred and individual/group performance.

Information transfer is a process by which knowledge developed in one location (source) is identified, acquired, and implemented by individuals in another location (receiver). In their study of information transfer, Roosenbloom and Wolek (1970) differentiated between internally and externally available information and between design engineers and research engineers (i.e. scientists). They found that engineers work with and depend on information internal to the firm to a larger extent than scientists. Engineers in a product design or development function tend to work with internal information relatively more than engineers assigned to research positions in a central laboratory. When the work effort was toward the development of an emerging body of knowledge, engineers relied on more formal, external sources (e.g. journal publications, conference presentations, patents, etc.). When the work effort was focused on ongoing operations, the engineers depended more on informal, face-to-face interaction (a medium that may convey information that is not written or put into words). In contrast, research engineers tend not to rely on face-to-face communication. Written information is perceived as more objective and substantiated, which increases the credibility of the transferred information.

Allen (1971, 1977) also found that engineers and scientists differ in their information styles. Scientists tend to rely more on the scientific literature, personal experience, and external colleagues, while high performing engineers spent more time in face-to-face communication with their colleagues within the firm. Scientists or engineers working on emerging bodies of knowledge thus tend to depend on and work with more explicit, codified, theoretical knowledge than their more design-oriented engineering counterparts. Scientists and research engineers, by the nature of their work, develop their ideas into articulated concepts, which they then use to theorize, hypothesize, and explain. The product of such effort is often an explicit theory and hypothesized set of relationships. Engineers working on product design or process improvements, on the other hand, may tend to work to a larger extent in groups and to focus on achieving "incremental" technical improvements within existing technology.

Specific organizations have characteristic knowledge development and application processes that depend both on their research or design orientations and on their information styles in each activity. Most organizations have specific biases toward theoretical knowledge codification or toward tangible knowledge integration. Organizations that tend toward theorizing and codification processes may identify and develop know-why levels of knowledge more quickly than tangible knowledge integrators who are focused on building up know-how levels of knowledge. They may therefore be the first-to-market with emerging technologies and product innovations. Organizations that are based on tangible integration processes, on the other hand, may have to obtain emerging theoretical knowledge and technology in embedded forms (like new machines) from external sources. However, these organizations may be more adept at incrementally improving product and process technologies.

Organizational competences may therefore reflect asymmetrical accumulations of knowledge and capabilities that distinguish a firm from its competitors. These accumulations of knowledge and capabilities may be sources of competitive advantage when they are difficult to transfer and imitate. A firm's accumulated knowledge and capabilities also enable and constrain a firm's ability to develop new competences in specific areas such as product development. Depending on the degree to which a firm is biased toward developing know-how or know-why levels of knowledge, the firm will tend to be better at certain kinds and aspects of new product development than others.

New Product Development

Stages of Development

The new product development practices of innovating firms have been widely studied in recent years. An important aspect of new product development is the degree to which various required tasks can be partitioned (von Hippel, 1994; Sanchez and Mahoney, 1995) into separate and distinct activities. Much of the literature has described the tendency for firms to separate these activities into various discrete steps or stages (Urban and Hauser, 1993; Griffin, 1993; Saren, 1984; Crawford, 1983; Cooper and Klienschmidt, 1986; Cooper, 1990). In many firms, new product development consists of a set of sequential stages, each stage consisting of specific, multi-functional parallel activities. Cooper (1990, 1994) refers to these as "stage-gate" processes, because progression to each stage requires passing through a "gate" which is a formal decision-making process for controlling the development process.

One of the most cited product development stage models is that developed by consultants Booz, Allen and Hamilton, Inc. In their model, the development process begins with new product strategy development, then proceeds through idea generation, idea screening, business analysis, testing, development, and product launch. Although many descriptions of this process agree in terms of stages (Sanchez (1996a) adds a further partitioning of "development" into stages of product definition, product design, and component development), there is little consensus on the importance and duration of each stage. There is also debate about whether all steps must be completed in sequence or can be carried out in parallel or in overlapping steps. There is evidence that some firms are undertaking the stages in overlapping steps in order to bring their products to market ahead of their competitors (Takeuchi and Nonaka, 1986), while others are achieving concurrent parallel stages (Sanchez and Mahoney, 1995). Some authors are arguing that product development is by its very nature a creative process of convergent and divergent activities that does not lend itself to strictly sequential, predetermined stages of activities. Cooper (1994) describes what he sees as an emerging "third-generation new product process" in which stages are connected with "fuzzy gates" that are conditional, situational, and can be omitted or bypassed as need dictates.

Interviews I have conducted with engineers in the semiconductor industry suggest that the new product development process proceeds through a series of phases that consist of clearly defined tasks and activities. These phases were in most cases sequential, but were usually overlapping and in some cases were performed in parallel. Phases vary in duration by product and are not always separated by formal decision-making "gates". Engineers described these phases by the sets of activities contained within each phase. Engineers usually identified ending points of each phase in terms of the *completion* of a critical activity, rather than the occurrence of a formal decision process or gate.

The new product development process in the semiconductor industry typically begins with a general analysis of the feasibility of a project and then proceeds to the basic conceptualization of a new product and its basic decomposition into functional subsystems. A detailed design is then developed and a working prototype manufactured. The working prototype is then used to test the product under varying conditions and, when necessary, redesigned to meet customer specifications. Once those specifications are met, a manufacturing process is then "characterized" to define the capabilities to produce the new product to customer specifications. Once the characterization of the manufacturing process is complete, a production line is configured, and the product is manufactured, marketed and shipped. These activities can be separated into six basic phases: feasibility, concept development, prototype development, prototype testing, manufacturing ramp-up, and full-scale manufacturing.

PRODUCT DEVELOPMENT COMPETENCE

Product design. Within the phases of new product development in the semiconductor industry, there are three dimensions along which firms are currently developing strategically important capabilities: product design, process development, and manufacturing engineering. Some firms may emphasize product design and system integration—capabilities requiring highly skilled design engineers. In the 1970s, few engineers had the requisite skills, training, and experience to design complex integrated circuits. These design engineers were usually mobile and able to command high salaries. Indeed, many of the start-up semiconductor companies of the 1980s were begun by design engineers who left established Silicon Valley firms. Product design in this industry requires an ability to define the intricate patterns of circuits on individual layers of silicon (in two dimensions) and then to combine these layers in the form of a manufacturable integrated circuit (in three dimensions) that meets customer specifications or industry standards. The work of design engineers can therefore be thought of as translating customer specifications into a circuit design. Each design represents an explicit expression of a designer's codified knowledge about electronic circuitry. Thus, we can expect that in general, firms with strong knowledge codification processes will have an advantage in the development of new product designs.

Recent advances in digital computers and information technology have been made possible by achievements in semiconductor design and technology. The increasing density of integrated circuits (ICs) is paralleled by increases in the complexity of the system functions which a chip must perform. As ICs become larger, more dense, and more complex, they demand new capabilities from design, circuit, and manufacturing engineers. The large amount of complex information that IC designs now encompass can no longer be comprehended by individual designers and developers.

The increasing complexity of ICs has induced researchers and companies to search for methods and tools which can go beyond the design capabilities of individual human designers (see Gilder, 1986). This effort has led to the creation of systems for automating product design. Product design automation enables companies to use software to generate electronic circuits appropriate to a given set of design requirements. There are two basic approaches to IC design automation: the algorithmic approach and the knowledge-based approach. The algorithmic approach defines a fixed preprogrammed sequence of steps that will ultimately lead to a design solution. This approach seeks to automate the design process to the maximum extent possible so that human-introduced limitations, errors, and delays are avoided. The knowledge-based approach seeks to codify knowledge (in the form of heuristics and rules) acquired by designers over many years of experience. The codified knowledge (in the form of specific design practices and rules) is stored in a knowledge base and a reasoning/logic procedure is then incorporated into the system to operate on the knowledge base. This approach is now often known as "expert systems". Except for some specific applications and for laying out design structures, full automation from initial design concept to chip production is not often attained. Several project leaders interviewed have even suggested that human intervention at appropriate stages of the design cycle may always be desirable.

The advent of very large scale integrated circuits (VLSI) and improved IC design automation capabilities has brought with it the concept of a system-on-a-chip. Increasingly complex logic systems can be integrated on a very small silicon chip. As a consequence, the prior difference between a system designer's task and a circuit designer's task is becoming blurred. Further, to be sure that what is designed can in fact be made, circuit designers need to be aware of all aspects of the development cycle from system design to manufacturing process design to actual manufacturing. Of course, not everyone involved in IC product development must be involved in everything. There is still a need for system designers, circuit designers, device engineers, and chip manufacturers who are experts in their own fields. However, having basic knowledge of the entire development cycle facilitates effective interactions across specialists, functions, and tasks. Thus, interviewees suggested that the combination of increasing IC complexity and accelerating technological change has created a new scarcity: IC designers who can perform this integrative, multidisciplinary role. Design groups that develop the common understanding and language needed to achieve this integration create and use a knowledge base which may not be readily imitated, potentially making the capabilities of such a group a source of competitive advantage.

Thus it appears that the chance of new product success may be an increasing function of firm-specific design capabilities in particular groups. In addition, new product success may be an increasing function of the extent to which a firm can facilitate flows of knowledge across boundaries between various product and process design groups.

Process development. The second strategically important capability found in new product development is process development. The primary task of process development is to analyze and predict how different technical choices at the design stage will influence manufacturing performance. The state of prior knowledge about a process technology influences the steps a process engineer will take in developing a specific new manufacturing process. In some cases, a process engineer can draw on already existing process models, simulation tools, and techniques to provide reliable information about alternative process choices. In other cases, prior knowledge may be limited, and process engineers may be forced to develop new theoretical models, design new simulation tools, and create new heuristic techniques to develop radically new process technology.

Process development begins with a full product description (i.e. a full set of product specifications). Process development ends with the completion of a prototype (e.g. a silicon chip) of the product and a clearly defined organizational routine for efficient production. Process development engineers must define the organizational routines needed to assure consistent high quality production. Much of the process knowledge needed to produce a chip will be reflected in the actual product design. Process development is thus a "silicon-based capability"; it develops the sequence of process steps necessary to lay multiple layers of circuits on a silicon chip. Process development engineers often develop and introduce new process equipment and materials that improve chip manufacturing capability, and process development engineers often speak of success in their work in terms of process innovations and technical sophistication. Since process development may be important to competence in creating new products, we would expect that much new product development success depends on firm-specific process development capabilities in a number of specific manufacturing technology areas. In addition, new product success should be greater to the extent that a firm can integrate specific design and process development capabilities.

Manufacturing engineering. Manufacturing engineering "translates" a given design into a configuration of machines that is capable of maintaining a high production yield and quality level. Manufacturing engineers review a circuit design in the context of their current process technology and define production line configurations capable of achieving high levels of reliability. Manufacturing engineers often describe success in their work in terms of process stability and high manufacturing yield rates. Much of the knowledge needed to configure processes successfully is developed through tangible integration processes using various production machines over periods of time. Thus, we expect that firms with strong tangible integration processes will have superior manufacturing engineering capabilities. Firms with firm-specific manufacturing engineering capabilities in particular manufacturing technology areas may achieve some competitive advantage. Further, new product success should improve when firms facilitate an integration of firm-specific process development and manufacturing engineering capabilities.

DRAMs, SRAMs, and Logic ICs: A Comparison of Knowledge Creation Processes

Semiconductor devices can be categorized into two basic groups: discrete semiconductors and integrated circuits (ICs). Discrete devices such as transistors and diodes are relatively simple one-function products. Integrated circuits have experienced the most growth and competition in the last 20 years. By the end of the 1970s, there were thousands of IC products that varied by function, speed, density, power consumption, and price. Integrated circuits can be further categorized into two groups: bipolar ICs and metal-oxide semiconductors (MOS). In the early 1970s, bipolar technology used existing manufacturing technology to produce very fast chips that consumed relatively large amounts of power. The alternative metal-oxide technology produced chips that were slower but had lower power consumption.

Integrated circuits can be used in both analog and digital applications. Analog integrated circuits were designed primarily for radio, television, and analog communication systems. Digital integrated circuits, which are used in devices from computers to watches, can be divided into memory and logic chips. DRAMs, SRAMs, and EPROMs (DRAMs are dynamic random access memory devices, SRAMs are static random access memory devices, and EPROMs are erasable programmable read only memory devices) are the most widely used memory ICs. Memory devices consisting of large numbers of identical elements are designed to store information. Logic integrated circuits, however, are designed to process information and can be programmed to perform various tasks. Because of their functional flexibility, logic ICs are often designed for very specific functions and applications.

DRAMS, SRAMS, AND EPROMS

An important difference between memory ICs and logic ICs is that in memory devices, industry standards or "dominant designs" emerge relatively quickly, while dominant designs in various logic devices emerge much slower, if at all. Memory devices tend to have standardized interfaces that make them functionally interchangeable. Most competitors use the same packaging and pin configuration so that one firm's DRAM chip could be substituted for a competitor's DRAM chip of the same capacity with little or no perceived difference to the customer.

Memory devices may have various characteristics, but one key difference is between volatile and non-volatile devices. When power is removed from a volatile memory device, the information stored is lost. Non-volatile memory devices, however, retain information without a continual source of power. The most common volatile memory device is random access memory (RAM). Random access memory generally comes in two forms: dynamic random access memory (DRAM) and static random access memory (SRAM). Random refers to the ability of the chip to give back the exact information requested by the computer wherever it is located in the computer memory. Memory devices are highly regular in structure, consisting of rows and columns of identical transistors. Every transistor can be addressed separately in order to read the current contents or to write new contents.

DRAMs account for about one-half of the value of MOS memory ICs sold on the open market. The three primary qualities that design engineers seek in a DRAM device are: density (the number of bits per chip), address-access time, and power dissipation. The race to meet and exceed current requirements has driven DRAM design and processing to very high levels of technology complexity. DRAM competitors try to use the most advanced state-of-the-art process equipment in the manufacture of DRAM devices.

One drawback of DRAMs is that they can store information only for a fraction of a second and then information has to be refreshed or rewritten. SRAMs, however, do not require refreshing or rewriting to store information. SRAMs have a lower packing density and require many more transistors to store an equivalent amount of information, but once information is stored in the chip, it will stay as long as the power remains on.

Common non-volatile memory devices are ROMs, PROMs and EPROMs. ROM stands for "read only memory". ROMs are designed to store and give back information, and any information required from a ROM chip is designed into the chip during fabrication. PROM stands for "programmable read only memory". PROMs are designed to allow a user to program a memory circuit. Once programmed, a PROM functions like a ROM chip. EPROM stands for "erasable programmable read only memory". EPROMs are designed to allow information to be deleted by shining ultraviolet light on the chip. Erasing the programming allows the chip to be reprogrammed by an external programming machine. Most EPROMs can be reprogrammed up to ten times.

The DRAM market greatly exceeds the EPROM market in terms of the number of bits sold. A new DRAM generation emerges every three years, while a new EPROM generation emerges every 18 months. However, memory capacity from one DRAM generation to the following typically increases by a factor of four, while the increase in memory between generations of EPROMs is closer to a factor of two. Thus, a generation of DRAMs is both a much larger market and lasts for almost twice as long as a generation of EPROMs.

It is not uncommon to find older generations of EPROMs in demand for certain applications even though higher density EPROMs are available on the market. In fact, several different generations of EPROMs typically coexist and compete in the same market. In contrast, demand for DRAMs is strongly weighted toward the greatest density chip available, with rarely more than the two latest generations claiming a significant share of the market at the same time. Each new EPROM generation is therefore smaller than DRAMs in terms of market size and they succeed each other relatively quickly. As a result, EPROM producers typically do not redesign production processes for each new generation.

The primary application for DRAMs is computer memory boards. DRAM pin configurations, functions, and size are highly standardized so that most computer manufacturers can replace one DRAM manufacturer's chip with another firm's chip with little to no change to the computer board or the overall system functions. Demand for EPROMs has remained relatively stable, and EPROMs have not become as standardized across companies or across generations as DRAMs. Once a given generation of EPROMs is designed into a computer, it may become costly to replace an existing chip with a new generation chip. In this sense, EPROMs are similar to logic ICs. Both products are relatively design specific, and switching costs often make changes from one chip to another prohibitively costly. This explains why demand may be high for several generations of EPROMs at the same time.

LOGIC DEVICES

Semiconductor firms often design logic devices with unique instruction sets and operating languages. Once a company designs a given semiconductor firm's logic device into its machine, switching to another logic chip could be costly. Logic devices are therefore the most differentiated of integrated circuit products.

As a result of the differences between memory ICs and logic ICs, the nature of competition in design and process capabilities across the two market segments differs significantly. Design cost varies greatly with the complexity of the design of a chip. In the early 1970s, a few engineers could design a memory device within a few months; by contrast, dozens of engineers working for a few years might be needed to complete a microprocessor design. Once put into production, memory chips become commodity devices for which quality and cost control become critical to competitive success. Although manufacturing is also important for logic devices, design is the critical factor in the market success of microprocessors (Dorfman, 1987). Success in memory chips, however, is derived from process technology, while in logic chips product design is critical to success.

In researching capabilities critical to success in markets for logic ICs, we expect to find a positive relationship between a firm's market success and (1) its design competence and (2) its ability to integrate design and process development capabilities. On the other hand, in memory chip markets, we expect to find a positive relationship between a firm's market success and (1) its manufacturing engineering competence and (2) its ability to integrate process development capabilities and manufacturing engineering capabilities.

DISCUSSION AND CONCLUSION

Firms develop biases in their knowledge development processes, and tend to develop strengths in either knowledge codification skills or tangible integration skills. It is relatively rare to find companies that are good at both. These biases lead to strengths and weaknesses in their product development processes. Knowledge codifiers and tangible integrators tend to attack product development differently. Knowledge codifiers develop distinctive competences in product and process design. Because of their strengths in knowledge articulation and codification, they will be biased toward radical product and process redesigns. In contrast, tangible integrators develop competences in product characterization and continuous process improvement. Because of their strengths in tangible integration and coordination, they will be biased toward incremental product and process redesigns.

The evolution of the memory segment of the semiconductor industry helps to make clear the role of knowledge biases in a firm's ability to develop competence in product design, process development, and manufacturing. Two well-known examples from the semiconductor industry, Intel and NMB, illustrate these phenomena.

Throughout its history, Intel has maintained a clear strength in the articulation and codification of knowledge. In the early 1970s, the company maintained a leadership position in memory chips by pioneering both product design and process development technology. In 1969, it developed a semiconductor process technology called metal-on-silicon (MOS) which quickly became the process standard in the memory market. In 1970, it launched the first DRAM chip. With the 4K DRAM, Intel established the dominant design of the DRAM market.

Once the dominant design was established, the differences between competitors' product designs quickly disappeared. Process development and manufacturing gradually became critical sources of success. The minimum feature size of DRAM devices shrank by at least one-third every three years from 1970 to 1988. The number of bits stored on a DRAM device quadrupled every three years during the same time period. The same consistent progress can be found across a number of performance criteria such as power consumption and access time. Even though continual performance improvement like this is partially due to design engineering, process development and manufacturing increasingly play a central role.

In a recent article, Burgelman (1994) describes Intel Corporation's exit from DRAM design and manufacturing in 1984–1985, and EPROM manufacturing in 1991. In the early stages of the memory industry, production volumes and manufacturing yield levels were low. The concerns and activities of process and manufacturing engineers were similar. Intel specifically viewed process development as its distinctive competence.

Burgelman argues that the changing basis of competition in the memory business strained the relationships between Intel's process development and manufacturing engineers. The process development engineers "continued to see their task in terms of process innovation, revolutionary change, and technical elegance". With every new generation of DRAM product, Intel would radically redesign the process along with the new product. In contrast, the manufacturing engineers "increasingly saw their task in terms of stability, incremental change, and technical simplicity in order to reach higher yields". Intel found it difficult to shift from an emphasis on product design and process development to an emphasis on large-scale manufacturing.

As the memory segment evolved from 64K to 256K several competitors continued to follow Intel's lead and attempted to redesign their processes with each new product generation, entering each new product generation with a complete new product and process designs. However, several competitors began pursuing a different development strategy by developing a "shrink" version of the 64K DRAM and continuing to work on yield improvement with an incremental variation of their original 64K design. When the 256K DRAM market began to emerge, these competitors entered the market with 256K chips that were simply four 64K designs placed on the same piece of silicon. Thus emerged the difference between 4 × 1 and 1 × 4 chip designs. Competitors that had incrementally developed manufacturing competences used the "shrink" design strategy to enter each new generation with higher yield rates, lower costs, and equivalent performance.

Intel's knowledge development bias (knowledge codification) may have precluded it from developing a competence in large-scale manufacturing. The early technical heroes at Intel were product design and process development scientists who could codify fundamental physical phenomena in terms of scientific problems and resolve the problems in terms of product prototypes. This original knowledge development bias both enabled and constrained Intel in its product development capabilities. Intel gradually shifted its strategic priorities from memory devices to microcontrollers and microprocessors where the source of advantage is derived from product design, and today the company dominates a majority of the microprocessor and microcontroller markets.

By the end of 1985, Intel had exited the DRAM market. By this time, the production of 256K DRAM chips had surpassed the previous generation of 64K DRAM. Of the 12 remaining participants in the DRAM market, six Japanese manufacturers accounted for approximately 90% of the 256K market. They, together with all but one of the American manufactuers, had all adopted designs based on a standard NMOS technology. Inmos, a knowledge codifier, tried to enter the 256K DRAM market with a radically new product and process design. Even though they were slightly late, their 256K DRAM device was twice as fast and consumed one-eighth the power of the other devices on the market. The Inmos device was the first memory product based on CMOS process technology. Inmos was never able to produce their new design in volume and licensed their new product and process technology to two start-up manufacturers: NMB Semiconductor of Japan and Hyundai of Korea.

NMB (a tangible integrator) was a new venture created by a miniature ball bearing manufacturer in May 1984. The first NMB DRAM plant was completed in February 1985. The plant was brought to full operation in May 1985. NMB negotiated a series of design changes with Inmos and entered into full production in March 1986. By December 1986, NMB was producing one million chips per month, a scale that was considered the minimum efficient level for survival at the time. By 1988, NMB was ranked as the sixth largest producer of 256K DRAM worldwide. The differences between Intel and NMB are too complex to be explained by a single factor. However, the achievement of NMB Semiconductor may have some relationship with its existing process and manufacturing competences, its capabilities in process automation, and a company culture of continuous improvement and rapid incremental change. I argue that NMB is biased in its knowledge development process. The manufacture of miniature ball bearings requires high levels of process quality and yield capacity, and ball bearing design does not change from generation to generation. The bias for a tangible integration knowledge development process of the parent company may have transferred to the subsidiary unit.

In conclusion, this chapter expands the literature on the role of competences in the new product development process. I have examined the dynamic nature of competence development in the semiconductor industry and suggested ways in which different forms of organizational learning may lead to different competences and different sources of competitive advantage. I have proposed a framework for identifying specific forms of knowledge and learning capabilities that serve as the bases for competences and suggested that managers are both enabled and constrained by their firms' knowledge development processes. Because organizational biases in knowledge development systems lead to different product development competences and competitive advantage, companies within the semiconductor industry tend to demonstrate distinctive competences in one or more of the following three areas: product design, process development, and/or manufacturing engineering.

The idea that unique capabilities in R&D and new product development are sources of strategic competence is not new. Several studies have observed persistent differences across firms in their R&D and new product development capabilities (Clark and Fujimoto, 1991; Leonard-Barton, 1992). The primary contribution of this chapter is to compare and contrast the logic IC with the memory IC segments and how the sources of advantage differ over time and across the two segments, and to suggest how the competences needed to compete in these segments is both enabling and constraining firms in their efforts to compete over time.

REFERENCES

Allen, T. J. (1971). "Communications, technology transfer, and the role of technical gatekeeper", *R&D Management*, **1**, pp. 14–21.
Allen, T. J. (1977). *Managing the Flow of Technology*, Cambridge, MA: MIT Press.

Boisot, M., D. Griffiths and V. Moles (1996). "The dilemma of competence: Differentiation versus integration in the pursuit of learning", this volume, *Strategic Learning and Knowledge Management*, Chichester, UK: John Wiley & Sons.

Buchanan, D. A. and J. Bessant (1985). "Failure, uncertainty, and control: The role of operators in a computer-integrated production system", *Journal of Management Studies*, **22**, pp. 292–308.

Burgelman, Robert, A. (1994). "Fading memories: A process theory of strategic business exit in dynamic environments", *Administrative Science Quarterly*, **39**, pp. 24–56.

Clark, K. and T. Fujimoto (1988). "Overlapping problem solving in product development", in K. Ferdows, editor, *Managing International Manufacturing*, Amsterdam: North Holland.

Clark, K. and T. Fujimoto (1991). *Product Development Performance, Strategy, Organization and Management in the World Auto Industry*, Boston, MA: Harvard Business School Press.

Cooper, R. G. (1990). "New products: what distinguishes the winners?" *Research & Technology Management*, **33**(6), pp. 27–31.

Cooper, R. G. (1994). Third-generation new product processes', *Journal of Product Innovation Management*, **11**, pp. 3–14.

Cooper, R. G. and E. J. Kleinschmidt (1986). "An investigation into the new product process: Steps, deficiencies, and impact", *Journal of Product Innovation Management*, **4**, pp. 169–183.

Crawford, M. C. (1983), *New Product Management*. Homewood, IL: Irwin.

Dorfman, Nancy C. (1987). *Innovation and Market Structure: Lessons from the Computer and Semiconductor Industries*, Cambridge, Massachusetts: Ballinger Publishing Company.

Gilder, G. (1986). *Microcosm*, New York, NY: Simon and Schuster.

Griffin, A. (1993). "Metrics for measuring product development cycle time", *Journal of Product Innovation Management*, **10**(2) (March), pp. 112–125.

Griffin, Abbie and John R. Hauser (1994). "Integrating mechanisms for marketing and R&D", *Marketing Science Institute Report, No. 94–116* (October), Cambridge, MA: Marketing Science Institute.

Leonard-Barton, D. (1992). "Core capabilities and core rigidities: A paradox in managing new product development", *Strategic Management Journal*, **13** (summer), pp. 111–125.

McCann, Joseph and J. R. Galbraith (1981). "Interdepartmental relations", *Handbook of Organization Design*, Vol. 2, pp. 60–84.

Page, A. L. (1993). "Assessing new product development practices and performance: Establishing crucial norms", *Journal of Product Innovation Management*, Vol. 10, pp. 273–290.

Roosenbloom, R. S. and F. W. Wolek (1970). *Technology and Information Transfer.* Boston: Division of Research, Graduate School of Business Administration, Harvard University.

Sanchez, R. (1995). "Strategic flexibility in product competition", *Strategic Management Journal, (Special Issue)* (summer).

Sanchez, R. (1996a). "Strategic product creation: Managing new interactions of technology, markets, and organizations", *European Management Journal*, **14**(2) (April).

Sanchez, R. (1996b). "Managing articulated knowledge in competence-based competition", this volume, *Strategic Learning and Knowledge Management*, Chichester, UK: John Wiley & Sons.

Sanchez, R. and J. Mahoney (1995). "Modularity, flexibility, and knowledge management in product and organization design", University of Illinois working paper, Champaign, IL.

Saren, M. A. (1984). "A Classification and review of the intra-firm innovation process", *R&D Management*, **14**, pp. 11–24.

Souder, William, E. (1987). *Managing New Product Innovations*, Lexington, MA: Lexington Books.

Takeuchi, H. and I. Nonaka (1986). "The new product development game", *Harvard Business Review*, **1** (January–February), pp. 137–146.

Urban, G. L. and J. R. Hauser (1993). *Design and Marketing of New Products*, 2nd edn, Englewood Cliffs, N.J.: Prentice-Hall, Inc.

von Hippel, Erik (1994). "Sticky information and the locus of problem solving: Implications for innovation", *Management Science*, **40**, pp. 429–439.

Wind, Y. (1981). "Marketing and the other business functions", in pp. 237–264, *Research in Marketing*, Vol. 5, J. N. Sheth, editor, Greenwich, CT: JAI Press.

Wind, Y. (1982). "Product policy: Concepts, methods, and strategy", Reading, MA: Addison-Wesley.

Section III

Strategic Learning Between Organizations

The building of new competences in the biotechnology industry is studied by Klavans and Deeds. Their study investigates the different ways in which firms can learn from a perspective that assesses the impact of different approaches to learning on the ability of a firm to create value in a knowledge-intensive competitive environment. Using the value of initial public offerings of shares in biotechnology firms, Klavans and Deeds assess the effectiveness of three different avenues to building new competences: basic scientific discovery, technology development (conversion of scientific knowledge into products and processes), and absorptive capacity (the ability to recognize valuable information outside the firm, obtain it, and redeploy existing resources to use it effectively). Their study suggests that in the context of the biotechnology industry in the United States, both technology development and absorptive capacity modes of knowledge creation can be effective in creating new competences of significant strategic value.

Close interactions between business service firms and clients in knowledge-intensive industries (e.g. in consulting engineering services) may create many opportunities for service-providing firms to expand their knowledge bases and improve their competences. Sivula, van den Bosch and Elfring study knowledge transfer processes in service provider–client relationships to develop a model for better knowledge management of vertical alliances within an industry.

A firm's current knowledge-creating capabilities constrain its ability to build competences, and thus a firm's potential for building new competences is path dependent. Quélin suggests that developing means for integrating external knowledge into the firm may open important new avenues for overcoming path dependency and allow more rapid acquisition of new competences through strategic alliances. He discusses mechanisms which can improve the acquisition and integration of external knowledge in three types of strategic alliances: alliances to access existing competences, alliances to combine complementary assets, and alliances to create new capabilities.

6

Competence Building in Biotechnology Start-ups: The Role of Scientific Discovery, Technical Development, and Absorptive Capacity

RICHARD KLAVANS, DAVID L. DEEDS

INTRODUCTION

Why do some firms succeed while others fail? This is the defining issue for the field of strategic management. Initial answers to this question were found in the structure–conduct–performance paradigm of industrial organization economics (Bain, 1956; Porter, 1980, 1985). Recent work in the field has focused on the role of firm-specific resources (Barney, 1986, 1991; Dierickx and Cool, 1989; Wernerfelt, 1984) and capabilities (Hill and Deeds, 1995; Kogut and Zander, 1992; Prahalad and Hamel, 1990; Teece, Pisano and Shuen, 1990). Strategic management has also examined the process of value creation, especially the creation of valuable resources or capabilities (Henderson and Cockburn, 1994; Levinthal and Myatt, 1994; Rao, 1994; Sanchez, Heene and Thomas, 1996).

Strategic Learning and Knowledge Management.
Edited by Ron Sanchez and Aimé Heene.

This chapter builds on the recent interest in creating value from intangible resources and capabilities.

The goal of this study is to extend our understanding of how value is created in knowledge-intensive environments. The initial public offering (IPO) of biotechnology firms provides a unique opportunity to study this process. The value created (e.g. the market value from the IPO) can be traced to three competence-building activities: scientific discovery (increasing the stock of scientific knowledge in the firm); technology development (converting scientific knowledge into viable products and processes) and absorptive capacity (the ability to recognize the value of external information, assimilate it, and use this knowledge to reallocate discovery and development efforts).

One can characterize the differences between these three activities by examining the locus of knowledge generation and the flow of knowledge across organizational boundaries in each activity (see Figure 6.1). In scientific discovery, scientific knowledge is co-generated by the firm, competitors, and public institutions and tends to flow relatively freely across organizational boundaries. In technical development, technical knowledge is generated in the firm, and policies are often established to impede the flow of technical knowledge beyond the boundary of the firm. In absorptive capacity, scientific and technical knowledge is generated outside the firm and flows into the firm.

A key issue for the development of a dynamic theory of competence-based competition is understanding how a particular learning capability creates value within a specific context. This chapter will address this issue by examining which, if any, of these learning capabilities create value within the context of the biotechnology industry. The chapter is composed of three sections. The first section focuses on developing theory and hypotheses relating a firm's capabilities in scientific discovery, technical development, and absorptive capacity to value creation from R&D activities in the biotechnology industry. The second section presents the methodology used to test the hypotheses including specification of the model, description of the sample and data sources, and a description of our measures. Finally, we discuss the results from an analysis of 103 biotechnology firms.

THEORY AND HYPOTHESES

DISCOVERY CAPABILITIES

Scientific discovery is the process of discovering or generating new information about some phenomena of interest. The goal of scientific discovery is the creation of new knowledge about, or an enhanced

Scientific Discovery

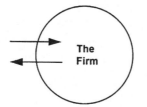

Technical Development

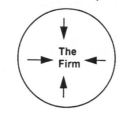

Absorptive Capacity

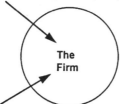

FIGURE 6.1

understanding of, our world. Participation in this process requires the dissemination of new knowledge through publications or conference presentations (Dasgupta and David, 1994). The process of scientific discovery may provide the basis for the development of new products and technologies. Development is usually viewed as a spillover, not a goal, of the scientific discovery process.

Scientific discovery is an example of the development of a firm-addressable competence, because scientific discoveries can rarely be owned or tightly controlled by an individual firm. The value created by a competence based on this particular form of learning may be difficult for an individual firm to capture. The tendency for scientific discovery to diffuse throughout the scientific community is well documented (Arrow, 1962; Mansfield, 1985; Nelson, 1959), and may be one reason why the vast majority of discovery activities occur in public institutions.

The reputation of the firm's scientists may be used to indicate the discovery capability of the firm. A firm with Nobel-laureate scientists would, for example, be thought to have scientific capability. Firms that have these Nobel-laureate scientists should therefore find it easier to raise money for future research. Biotechnology firms always provide the names of their top scientists and a brief personal history in the prospectus of the IPO. This information is included to convince investors that the firm has necessary research capabilities.

One way to measure the reputation of a firm's scientists is to examine citation patterns (Debackere and Rappa, 1994). Citations (i.e., researchers citing a research paper) are a rough measure of the importance of a research paper. The number of citations to the body of literature published by a scientist is a common surrogate for the influence and reputation of that scientist. These citation counts are commonly used in the promotion and tenure decisions of universities. Scientists without a critical mass of citations are suspect—additional evidence is needed to make the case that they are world-class scientists. Therefore, firms lacking scientists without a critical mass of citations may be perceived as lacking adequate research capability. This leads to our first hypothesis:

Hypothesis 1: The discovery capability of a firm (as indicated by the number of citations referring to papers by its scientists) will be positively related to the market value of the firm's equities.

TECHNICAL DEVELOPMENT CAPABILITY

One of the key challenges of innovation is not simply the discovery of a new idea, process, or means of organizing, but technically developing a product or process to the point where it can be produced at a commercially viable level (Pisano, 1994). Technology development is an example of the building of a competence that is more firm-specific. There are two types of capabilities normally associated with technology development. Some researchers suggest that development capabilities are embedded in behavioral procedures (Henderson and Cockburn, 1994). Other researchers suggest that development capabilities require areas of substantive technological expertise (Kandel *et al.*, 1991). Both groups emphasize that this capability is firm-specific.

Within the biotechnology industry technical development encompasses the processes of moving the recently discovered protein or therapeutic compound into the clinic and through various trials to regulatory approval. The skills required to develop the basic biologically active compound into a usable therapeutic or diagnostic include the development of manufacturing processes capable of producing the amount of the compound required for testing and commercial usage and the creation of a testing protocol that will be acceptable to the appropriate regulatory body. In this regard, the development of new products depends on the firm's technical development capability, not its scientific discovery capability. This leads to our second hypothesis:

Hypothesis 2: The technical development capability of a firm (as indicated by the number of products in preclinical and clinical trials) will be positively related to the market value of the firm's equity.

ABSORPTIVE CAPACITY

Cohen and Levinthal (1990) introduced the concept of absorptive capacity to the field of strategy. The concept comes from economic theories (primarily Schumpeterian) that examine the role of R&D in economic performance. In the first half of the twentieth century, Schumpeter argued that economic growth is rooted in technological innovation. Adding to the dominant focus in industrial organizational economics on price competition and allocative efficiency, Schumpeter's argument was picked up in the second half of the twentieth century with some compelling evidence that R&D had a significant effect on economic growth (Solow, 1957). The stream of literature that emerged from these Schumpeterian roots is quite broad—covering a variety of issues critical to the question of R&D and economic performance (for reviews, see Scherer, 1980; Kamien and Schwartz, 1982; Baldwin and Scott, 1987).

The concept of absorptive capacity has evolved from prior research on organizational learning. Organizational learning has been defined as the growing insights into and successful restructuring of organizational problems (Simon, 1969), the process of improving actions through better understanding (Fiol & Lyles, 1985), and the ability of the firm to assess and act upon internal and external stimuli in a cumulative, interactive and purposeful manner (Meyers, 1990). There is a marked similarity between these definitions and the definition of absorptive capacity.

The distinguishing feature of the absorptive capacity of an organization is that it is posited to be a function of the level of a firm's prior related knowledge. A firm's prior related knowledge enables it to recognize valuable new information, assimilate it and apply it to commercial ends. A firm which has a well-developed knowledge base in a particular field will have a high absorptive capacity and is better prepared to evaluate and act on any new information or ideas developed in the field. In contrast, a firm which has little or no knowledge of a particular field will be less able to evaluate and act on new information that is important to their products or markets. In fact, this firm is unlikely even to recognize that valuable new information or ideas have been developed. In competence-based competition the ability of management to recognize the type of assets and capabilities that will be most useful in the future becomes critical to firm success (Sanchez, Heene and Thomas, 1996). Clearly, a firm with superior absorptive capacity has an advantage in an environment in which competition is competence-based.

Absorptive capacity is qualitatively different from scientific discovery and technology development. Absorptive capacity involves learning and acting on the scientific discoveries and technical activities occurring outside the boundaries of the firm. Scientists in a firm learn about their external environment by participating in scientific communities through attendance at conferences, publishing papers, involvement in professional societies, etc. Additionally, management can expand a firm's absorptive capacity by collecting competitive intelligence. The information gathered from outside the firm is then used to redirect scientific discovery and technology development activities inside the firm.

Investments in competences can be viewed as creating strategic options (Sanchez, 1993) for the firm and have been shown to be an important component of a firm's market value in dynamic competitive environments (Sanchez and Thomas, 1996). In a subsequent article, Cohen and Levinthal (1994) illustrate how absorptive capacity would result in more effective R&D expenditures, if R&D activities are modeled as investments in options. Absorptive capacity reduces the gap between the firm's valuation of the R&D option and the true value of the option. Firms with greater absorptive capacity have smaller gaps. If the gap increases because the value of the R&D option changes due to external conditions, firms with absorptive capacity may close the gap more quickly because they are more likely to recognize this change. Viewing R&D expenditures as creating strategic options, and the firm's absorptive capacity as a significant determinant of the gap between the true versus perceived value of these options leads to our third hypothesis.

Hypothesis 3: The absorptive capacity of the firm (as indicated by the number of research communities that the firm participates in) will be positively related to the market value of the firm's equities.

METHODOLOGY

THE MODEL

Competence building has been defined as any process by which a firm qualitatively changes its existing stock of assets and capabilities, or creates new abilities to coordinate and deploy new and existing assets and capabilities in ways that help the firm achieve its goals (Sanchez, Heene and Thomas, 1996). The processes of interest in this chapter—scientific discovery, technical development, and absorptive capacity—are all competence-building processes. Therefore, our model investigates the impact of each of these competence-building processes on the market value of the equity of new biotechnology firms (cf. Sanchez and Thomas, 1996). This concept is represented as a linear model in which the dependent variable is a stipulated organizational goal (the creation of equity value from R&D activities), and the independent variables are discovery capability, development capability and absorptive capacity.

Value creation from R&D activities =
B_0 + B_1 (discovery capabilities)
+ B_2 (development capabilities)
+ B_3 (absorptive capacity)
+ B_4 (control variable)

THE SAMPLE

The sample of firms in this study is homogeneous along the three key dimensions of competence suggested by Sanchez, Heene and Thomas (1996): organization, intention and goal attainment. All of the firms are involved in scientific discovery and technical development. All of the firms collect and intend to use scientific and technical knowledge to decide which research options to pursue. All of the firms have the (interim) goal of an initial public offering. This sample of firms allows us to examine which factors may be more important to goal attainment: scientific discovery, technical development or absorptive capacity.

The sample used in this study consists of 103 biotechnology companies which made an IPO between 1982 and 1993. The sample was gathered from the total population of 225 publicly held biotechnology firms (Burrill and Lee, 1993). The sample was limited to firms which had gone public since 1982. This limited our sample to 218 firms. All 218 were contacted by phone and a copy of the prospectus from their initial public offering was requested. One hundred and five companies were able to provide a prospectus. Two companies were excluded from the sample because warrants for shares in their parent company were included in the IPO. Therefore, we had a response rate of 47%.

To test for biases in our sample we compared the average total assets and total liabilities of the firms in our sample to the average total assets and liabilities reported by Burrill and Lee (1993) for all 225 public firms.

Our sample averaged $11 123 000 in total assets and $3 515 000 in total liabilities. Burrill and Lee (1993) reported the average total assets for the 225 public biotechnology firms to be $11 377 000 and total liabilities to be $3 313 000. In addition, the percentage of non-pharmaceutical healthcare companies in our sample was 15% and the industry-wide percentage, as reported by Burrill and Lee (1993), was 17%. Based on these comparisons and the size of our sample, we believe we have analyzed a fairly representative sample of the publicly held biotechnology companies.

DATA SOURCES

The data used in our analysis were gathered from four sources. The dependent variable came from the Center for Research in Security Prices (CRSP) tapes. The CRSP tapes have been used in numerous studies in multiple fields and have proven to be a reliable source of information on firms' stock price and market value. The citation counts came from the Institute for Scientific Information's (ISI) Science Citation Index. This index identifies the articles published each year which cite the prior work of individual researchers. The Center for Research Planning (CRP) provided data on the research communities that these 103 biotechnology firms participated in. This data came from yearly analyses of bibliographies of worldwide scientific publications using a technique called co-citation analysis (Garfield, Sher and Torpie, 1964; Small and Griffith, 1974). The particular algorithms developed by CRP build on the theoretical insights of Price (1963), additional theoretical developments by Kuhn (1970), and overcome some of the commonly known problems associated with co-citation analysis of the scientific literature (Hicks, 1987; Leydesdorff, 1986; Mombers *et al.*, 1985). An independent assessment of CRP's model can be found in Franklin and Johnston (1988). The prospectus for each of the initial public offerings by the firms in our sample was used to identify the firm's top scientists and the number of products in clinical and preclinical trials.

THE DEPENDENT VARIABLE

Market value of R&D endeavors. The market value of the equity of start-up biotechnology firms is used to indicate the market value of a bundle of R&D activities. These firms generally have no products on the market, are sustaining significant accounting losses, and have few if any tangible assets of any significant value (Burrill and Lee, 1993). In essence, the market value of a new biotechnology firm's equity must reflect the market evaluation of the intangible scientific and technical knowledge and competences of the firm, since these are the only apparent assets and are the key to the firm successfully developing the new products required to create a stream of revenues.

The measure of market value is based upon the work of McGuinness (1993) and Ritter (1991). The market value of the firm's equity was chosen as the dependent variable because initial returns to IPOs are misleading. The IPO price is not determined by the market, but rather by agreement between the owners and underwriters. Therefore, the appropriate measure of firm value is the total market value of the firm's equity after the market has had a chance to react to the offering.

The total market value of the offering firm's equity (1990 dollars) is measured at the end of the first day of trading, the end of the first week of trading and the end of the first month of trading. We choose these three periods in order to maximize the market's ability to react to the offering and minimize any possible threats to validity. Market value at the end of the first day of trading has been used in numerous studies of IPOs (Downs and Heinkel, 1982; McGuinness, 1993; Ritter, 1984a; Ritter, 1984b; Titman and Trueman, 1986). Due to the small size of some of the offerings in our sample we present results for the end of the first week of trading and the end of the first month of trading to maximize the market's ability to evaluate the offering while still minimizing any potential threats to validity (Peterson, 1989; Salinger, 1992). A logarithmic transformation was used to control for the skewness of the distribution.

INDEPENDENT VARIABLES

Discovery capabilities. We use citation analysis as an indication of the quality of the firm's discovery capabilities. The names of the top scientists employed by each firm were gathered from the prospectus of the firm's initial public offering. Only full-time employees were included in the list in order to control for biases created by firms attempting to increase their visibility/ legitimacy by hiring a long list of scientific advisors or consultants. Names of all scientific personnel listed in the prospectus as well as top executives were compiled. We then used the Science Citation Index to gather the total number of citations for each scientist in the firm during the year in which the IPO was issued. These citations were then totaled to create a measure of the quality of the scientific team employed by the biotechnology firm at the time of its initial public offering. A logarithmic transformation was used to control for a skewed distribution.

Technical development capability. Measures of technical capability focus on the participation of the firm's scientific and technical employees in technical development groups. These groups of people within the organization are organized to commercialize a scientific and/or technical development. Cumulative employee hours have been used to characterize capabilities by type of group (Pisano, 1994). But most indicators of technical capability are based on the outcomes of these groups, such as patent applications, patents, or new products.

Two indicators of development capability are used: the number of new products in preclinical trials and the number of new products in clinical trials. These indicators represent different stages of the development process. A stream of new products in preclinical and clinical trials indicates that the firm has the development capabilities required to achieve at least some initial success. Biotechnology firms reveal information about these products in order to convince investors that the firm has a full development pipeline. A logarithmic transformation was used to control for the skewness of both distributions.

Absorptive capacity. The number of research communities that the firm's scientists and engineers participate in is used to indicate absorptive capacity. This measure of absorptive capability is based on participation of the firm's scientists and engineers in research communities and development communities whose members are primarily "outside" the boundary of the firm. Research communities (communities of scientists in laboratories around the world) are considered the source of scientific progress (Price, 1963; Kuhn, 1970). Participation in these research communities can be indicated by raw publication counts or (as used in this study) publication activity organized by the research community (Klavans, 1994). A logarithmic transformation was used to control for the skewness of the distribution.

CONTROL VARIABLE

Hot markets. Ibbottson and Jaffe (1975) first documented the existence of a number of "hot markets" for IPOs during the last 20 years. These "hot markets" are characterized by a high volume of IPO activity. During these periods both the number of IPOs brought to the market and the average value of the IPOs brought to market are significantly higher than during a normal period. In addition, Ritter (1984b) documents that the 1980 "hot market" was really a hot market for natural resource issues, establishing that certain market segments may experience "hot markets" independent of the broader market.

We examined the number of IPOs per year to identify "hot markets". In the case of biotechnology the years 1986, 1991 and 1992 show all the characteristics of a "hot market". Table 6.1 presents the number of IPOs in our

TABLE 6.1   Frequency and Size of IPOs by Year

Year	Number of IPOs in Sample	Average Value of Offering Firm in Sample (in Millions)	Total Capital Raised by Biotechnology (in Billions)
1982	2	$85 571	N/A
1983	3	$70 159	$1.1
1984	0	$0	$0.1
1985	1	$14 699	$0.3
1986	16	$102 943	$1.3
1987	8	$42 111	$0.6
1988	1	$103 056	$0.2
1989	5	$57 363	$0.6
1990	5	$38 214	$0.8
1991	37	$108 009	$4.0
1992	24	$112 543	$2.8
1993	2	$63 558	N/A

sample for each year, the average market value of the offering firm in our sample in each year, and the total capital raised through biotechnology offerings each year (Burrill and Lee, 1993). The data clearly show that the amount of capital raised, the average market value of each offering firm, and the number of offerings in 1986, 1991 and 1992 at least doubled during the hot years. Therefore, to control for the "hot market" phenomena a dummy variable was created which was coded 1 for all offerings during 1986, 1991 and 1992 and was coded 0 for all other offerings.

RESULTS AND CONCLUSIONS

Descriptive statistics are presented in Table 6.2. All of the variables were log transformed to address problems of extreme skewness. Log transforms are commonly used in these types of data.

The average market value of the equity of the firms in our sample was $62 794 000 after the first day of trading, $61 681 000 after the first week of trading and $62 040 000 after the first month of trading. The comparabilities of the market values suggests that the market value largely stabilizes by the end of the first day of trading. The work of the average firm's scientists had been cited in the literature 125 times. The average firm had 1 product in clinical trials and 2.11 products in preclinical trials, and participated in 9.67 research communities, although 32 firms participated in no research communities. One firm participated in 95 research communities. Seventy-six of the IPOs were issued during "hot markets".

TABLE 6.2   Descriptive Statistics

Variable	Obs	Mean	Std. Dev.	Min.	Max.
Valday*	103	10.756	0.809	8.63	12.6
Valweek*	103	10.736	0.812	8.64	12.6
Valmon	103	10.737	0.836	8.54	12.5
SciCap*	103	3.997	1.747	0	7.31
TechPre*	103	0.790	0.738	0	2.64
TechCli*	103	0.407	0.654	0	2.40
AbsCap*	103	1.528	1.341	0	4.57
Hot	103	0.738	0.442	0	1

* Log transforms.

In Table 6.3, the correlation matrix for the alternative dependent variables (value after one day, value after one week and value after one month) shows that the values are highly intercorrelated. Any results should not depend on an arbitrary choice of dependent variable.

Table 6.3 also shows the correlation between the dependent variable (value after one day) and the independent variables listed in Table 6.2. The dominant relationship appears to be between absorptive capacity and value (significant at the 0.001 level). There is also a strong intercorrelation between absorptive capacity and the number of drugs in preclinical development (significant at the 0.001 level). This may indicate that these two variables are interrelated. In a regression equation, this strong intercorrelation may suppress the influence of preclinical product development capability and heighten the influence of absorptive capacity.

Discovery capability and "hot market" have marginal relationships with value (both are significant at the 0.05 level). Discovery capability seems to have an indirect effect on value; the primary link is to

TABLE 6.3   Correlation Matrices

	Valday	Valweek	Valmon
Valday	1.0000		
Valweek	0.9778	1.0000	
Valmon	0.9421	0.9771	1.0000

	Valday	SciCap	TechPre	TechCli	AbsCap	Hot
Valday	1.0000					
SciCap	0.2275	1.0000				
TechPre	0.4217	0.3626	1.0000			
TechCli	0.3080	0.1247	0.4470	1.0000		
AbsCap	0.5200	0.3423	0.4666	0.0662	1.0000	
Hot	0.2468	0.1136	0.1864	0.0762	0.2283	1.0000

absorptive capacity and preclinical development (significant at the 0.01 level). The relationship between "hot market" and absorptive capacity is consistent with the hypothesis that research activities occur in "waves". The flurry of IPO activity could be the result of an underlying flurry of research activity with development possibilities.

The regression results are presented in Table 6.4. The adjusted R^2 is 0.3316 and the F-statistic for the model is 11.12 ($p < 0.0001$) indicating that our model explains a significant amount of the variance in the market value of the equity of the firms in our sample. The regression results suggest that the two dominant factors in creating value from investments in R&D are absorptive capacity and development capability. The influence of scientific capability, preclinical development capability and a "hot market" do not appear to be significant.

Preclinical development capability seems to have an insignificant influence due to the high intercorrelation with absorptive capacity. When this variable is dropped from the regression equation, the overall adjusted R^2 increases slightly (due to the decrease in the number of degrees of freedom), and the T-statistics for clinical development capability and absorptive capability increase (3.2 and 5.3, respectively). Absorptive capacity still remains the dominant influence. All other independent variables continued to have an insignificant influence on value.

TABLE 6.4   Regression Results
(Dependent Variable: Value at End of First Day of Trading)

Source	SS	df	MS	
Model	24.33648	5	4.86729538	
Residual	42.45421	97	0.437672272	
Total	66.79069	102	0.654810659	

	Coef.	Std. err	t	$P > \lvert t \rvert$
SciCap	0.00150	0.04116	0.037	0.971
TechPre	0.10475	0.11692	0.896	0.372
TechCli	0.28163	0.11385	2.474	0.015
AbsCap	0.26163	0.05808	4.505	0.000
Hot	0.20555	0.15296	1.344	0.182
Constant	10.001	0.18901	52.911	0.000

Number of obs = 103
$F(5, 97)$ = 11.12
Prob > F = 0.0000
R^2 = 0.3644
Adj R^2 = 0.3316
Root MSE   = 0.66157

TABLE 6.5   ility of T-Statistics
(Partial Correlation of Valday, Valwe.. and Valmonth with Independent Variables)

Variable	Valday (Pcorr. Sig.)	Valweek (Pcorr. Sig.)	Valmonth (Pcorr. Sig.)
SciCap	0.0037	0.0417	0.0181
	0.971	0.682	0.8590
TechPre	0.0906	0.0553	0.0560
	0.372	0.587	0.5820
TechCli	0.2436	0.2411	0.2471
	0.015	0.016	0.014
AbsCap	0.4159	0.4042	0.4055
	0.000	0.000	0.000
Hot	0.1352	0.1597	0.1422
	0.182	0.114	0.160

The T-statistics in the regression table do not change appreciably if one uses the different measures of value (Table 6.5). Absorptive capacity remains the dominant factor. The influence of preclinical development capability is not significant but this may be due to the intercorrelation with absorptive capacity. The influence of clinical development remains important when either preclinical or absorptive capacity are included in the model. Neither the reputation of scientists nor the existence of a "hot market" have any significant influence on the value of the equities of the sample of biotechnology firms.

The results support the hypotheses that development capability and absorptive capacity improve a firm's ability to create value from R&D activities. The measure of absorptive capacity is correlated with all of the variables except clinical product development which may explain our failure to gain any support for hypothesis 1. However, given the strength of our results absorptive capacity appears to play a key role in the development of competence among biotechnology start-ups.

Our results provide evidence to support the capabilities position in the current debate between the industry structure and resources/capabilities schools within the field of strategy. Firm-specific capabilities in absorptive capacity and technical development were significantly positively related to the value of a firm's equities. In addition, the magnitude of the coefficients indicate that increases in absorptive capacity and development capabilities significantly increase the value created from a firm's investment in R&D. A 1% increase in absorptive capacity and development capabilities increases the market value of the firm's equity by 0.54%. In the case of the average biotechnology firm in our sample this is an increase of over \$320 000 in the market value of the firm's equities.

Our results suggest that both technical development capabilities and absorptive capacity are very important in the value creation process of biotechnology firms. We believe these results are due to the fact that, in contrast to scientific discovery, both of these capabilities provide appropriable benefits to the specific firm within the context of the biotechnology industry. Technical development capability is clearly appropriable because it facilitates the advance of the products which are owned by the organization into the regulatory process and hopefully on to the market. Successfully developing a product allows the firm to gain both desperately needed cash flows and credibility in the broader business environment.

Absorptive capacity creates appropriable benefits for the firm by increasing the productivity of the firm's R&D investments. Continually absorbing information from beyond the boundaries of the firm allows the firm to continually re-evaluate its portfolio of R&D projects based on this information. This process improves the odds of success by decreasing the gap between the perceived value of the firm's R&D options and the real value of the options. Decreasing this gap allows a firm more accurately to allocate scarce resources among its portfolio of R&D projects. This is critical in a rapidly developing highly technical field such as biotechnology. The knowledge base of the field is relatively immature and developing rapidly (Pisano, 1994). Under these circumstances the costs and possibility of failure are high and the relative merits of potential avenues of exploration are unclear. Under these conditions, absorptive capacity improves the firm's ability to recognize unprofitable avenues of exploration and allows a firm to adjust its portfolio of R&D projects to reduce the chance of failure by avoiding repetition of the failures and dead ends of competitors and other research organizations in the field. Therefore, as the absorptive capacity of the firm increases, the return on its R&D investments ought to increase.

While our results provide strong statistical support for our conclusions, we must also acknowledge that our focus on biotechnology raises questions about the generalizability of our study beyond this industry. Biotechnology has several unique characteristics, including a long product development and approval cycle, heavy reliance upon basic scientific research and a very expensive product development process.

However, in spite of these unique characteristics, we still believe that our results are generalizable beyond the biotechnology industry. The importance of absorptive capacity in R&D may be one reason for the emergence of the competitive intelligence profession—a profession which is aimed at developing tools and techniques for absorbing information that is external to the firm.

While we have found strong empirical support for our model it should also be noted that there is still a significant amount of variation in the value of the equities of the firms in our sample which remains unexplained. Obviously, there remain other variables of potential interest which demand further study. Some of this may be due to the quality of our measures of learning capabilities. It is clear that further work needs to be done to refine and expand our ability to measure the various aspects of learning in creating R&D competence.

REFERENCES

Arrow, K. J. (1962). "Economic welfare and the allocation of resources for invention", in R. R. Nelson, editor, *The Rate and Direction of Inventive Activity: Economic and Social Factors*, Princeton, NJ: Princeton University Press.
Bain, J. (1956). *Barriers to New Competition*, Cambridge, MA: Harvard University Press.
Baldwin, W. L. and J. T. Scott (1987). *Market Structure and Technological Change*, Chichester: Harwood.
Barney, J. B. (1986a). "Strategic factor markets: expectations, luck and business strategy", *Management Science*, **32**, pp. 1231–1241.
Barney, J. B. (1986b). "Organizational culture: Can it be a source of sustained competitive advantage?" *Academy of Management Review*, **11**, pp. 791–800.
Barney, J. B. (1986c). "Types of competition and the theory of strategy: Toward an integrative framework", *Academy of Management Review*, **11**, pp. 791–800.
Barney, J. (1991). "Firm resources and sustained competitive advantage", *Journal of Management*, **17**(1), pp. 99–120.
Burrill, Steven G. and Kenneth B. Lee (1992). *Biotech 92: Promise to Reality*, San Francisco: Ernst & Young.
Burrill, Steven G. and Kenneth B. Lee (1993). *Biotech 93: Accelerating Commercialization*, San Francisco: Ernst & Young.
Burrill, Steven G. and Kenneth B. Lee (1994). *Biotech 94: Accelerating Commercialization*, San Francisco: Ernst & Young.
Cohen, W. and D. Levinthal (1990). "Absorptive capacity: A new perspective on learning and innovation", *Administrative Science Quarterly*, **35**, pp. 128–152.
Cohen, W. and D. Levinthal (1994). "Fortune favors the prepared firm", *Management Science*, **40**(2), pp. 227–241.
Dasgupta, P. and P. David (1994). "Toward a new economics of science", *Research Policy*, **23**, pp. 487–521.
Debackere, K. and M. A. Rappa (1994). "Technological communities and the diffusion of knowledge: A replication and validation", *R&D Management*, **24**(4), pp. 355–371.
Dierickx, I. and K. Cool (1989). "Asset stock accumulation and sustainability of competitive advantage", *Management Science*, **35**, pp. 1504–1513.
Downes, D. H. and R. Heinkel (1982). "Signaling and the valuation of unseasoned new issues", *Journal of Finance*, **37**(1), pp. 1–10.
Fiol, M. and M. Lyles (1985). "Organizational learning", *Academy of Management Review*, **10**(4), pp. 803–813.
Franklin, J. J. and R. Johnston (1988). "Cocitation bibliometrics as a tool of S&T and R&D management: Issues, applications and developments", in A. F. J. van Raan, editor, *The Handbook of Quantitative Studies of Science and Technology*, Amsterdam, The Netherlands: North Holland.

Garfield, E., I. Sher and R. J. Torpie (1964). "The use of citation data in writing the history of science", Philadelphia, Pa: Institute for Scientific Information.

Henderson, R. & I. Cockburn (1994). "Measuring competence? Exploring firm effects in pharmaceutical research", *Strategic Management Journal*, **15** (Special Issue), winter, pp. 63–84.

Hicks, D. (1987). "Limitations of co-citation analysis as a tool for science policy", *Social Studies of Science*, **17**, pp. 295–316.

Hill, C. W. L. and D. L. Deeds (1995). "The importance of industry structure for the determination of firm profitability", Working Paper, University of Washington.

Ibbotson, R. G. and J. J. Jaffe (1975). " 'Hot issue' markets", *Journal of Finance*, **30**, pp. 1027–1042.

Kamien, M. I. and N. L. Schwartz (1982). *Market Structure and Innovation*, Cambridge: Cambridge University Press.

Kandel, N., J. P. Remy, C. Stein and T. Durand (1991). "Who's who in technology: Identifying technological competence within the firm", *R&D Management*, **21**(3), pp. 215–228.

Klavans, R. (1994). "The measurement of a competitor's core competence", in G. Hamel and A. Heene, editors, *Competence-Based Competition*, New York: John Wiley & Sons.

Kogut, B. and U. Zander (1992). "Knowledge of the firm, combinative capabilities and the replication of technology", *Organization Science*, **3**(3), pp. 383–396.

Kuhn, T. (1970). *The Structure of Scientific Revolution*, Illinois: University of Chicago Press.

Levinthal, D. and J. Myatt (1994). "Co-evolution of capabilities and industries: the evolution of mutual fund processing", *Strategic Management Journal*, **15**, pp. 45–62.

Leydesdorff, L. (1986). "The development of frames of references", *Scientometrics*, **9**, pp. 103–125.

McGuiness, P. (1993). "The market valuation of initial public offerings in Hong Kong", *Applied Financial Economics*, **3**, pp. 267–281.

Mansfield, E. (1985). "How rapidly does new technology leak out?" *Journal of Industrial Economics*, Vol. 34, No. 2, December, pp. 217–223.

Meyers, P. (1990). "Non-linear learning in large technological firms: Period Four implies Chaos", *Research Policy*, **19**, pp. 97–115.

Mombers, C., A. von Heeringer, R. van Venetie and C. le Pair (1985). "Displaying strengths and weaknesses in national R&D performance through document cocitation", *Scientometrics*, **7**, pp. 341–356.

Nelson, R. R. (1959). "The simple economics of basic scientific research", *Journal of Political Economy*, **67**.

Peterson, P. P. (1989). "Event studies: A review of issues and methodology", *Quarterly Journal of Business and Economics*, **28**, pp. 36–66.

Pisano, G. (1994). "Knowledge integration and the Locus of Learning: An empirical analysis of process development", *Strategic Management Journal*, **15** (Special Issue), winter, pp. 85–100.

Prahalad, C. K. and G. Hamel (1990). "The core competence of the corporation", *Harvard Business Review*, May–June, pp. 79–91.

Porter, M. E. (1980). *Competitive Strategy*, New York: Free Press.

Porter, M. E. (1985). *Competitive Advantage*, New York: Free Press.

Price, D. J. de Solla (1963). *Little Science, Big Science*, New York: Columbia University Press.

Rao, H., (1994). "The social construction of reputations: certification contests, legitimation and the survival of organizations in the American automobile industry: 1985–1912," *Strategic Management Journal*, **15**, pp. 29–44.

Ritter, J. A. (1984a). "Signaling and the valuation of unseasoned new issues: A comment", *Journal of Finance*, **39**(4), pp. 1231–1237.

Ritter, J. A. (1984b). "The 'hot issue' market of 1980", *Journal of Business*, **57**, pp. 215–240.

Ritter, J. A. (1991). "The long-run performance of initial public offerings", *Journal of Finance*, **46**(1), pp. 3–27.

Salinger, M. (1992). "Value event studies", *Review of Economics and Statistics*, **74**, pp. 671–677.

Sanchez, Ron (1993). "Strategic flexibility, firm organization, and managerial work: A strategic options perspective," *Advances in Strategic Management*, **9**, pp. 251–291.

Sanchez, R., A. Heene and H. Thomas (eds) (1996). *Dynamics of Competence-Based Competition*, Oxford: Elsevier.

Sanchez, R. and H. Thomas (1996). "Strategic goals" in theory and practice of competence based competition: From industry studies to a new theory of competitive dynamics, R. Sanchez, A. Heene and H. Thomas, editors, Oxford: Elsevier.

Scherer, F. M. (1980). *Industrial Market Structure and Economic Performance*, 2nd edn, Chicago: Rand McNally.

Simon, H. A. (1969). *Sciences of the Artificial*, Cambridge, MA: MIT Press.

Small, H. G. and B. C. Griffith (1974). "The structure of scientific literature, I: Identifying and graphing specialities", *Science Studies*, **4**.

Solow, R. (1957). "Technical change and the aggregate production function", *Review of Economics and Statistics*, August.

Teece, D. J., G. Pisano and A. Shuen (1990). "Firm capabilities, resources and the concept of strategy', Working paper, University of California, Berkeley.

Titman, S. and B. Trueman (1986). "Information quality and the valuation of new issues", *Journal of Accounting and Economics*, **8**, pp. 159–172.

Wernerfelt, B. (1984). "A resource based view of the firm", *Strategic Management Journal*, **5**, pp. 171–180.

7

Competence Building by Incorporating Clients into the Development of a Business Service Firm's Knowledge Base

PETTERI SIVULA, FRANS A. J. VAN DEN BOSCH, TOM ELFRING

In a business service context, client alliances may provide an important way to build the competences of the service firm. The close interaction with the client in service delivery offers an opportunity for a business service firm to absorb knowledge from the client. This chapter adds to our understanding of managing the process of learning and knowledge transfer by looking at how clients can contribute to the development of the knowledge base of knowledge-intensive business service firms. Combining insights from the resource-based literature, this chapter develops a model of competence building through knowledge management in downstream alliances.

1 INTRODUCTION

The development and deployment of knowledge allow firms to gain competitive advantage by serving as the foundation of their capabilities

Strategic Learning and Knowledge Management.
Edited by Ron Sanchez and Aimé Heene.
Copyright © 1997 John Wiley & Sons Ltd.

and competences. The ability to develop a knowledge base is increasingly seen as a fundamental process of competence building. Business service firms in particular rely on their knowledge base, because in addition to transforming production factors to services, specific forms of knowledge may often be an input and an output in service delivery processes. Therefore, both scholars and managers need to understand how firms, and in particular business service firms, can develop their knowledge bases more effectively.

The knowledge base of a company can be examined at two levels: knowledge as a specific *content* resource, and knowledge that serves as the basis for the firm's ability to integrate the *processes* of knowledge creation and development. Resource base, dynamic capabilities and competence-based competition theory address various aspects of this issue. Resource-based theory suggests the properties that are required for knowledge to become a rent-generating resource (Dierickx and Cool, 1989; Peteraf, 1993). Dynamic capabilities theory views the development of a knowledge base as a learning process (Lane, 1994; Teece, Pisano and Shuen, 1994). Competence-based competition theory extends both of these theories by incorporating managers' ability to manage knowledge effectively in building and leveraging competencies (Sanchez, Heene and Thomas, 1996). These theories jointly contribute to our understanding of the development of a knowledge base. They suggest that the knowledge base can be developed both internally and within an alliance (Penrose, 1959; Cohen and Levinthal, 1990; Badaracco, 1991; Hamel, 1991). The internal development of knowledge, organizational learning and the use of external knowledge are all being actively researched.

Some research has focused on learning in alliances with other firms, but little is known about learning from clients. There is some evidence that users or clients can be an important source of innovation (Von Hippel, 1988; Rothwell, 1986). The research on marketing of services has revealed that durable relationships between business service firms and clients provides opportunities for the service provider to absorb and utilize the client's knowledge (Sharma, 1991). Given the importance of the development of a knowledge base in business service firms, it is remarkable that the client, as an important source of knowledge, has largely been neglected. The often active role of clients in service delivery suggests that a client might be an important source and partner in the development of a knowledge base. This is already recognized in some of the leading business service firms (e.g. Fluor Daniel, Annual Report, 1992). However, in present theories, this competence-building routine has not been adequately recognized. In this chapter we attempt to remedy this situation.

The main aim of this chapter is to analyse the role of client alliances in the development of a knowledge base and from this analysis to propose a model of knowledge management for business service firms aimed at creating new capabilities in knowledge base development. Combining insights from the above-mentioned theories with research on knowledge, learning, innovation and relationships, this chapter examines how the development and deployment of the knowledge base can be of strategic importance to business service firms (Section 2); proposes a preliminary model of knowledge management in downstream alliances (Section 3); and summarizes the opportunities for creating new capabilities by incorporating clients into the development of the business service firm's knowledge base (Section 4).

2 DEVELOPMENT AND DEPLOYMENT OF KNOWLEDGE IN BUSINESS SERVICE FIRMS

Knowledge has been suggested to be the most important resource that contributes to the success of the firm (Grant, 1994). However, it is not only knowledge as a resource that contributes to the success of the firm. Managerial knowledge also *coordinates* the knowledge processes of a firm (creation, development, maintenance and deployment of knowledge). This implies that the knowledge base of the company may be viewed at two levels, namely, knowledge as a specific content resource and knowledge as a capability that integrates the activities of the firm at the organizational level and influences the processes of knowledge creation and development.

There are a number of ways to classify and describe the characteristics of the knowledge of the firm. A common way of describing the characteristics of knowledge is to divide it into explicit and tacit knowledge as classified by Polanyi (1966). Hayek (1945) provided a similar classification by dividing knowledge into scientific and practical knowledge of "time and place". Penrose (1959) made a distinction between objective and experiential knowledge, whereas Badaracco (1991) discerns migratory and embedded knowledge. These four classifications point out the difference between codified knowledge and other forms of knowledge that has tacit (difficult to articulate), circumstantial (context dependent) or experiential (acquired or transferred by active participation) characteristics. Explicit knowledge is more easily acquired and transferred than tacit knowledge (Sanchez 1996, in this volume). Explicit knowledge may be associated with the notion of information as "organized data" (Davis and Botkin, 1994) and may be found in tangible sources: databanks, manuals, directives or professional journals. Tacit knowledge, on the other hand, is closer to a notion of knowledge as an applied, context-dependent source of information. It is typically difficult to articulate and codify and thus difficult to transfer. The transfer of tacit knowledge requires activity and participation (Nonaka, 1994; Nonaka and Takeuchi, 1995). Tacit knowledge is thus people dependent (Hall, 1992) and it may be embedded in the skills and expertise of the employees. Tacit knowledge has also been suggested to be stored in organizational routines (Nelson and Winter, 1982). Cooperation between partners may also create routines that embody tacit knowledge from previous engagements. The knowledge embodied in the members of both organizations participating in service delivery together forms a part of the network knowledge base (Sharma, 1992).

Sharma (1992) has argued that the major source of tacit knowledge in a business service firm may be its activities in networks. Network knowledge may be (1) industry specific, (2) technology specific, (3) function specific or (4) client specific. The tacitness of network knowledge and the tendency for membership in one network to limit membership in another competitive network (Sharma, 1992) suggests that network knowledge has the properties of being difficult to imitate by competitors and difficult to acquire from factor markets. These properties of network knowledge may make it a strategically important resource that has all the properties required for a rent-generating resource: (1) idiosyncrasy (firm specific or network specific, unique), (2) non-imitability, (3) superiority (low cost, high quality) (Teece, Pisano and Shuen, 1994), (4) scarcity (Peteraf, 1993) and (5) non-tradeability (resource endowments do not equilibrate through factor markets) (Dierickx and Cool, 1989). Network knowledge may thus allow a firm to gain a competitive advantage. To make this competitive advantage sustainable, the managers of a business service firm need to create a context that supports continuous processes for the absorption of network knowledge. The continuous enhancement of relationships with clients and the enlargement of client contacts may sustain the competitive advantage by offering opportunities for knowledge development and transfer. To achieve this requires superior managerial cognition, coordination ability and abilities to manage knowledge development effectively (Sanchez, Heene and Thomas, 1996).

Our *typology of knowledge-related activities* in a business service firm, shown in Figure 7.1, combines two dimensions: the type of activity and the locality of activity. The type of activity refers to either the deployment of the existing knowledge base or the development of the knowledge base of the company. The deployment of knowledge is affected by internal managerial services (Penrose, 1959) that influence the flow of knowledge within a business service firm and between firms that are linked by business relationships. The development of knowledge refers to changes in the knowledge base of the company (possessed by employees, embodied in services, or embedded in managerial systems). The second dimension, the locality of activity, makes a distinction between activities that take place within the boundaries of the organization and those that are taking place in an interface context with other firms, for example, clients. In managing interfaces it is interesting to recognize that different aspects of the activities presented in Figure 7.1 are interlinked. Cohen and Levinthal (1990) and others have proposed that the internal development of a knowledge base facilitates a firm's ability to absorb and exploit extramural knowledge. Internal linkages between transfer and development of knowledge (see some recent contributions, Bartlett and Ghoshal, 1993; Nonaka, 1994; Hedlund, 1994; Von Krogh and Slocum, 1994) are not considered here in order to focus on the development of the knowledge base of a firm by utilizing external sources of knowledge.

Internal managerial capabilities provide a context for the vertical and horizontal transfer of knowledge, and support everyday operations within the business service firm and in its service delivery. Service delivery activities may consist of: (1) extension (Hedlund, 1994) as a service that embodies components of knowledge that are transferred from a business service firm to a client and (2) the utilization of a client's knowledge in service delivery. In the first case, a more formal trade of knowledge takes place. This, however, does not diminish the knowledge base of the company, since knowledge, typically, does not deteriorate when

	LOCALITY OF ACTIVITY	
	internal	interface
transfer of knowledge	BACK OFFICE 1. vertical 2. horizontal	SERVICE DELIVERY 1. extension 2. utilization of client's knowledge in service delivery
development of knowledge base	INTERNAL DEVELOPMENT OF KNOWLEDGE BASE 1. R&D 2. Training	INTERFACE DEVELOPMENT OF KNOWLEDGE BASE 1. cooperative development 2. absorption 3. development by pressure

TYPE OF ACTIVITY

FIGURE 7.1   Typology of Knowledge-related Activities in a Business Service Firm

used (Dierickx and Cool, 1989). The second case implies a client's more active participation in service delivery through a combination of the business service firm's knowledge and the client's knowledge. Client participation in service delivery—for example by providing employees for project organization—does not necessarily influence the knowledge base of the business service firm directly.

As depicted in Figure 7.1, the knowledge base of the business service firm may be developed both internally and externally. R&D and training activities influence the development of the knowledge base internally. The horizontal integration of knowledge in an organization may further develop organizational knowledge (Bartlett and Ghoshal, 1993; Grant, 1994). The knowledge base of the company may be influenced by external sources in at least two ways: cooperative development of knowledge in alliances and the absorption of knowledge from a client. The second mode of knowledge development is the informal trading of knowledge (Von Hippel, 1988). The absorption of knowledge takes place simultaneously with the formal trading of knowledge (extension) as the employees of both firms intermingle in service delivery. This is due to the basic characteristic of services: the production and consumption of the service are often inseparable (Mills and Moberg, 1990). The research on marketing of services has revealed that the relationships between a business service firm and a client are often durable (Sharma, 1991) and thus may offer a basis for continuous knowledge exchange and learning.

Based on these arguments, close interaction with a client provides opportunities for (1) the utilization of a client's knowledge in service delivery, (2) the absorption of a client's knowledge, (3) the cooperative development of knowledge, and (4) learning-by-doing and other dynamic effects of business relationships. The last mode of knowledge development means that the business relationship with a client may have dynamic effects on the knowledge base of the company in addition to the effect of cooperation already mentioned. A demanding client, for example, may pressurize a business service firm to develop knowledge internally in order to satisfy the client. The last argument reflects Gardiners and Rothwell's (1985) proposition that "tough" clients may play a role in stimulating innovation. Rothwell (1986) suggested a more active role for the client in knowledge development and pointed out the need for greater recognition of the importance of users as active participants in innovation processes. The *active role of a client* in a service delivery situation suggests that a service client may be an even more important source of knowledge and partner for knowledge development than users of physical products in manufacturing industries.

It should be noted that as client alliances aim at providing cost efficient and high quality services for clients, knowledge absorption from the client alliance may be regarded by the business service firm's management as a mere by-product that does not directly contribute to the development of the knowledge base of the firm. As a firm's efforts to create new capabilities are guided by managers' cognitions, it is important to such managerial perceptions. To create new patterns of action, both employees and managers must be involved at all levels of analysis of the client relationship. In the model developed in the next section, we investigate the elements of a strategic logic (Sanchez and Heene, 1996) of learning from client relationships.

3   TOWARDS A MODEL OF KNOWLEDGE MANAGEMENT IN DOWNSTREAM ALLIANCES

In this section, key determinants of knowledge transfer in downstream alliances are identified. Second, we propose a model of knowledge management in downstream alliances.

DETERMINANTS OF KNOWLEDGE TRANSFER IN DOWNSTREAM ALLIANCES

Three factors influence the magnitude and the direction of knowledge flows in a downstream alliance: (1) the transferability of knowledge, (2) a client's willingness to share its knowledge, and (3) a business service firm's willingness and capacity to absorb external knowledge. The transferability of various forms of knowledge was commented upon earlier in this chapter. In this section we focus on the remaining two determinants of knowledge transfer. Some empirically grounded theories have been developed about knowledge transfer in horizontal alliances (Hamel, 1991) and the impacts of internal knowledge development on a firm's absorptive capacity (Cohen and Levinthal, 1990). Analogical similarities support the application of these results in our model. (For earlier approaches see Van den Bosch *et al.* 1994 and Sivula *et al.* 1995.) Hamel's (1991) research on the internalization of knowledge in alliances helps to identify the factors that determine the penetrability of a client's knowledge base. Cohen and Levinthal (1990), on the other hand, contribute to the issue by focusing on the internal determinants of knowledge absorption. *The determinants of a firm's absorptive capacity for external knowledge* will be formulated by combining Hamel's (1991) and Cohen and Levinthal's (1990) research on knowledge absorption from external sources, as summarized in Table 7.1.

TABLE 7.1   Dependent Variables of Model of Knowledge Management in Downstream Alliances

Dependent Variables	Determinants	Managerial Coordination

A INTERNAL
1. Receptivity (Hamel, 1991; Cohen and Levinthal, 1990)
	1.a. Active:
	  • development of prior knowledge
	  • organizational factors and mechanisms (team building and cross-functional linkages)
	  • communication systems
	1.b. Passive:
	  • learning specific factors
		1. Organizational incentives (Reve, 1990)
		2. Culture (Reve, 1990)
		3. Routines (Teece, Pisano and Shuen, 1994)
		4. Direction (Grant, 1994)
		5. Managerial roles (Bartlett and Ghoshal, 1993)

B INTERFACE
1. Transparency of client (Hamel, 1991)
	1.a. Active:
	  • gatekeeping
	  • number of people involved in a project
	  • restriction in collaboration agreement
	  • site selection
	1.b. Passive:
	  • social context
	  • tacitness of knowledge and skills
	  • relative pace of skill building
		1. Interorganizational incentives (Reve, 1990)
		2. Structure of cooperation
		3. Routines of cooperation

Sources: Bartlett and Ghoshal, 1993: Cohen and Levinthal, 1990; Grant, 1994; Hamel, 1991; Reve, 1990 and Teece, Pisano and Shuen, 1994.

Transparency of a partner affects the potential for learning (Hamel, 1991). In our model transparency is essentially a property of the client. Different types of clients may be distinguished by their mode of involvement, their knowledge base and their preference for different types of projects (piecemeal or whole). Also, the special nature of the relationship between the client and the business service firm may affect the opportunity for the absorption of knowledge from client alliances. Clients need to feel secure that client-specific knowledge will not be used in ways that could diminish their competitive position. This implies that there may be factors that limit the opportunity for knowledge absorption from client alliances. On the other hand, business services may be delivered in such a way that some components of knowledge based on experience from previous engagements may not be used to full effect for a new client, because the knowledge is a co-specialized asset useful in the context of a specific client's problems. In that sense, the deployment of knowledge from previous clients may not harm them, but may generally improve the service.

Hamel (1991) divided the determinants of transparency into active and passive factors. *Active factors* may be influenced by the client. A client may limit the transparency in a variety of ways. One or more individuals may be charged with monitoring knowledge flows across the boundaries of a firm (gatekeeping). This gatekeeping is an important activity of interface management from the client's perspective. The nature of joint tasks also affects the transparency. The more people involved with cooperation and the more intermingling needed in a service delivery, the more transparent an organization becomes. The scope of a collaborative agreement also affects the transparency. If only a narrow range of products or markets is involved in the joint task, the transparency will be limited. Site selection and control may also be used for limiting transparency. Performing the joint tasks at the client's site may increase the transparency of the client.

Passive factors are related to the social context of the client, tacitness of knowledge and the nature of the relationship (competition versus cooperation). Passive barriers to transparency may be even more efficient than active measures (Hamel, 1991). The business service firm may find it difficult to learn how to penetrate the client's social context, in which case different cultures and a defensive attitude towards outsiders may be barriers to transparency. Creating trust could mitigate this, and we touch upon the role of trust at the end of this section. As noted earlier, the nature of knowledge may also be a natural barrier to transparency. Tacit knowledge is more difficult to encode and transfer than more explicit knowledge (Hamel, 1991).

Receptivity determines the firm's capacity to learn (Hamel, 1991). This concept is close to Cohen and Levinthal's (1990) notion of absorptive capacity. Absorptive capacity, however, is defined more broadly to include the capacity to evaluate and utilize outside knowledge in addition to assimilating external knowledge. Receptivity of the firm has active and passive determinants similar to those affecting transparency. *Active determinants* of receptivity are related to the development of prior-related knowledge (R&D) and training that facilitates the absorption of external knowledge. Also, organizational factors like team building, the establishment of cross-functional linkages and communication systems will increase the receptivity of the firm internally (Cohen and Levinthal, 1990).

A competence perspective by the management of the firm may also contribute to the receptivity of the firm.

Hamel (1991) presented the *passive determinants* of receptivity in three paradoxes: (1) learning often requires unlearning, (2) a small crisis abets learning and a big crisis limits learning and (3) the greater the need to learn, the higher the barriers to receptivity (1991: 97). Hamel's third paradox is similar to Cohen and Levinthal's focus on prior-related knowledge in a firm's capability of absorbing extramural knowledge.

MODEL

Two central features in the resource-based view of the firm can be discerned: the firm as an integrator of resources and the firm as a developer of resources (Teece, Pisano and Shuen, 1994). These two features will be combined in our model. The integrating perspective will be adapted from Reve's (1990) model in which a firm influences its resource base and its business environment and combines its core resources with the partner's complementary resources by establishing strategic alliances. The downstream alliance is a meaningful arrangement for both parties if (i) the complementary resources and skills are needed in a service delivery or (ii) if these skills and resources facilitate cooperative knowledge development. We examine the development perspective by focusing on creating new capabilities in developing the knowledge base of the firm.

Before presenting the model of knowledge transfer, we will briefly identify four key *knowledge flows* between the business service firm and the client, as shown in Figure 7.2 (see arrows 1, 2, 3 and 4). At the organizational level, cooperative projects or client alliances contribute to the experience and the knowledge base of the business service firm (see arrow 1) through direct absorption of knowledge, the cooperative development of knowledge or the dynamic effects of a demanding client that induce the internal development of knowledge. Internal managerial services support and provide a context for the knowledge-intensive service delivery (see arrow 2). These are closely associated with the coordination mechanisms of the firm. At the project level, business services (embodying knowledge components) are provided in cooperation with the client (see arrow 3). This implies that a client's knowledge may be partly utilized in service delivery. The close interaction and the actual process of delivering a service offers an opportunity for knowledge absorption and learning-by-doing both at the level of the individual and the project team (see arrow 4). From a competence-based perspective, the managerial challenge in these four knowledge flows is to create *new capabilities* in developing the firm's knowledge base—that is, new abilities to sustain the coordinated development of knowledge assets in ways that help the firm achieve its goals (Sanchez, Heene and Thomas, 1996).

Figure 7.2 presents a model that shows the determinants of knowledge absorption from downstream alliances with clients and associated coordination mechanisms. *Three basic patterns of activities* for knowledge transfer and development for a business service firm may be identified: (1) the current knowledge base *supports* extension (a service that transfers knowledge), (2) internal development activities (training, R&D) *facilitate* the absorption of knowledge from downstream alliances and (3) internal development and the absorption of knowledge combine together to *develop* the knowledge base of the business service firm. Figure 7.2 depicts these three basic patterns of activities with corresponding arrows. The factor markets have also been suggested as being a source of knowledge for a business service firm (Sharma, 1992). However, the resource-based view of the firm suggests that in creating rent-generating

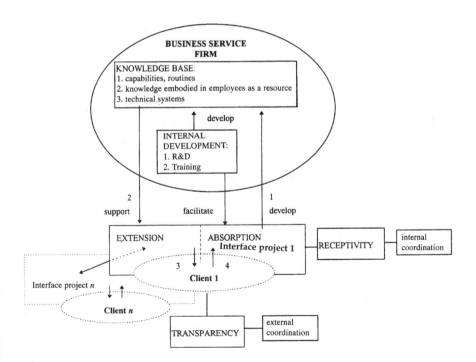

FIGURE 7.2   Model of Knowledge Management in Downstream Alliance

resources, market mechanisms for knowledge acquisition may be less effective than the internal development of resources.

The focus on downstream alliances suggests two ways of influencing the development of the knowledge base of the firm: the internal development of knowledge through the absorption of knowledge from alliances and the internal development of the firm's knowledge base (see the box within the business service firm in Figure 7.2) by the training of employees or by conducting R&D activities. Not only does this develop the knowledge base of the firm directly, but as indicated above, it indirectly facilitates the firm's absorptive capacity. Internal coordination mechanisms, see Table 7.1, include organizational incentives and culture (Reve, 1990). The focus on knowledge as a resource suggests at least three other mechanisms for the coordination of knowledge as well. First, the utilization of a firm's routines (Teece, Pisano and Shuen, 1994), second, direction in terms of rules, guidelines, standard operating procedures (Grant, 1994), and third, managerial roles (Bartlett and Ghoshal, 1993) in managing the knowledge flows and creating new patterns of action in the use of these flows (Sanchez, Heene and Thomas, 1996). The relationship with the client requires external coordination due to the lack of formal control. The interface coordination mechanisms, see Table 7.1, are mainly based on interorganizational incentives like negotiations (Reve, 1990). Negotiations between the potential partners that aim at achieving a contract that specifies the content and context of cooperation may be used for influencing the transparency of the client. Contracts that deal with a wide range of issues and give access to the client's employees, documents, site and other sources of information increase the client's transparency (Hamel, 1991). In this respect, interface coordination may also be used for influencing client's transparency. Even if a business service firm can only influence the transparency of the client indirectly, a firm may be able to identify the problems associated with transparency and try to reduce them. For instance, the passive factors in the transparency of the client, may require the development of commonly understood roles and interaction patterns. These routines of cooperation may facilitate the communication of tacit knowledge (Nelson and Winter, 1982).

For deliberately *creating new capabilities*, the creation of new patterns of action in combining existing knowledge with newly absorbed knowledge from the client is needed. The typology presented in Table 7.1 of determinants and managerial coordination mechanisms is *a first step towards theory building* regarding the managerial processes involved in creating new capabilities and competence building. These managerial processes deserve more attention in present theories of competence-based competition.

PROJECTS WITH CLIENTS

In case studies aimed at this kind of theory building in business service firms, *project management* to enhance competence building deserves close attention. In project management, managerial tools and instruments can be developed to facilitate new combinations of resources and capabilities scattered both *within the firm* and *in the variety of projects* performed with clients.

The *connections between projects*, for example between 1 and *n* as depicted in Figure 7.2, may be viewed to be *parallel* or *sequential*. In the first case, knowledge may be transferred through people or codified knowledge (Sanchez 1996, in this volume) between different projects that are related in some respect (horizontal integration of knowledge). This may support the extension or development of knowledge in the projects involved. The sequential case, however, refers to past or future projects. If the cooperative project *n* is with the same client 1, the earlier assignments and the associated learning from the cooperation may be argued to be beneficial for this client in terms of efficient and improved services. Prior knowledge about the client and industry and their established routines help to make cooperation smooth and fast. However, if the future cooperative project *n* is with a different client, client 1 may feel threatened, since the potential knowledge transfer to competitors may erode the competitive edge of client 1. The result may be the limitation of transparency or the refusal of repeat engagements. On the other hand, client 1 may also benefit from the service provider's earlier assignments with different clients. This is especially the case when relevant network knowledge is utilized, for example in the customization of services. As Elfring and Baven have noted: "Customization can be achieved faster and better when the service supplier has prior knowledge of the industry in which the customer operates. As a result, clients increasingly require a degree of knowledge from service suppliers about the industry concerned" (1994: 47). Finding the right balance between offering client benefits from network knowledge and creating the fear of diffusion of knowledge to competitors, is a dilemma facing providers of knowledge-intensive business services that is difficult to overcome, but has to be managed. A business service firm that is aiming at aggressive knowledge absorption may find it difficult to establish a downstream alliance if the client feels that the business service firm is exploiting client's resources. In this respect, a business service firm's managers and employees must be able to create trust (for a recent attempt to define trust, see Hosmer, 1995: 399) and consensus in client alliances about the mutual benefits from cooperative knowledge development and transfer.

Other factors that hinder the absorption of knowledge from client alliances may be *internal to the firm*. The employees of the business service firm may feel that they do not have anything to learn from the client. Alvesson (1994) provided interesting evidence for this. He studied Swedish advertising agencies and found that: "The advertising people seldom think of the client's suggestions as expressions of knowledge or insightful evaluation. The client is someone who is always wrong, if he is not in agreement with the advertising people" (1994: 549). Consequently, creating new capabilities in the knowledge base development of firms may require efforts to assume the attitude of a student rather than that of a teacher.

4   SUMMARY AND CONCLUSIONS

In this chapter we have analysed the development of the knowledge base of the knowledge-intensive business service firms with regard to client alliances. To this end, we identify determinants of knowledge transfer between a business service firm and a client. Based on these determinants we propose a preliminary model of knowledge management aimed at creating new capabilities in knowledge base development. The model contains the determinants of knowledge absorption from downstream alliances and associated managerial coordination mechanisms. We hope to contribute to the better management of knowledge-intensive business service firms by focusing on the context-specific source of competitive advantage: *developing the business service firm's knowledge base by learning from the close interaction with the clients.* This approach may help to overcome the problem of infinite regress in analysing capabilities or competences as sources of competitive advantage in general (Collis, 1994).

The first step in this theory-building effort was taken by proposing a typology of knowledge-related activities in client relationships. We use this typology to make a distinction between internal and interface activities on the one hand and between static and dynamic influences of knowledge-related activities on the other hand. The typology helped us to clarify these concepts by positioning them, showing their boundaries, and using this framework to suggest the usability of concepts from different streams of research. To show the relationships between the concepts, we propose a preliminary model for managing knowledge base development in client alliances. With the help of this model, we have identified a paradox in providing knowledge-intensive services and stressed the necessity of creating trust in client alliances to overcome a potential client dilemma in participating in the development of a business service firm's knowledge base.

However, further theoretical and empirical research is needed. Especially, the managerial aspects of our model and the building up of managerial coordination activities over time deserve more attention. Detailed longitudinal case studies in knowledge-intensive business service firms such as engineering consultancy firms and management consultancy firms are needed to improve the proposed model and to address the issues raised through further research. It will be a challenge for empirical research to discover managerial coordination mechanisms for knowledge transfer in client relationships and to determine whether the discovered mechanisms will be useful in a more general sense as well. However, the question arises if all service provider–client interactions are a fruitful platform for competence building?

In this connection we would like to stress the importance of (i) identifying *different types of clients* for the development of the knowledge base and competence building of the business service firm and (ii) strategies for dealing with these different types of clients. Looking at the client relationships from the perspective of competence building may provide a novel insight into practice. It may be useful for managers in knowledge-intensive business firms to analyse their client base as a source of knowledge and identify the potential learning partners. One way to approach the problem is to focus on the transparency of the client as an indication of learning potential. The other factor in analysing the client base that deserves attention is the position of the clients in terms of knowledge. The clients with leading positions in their industry, or which are otherwise known as innovative, may be the best sources of external knowledge. The competence-based competition between knowledge-intensive business service firms requires that managers have the ability to incorporate strategically important clients into knowledge base development and coordinate the knowledge transfer process in client alliances. Those knowledge-intensive business service firms that focus on more effective management of learning processes with clients may be building competitive advantage over others.

REFERENCES

Alvesson, M. (1994). "Talking in organisations: managing identity and impressions in an advertising agency", *Organisation Studies*, **15**(4), pp. 535–563.

Badaracco, J. L. (1991). *The Knowledge Link: How Firms Compete Through Strategic Alliances*, Boston, Mass: Harvard Business School Press.

Bartlett, C. A. and S. Ghoshal (1993). "Beyond the M-form: Toward a managerial theory of the firm", *Strategic Management Journal*, **14**, pp. 23–46.

Cohen, W. M. and D. A. Levinthal (1990). "Absorptive capacity: A new perspective on learning and innovation", *Administrative Science Quarterly*, **35**, pp. 128–152.

Collis, D. J. (1994). "Research note: How valuable are organizational capabilities", *Strategic Management Journal*, **15**, pp. 143–152.

Davis, S. and J. Botkin (1994). "The coming of knowledge-based business", *Harvard Business Review*, September–October, pp. 165–170.

Dierickx, I. and K. Cool (1989). "Asset stock accumulation and sustainability of competitive advantage", *Management Science*, 35(12), pp. 1504–1511.

Elfring, T. and G. Baven (1994), "Outsourcing technical services: Stages of development", *Long Range Planning*, 27(5), pp. 42–51.

Fluor Daniel (1992). Annual Report.

Gardiner, P. and R. Rothwell (1985). "Tough customers: Good design", *Design Studies*, 6(1), pp. 7–17.

Grant, R. M. (1994). *Organisational Capability Within a Knowledge-based View of the Firm*, Unpublished paper submitted to Amos Tuck Conference on Managing Hypercompetition.

Hall, R. (1992). "The strategic analysis of intangible resources", *Strategic Management Journal*, 13, pp. 135–144.

Hall, R. (1993). "A framework linking intangible resources and capabilities to sustainable competitive advantage", *Strategic Management Journal*, 14, pp. 607–618.

Hamel, G. (1991). "Competition for competence and interpartner learning within international strategic alliances", *Strategic Management Journal*, 12, pp. 83–103.

Hayek, F. A. (1945). "The use of knowledge in society", *American Economic Review*, 35, pp. 519–530.

Hedlund, G. (1994). "A model of knowledge management and the N-form corporation", *Strategic Management Journal*, 15, pp. 73–90.

Hosmer, L. T. (1995). "Trust: the connecting link between organizational theory and philosophical ethics", *Academy of Management Review*, 20, pp. 379–403.

Lane, P. J. (1994). *Internal Advantage from External Knowledge: Interorganizational Learning and Organizational Culture in the Capabilities Development Process*. Paper presented at the Academy of Management Meeting, Dallas.

Leonard-Barton, D. (1992). "Core capabilities and core rigidities: A paradox in managing new product development", *Strategic Management Journal*, 13 (Special Issue), summer, pp. 111–126.

Mills, P. K. and D. J. Moberg (1990). "Strategic implications of service technologies", in Bowen, D. E., R. B. Chase, T. G. Cummings and Associates, editors, *Service Management Effectiveness*, San Francisco: Jossey-Bass Inc. Publishers.

Nelson, R. R. and S. G. Winter (1982). *An Evolutionary Theory of Economic Change*, Cambridge, MA: The Belknap Press of Harvard University Press.

Nonaka, I. (1994). "A dynamic theory of organisational knowledge creation", *Organisation Science*, 5(1), pp. 14–37.

Nonaka, I. and H. Takeuchi (1995). *The Knowledge-creating Company*, Oxford: Oxford University Press.

Penrose, E. T. (1959). *The Theory of the Growth of the Firm*. Oxford: Basil Blackwell.

Peteraf, M. A. (1993). "The cornerstones of competitive advantage: A resource-based view", *Strategic Management Journal*, 14, 179–191.

Polanyi, M. (1966). *The Tacit Dimensions*, London: Routledge & Kegan Paul.

Reve, T. (1990). "The firm as a nexus of internal and external contracts", in Aoki, M., B. Gustaffson and O. E. Williamsson, editors, *The Firm as a Nexus of Treaties*, London: Sage.

Rothwell, R. (1986). "Innovation and re-innovation: A role for the user", *Journal of Marketing Management*, 2, pp. 109–123.

Sanchez, R. (1996) "Managing articulated knowledge in competence-based competition," in R. Sanchez and A. Heene, editors, *Strategic Learning and Knowledge Management*, Chichester: John Wiley & Sons.

Sanchez, R., A. Heene and H. Thomas (1996). *Towards the Theory and Practice of Competence-based Competition*, forthcoming.

Sharma, D. D. (1991). *International Operations of Professional Firms*, Lund, Sweden: Studentlitteratur.

Sharma, D. D. (1992). "Experiential network knowledge in international consultancy", in Forsgren, M. and J. Johanson, editors, *Managing Networks in International Business*, Philadelphia: Gordon and Breach, pp. 126–137.

Sharma, D. D. (1994). "Classifying buyers to gain marketing insight: A relationship approach to professional service", *International Business Review*, 3(1), pp. 15–30.

Sivula, P., F. A. J. van den Bosch and T. Elfring (1995). *Managing Interfaces by Incorporating Clients into the Development of Business Service Firm's Knowledge Base*, paper presented at The First European Academics of Management Conference on Managing Interfaces. Brussels, August 25–26.

Teece, D. J., G. Pisano and A. Shuen (1994). *Dynamic Capabilities and Strategic Management*, CCC Working Paper No. 94-9.

Van den Bosch, F. A. J., Ch. Baden Fuller and T. Elfring (1994). *Learning Alliances Between Business and Business Schools*, Paper presented at EDAMBA Euroconference on Partnership between Business and Business Schools, Erasmus University Rotterdam, April 28–29.

Von Hippel, E. (1988). *The Sources of Innovation*, New York: Oxford University Press.

Von Krogh, G., J. Roos and K. Slocum (1994). "An essay on corporate epistemology", *Strategic Management Journal*, 15 (special issue), pp. 53–71.

Voss, A. C. (1985). "The role of user in the development of applications software", *Journal of Product Innovation Management*, 2, pp. 113–121.

Winch, G. and E. Schneider (1993). "Managing the knowledge-based organizations: The case of architectural practise", *Journal of Management Studies*, 30(6), pp. 923–937.

8

Appropriability and the Creation of New Capabilities Through Strategic Alliances

Bertrand Quélin*

This paper analyzes the firm as a crucible of resources. It develops the point of view that the firm's competences and capabilities possess a strong organizational dimension. A framework for the organization of competences, which is at the core of the firm, is proposed. By emphasizing the constraint of the path dependence, the analysis shows that the firm, in order to develop new capabilities, must build alliances. Consequently, these alliances become important organizational mechanisms. The framework which we develop particularly examines three types of alliances. The advantages and limits of each are assessed and discussed. The resulting analysis shows which type of alliance may be best adapted to the building of new competences and capabilities.

* The author thanks Thanh-Hà Lê, Stephen Taylor, Howard Thomas and two anonymous reviewers for their helpful comments on an earlier draft. This research was supported by a grant from companies members of the HEC Foundation.

INTRODUCTION

Numerous works have, during the past decade, strived to renew Resource Theory. Principally issues pertaining to strategic analyses, these studies represent an important contribution to the theory of the firm. By distancing themselves from a contractual conception of the firm, the studies bring to light the fundamental nature of the firm in terms of resources. This research continues investigation of the relationship between asset specificity and firm specificity (Penrose, 1959; Wernerfelt, 1984; Rumelt, 1984; Barney, 1986; Prahalad and Hamel, 1990). Here, the firm is conceived as including both generic and specific assets. Some of these assets are essential to the central competences of the firm—that is, the mastery of an expertise and of specific capabilities at a given moment, expressed as a competitive advantage in relevant markets (Dierickx and Cool, 1989; Barney, 1991; Mahoney and Pandian, 1992; Teece, Pisano and Shuen, 1994; Hamel and Heene, 1994). In this chapter, we analyze the firm as a crucible of specific resources and competences, paying close attention to the critical function of the firm in the combination, integration, and absorption of competences. Once some basic principles are established, we develop an analysis arguing that cooperation efforts between firms are appropriate organizational mechanisms for gaining access to specific resources and for building new resources and competences. A framework is developed in order to distinguish three types of strategic alliances. Their respective advantages and limits are discussed. Finally, this analytical framework is utilized to understand the nature of the firm and the underlying logic behind strategic goals (Sanchez and Thomas, 1996).

THE FIRM: A CRUCIBLE OF SPECIFIC COMPETENCES AND CAPABILITIES

The resource-based conception of the firm emphasizes the deterministic role of competences accumulated during the development of the firm (Ghemawat, 1991). These competences are held to be idiosyncratic, specific, tangible or intangible assets of the firm. The most critical competences are based on capabilities that are developed internally and characterized as being highly collective and organizational (Winter, 1987; Grant, 1991; Amit and Schoemaker, 1993).

THE COMPETENCES AND CAPABILITIES OF THE FIRM

A "competence is an ability to sustain the coordinated deployment of assets in a way that helps a firm to achieve its goals" and capabilities are "repeatable patterns of action in the use of assets" (Sanchez, Heene and Thomas, 1996) to produce goods and/or services. The competences and capabilities create value for the firm only when connection and interaction among the assets occur through the exercise of distinct, central capabilities and competences (Selznick, 1957; Barney, 1989; Prahalad and Hamel, 1990; Sanchez, Heene and Thomas, 1996).

Capabilities are an important and special category of assets (Sanchez, Heene and Thomas, 1996). As a result, their specific characteristics need to be defined. On the one hand, capabilities can be of an individual (information, knowledge, know-how), as well as of an organizational, dimension. This latter dimension can be either formal (through instructions, prescriptions, procedure and guides) or a more tacit or informal (confidence, loyalty, routines, codes) (Itami, 1987; Winter, 1987). On the other hand, capabilities play a critical role in the redeployment of the firm's resources through informational exchanges and through organizational processes. Capabilities are thus perceived as being integrated both with the knowledge acquired by the employees and with the technical and informational systems of the firm.

To define capabilities and competences further, we distinguish four characteristics: they are rare; their transferability is limited or even uncertain (Williamson, 1985; Barney, 1986); they cannot be easily imitated (Lippman and Rumelt, 1982)[1]; their appropriability is less linked to the domain of property rights than to a long organizational learning process (Teece, 1986; Barney, 1986; Dierickx and Cool, 1989).

These characteristics lead to the idiosyncratic nature of the capabilities and certain resources of the firm. The capabilities and competences of the firm can thus be conceived as a group of differentiated knowledge, complementary assets, and routines that are at the root of the competitive advantage of the firm. They may therefore serve as a source of sustainable advantage for the firm in a specific activity (Teece, Pisano and Shuen, 1994). As tangible and intangible processes (Hall, 1992), they are developed by the firm over time and become specific to the firm.

The argument made here is that the competences and capabilities of the firm have a determining role in its management and development of resources. They are fundamental to the adaptation of the firm to its environment and, at the same time, they encourage the development and

---

[1] Sanchez and Thomas (1996) develop an interesting extension to the Lippman and Rumelt (1982) notion of causal ambiguity as a source of isolating mechanisms. According to the former authors, causal ambiguity can also orientate the perceptions and the focus of leaders and can even contribute to the negligence of market or development opportunities of the firm. Thus, this internal managerial dimension of causal ambiguity constitutes a promising path for research.

growth of the firm by integrating new resources and by redeploying existing resources. To complement this idea, we stress the organizational dimension of capabilities and competences, underlining the importance of their role in the interactions and building up of resources. In particular, we examine both their importance in the firm's choice of its organizational structure for the development of new competences and their role in strategic alliances.

INTEGRATION OF COMPETENCES

In order to understand the role of the coordination of resources and of their interaction in the value creation process, it is necessary to explore further the integration of capabilities and competences within the firm. The resource-based literature recognizes the accumulation of resources as a characteristic fundamental to the firm. However, the characterization of the specificity of the firm is often limited to a single dimension of resources and assets, and their combination and coordination are both neglected. Although the accumulation of competences is an essential characteristic of the resource-based nature of the firm, making it a crucible of resources and capabilities, it is necessary to deepen our knowledge of the linkages between firm assets and competences, since the existence and quality of the linkages established between assets determine the specificity of the firm (Rumelt, 1984; Williamson, 1985). Two possibilities are examined: the links between assets and competences which are internal to the firm and the capability of the firm to access and use external competences owned by other firms, defined by Sanchez and Heene (1996) as "firm addressable resources" in their systemic view of the firm.

ORGANIZATIONAL COMBINATION AND CREATION OF VALUE FROM RESOURCES

The firm possesses capabilities that extend beyond the individual resource level. Among these capabilities, the most important are those which allow for assets, resources, capabilities and systems to be combined. The richness and the diversity of these combinations depend on the accumulated knowledge and competences which the firm can mobilize.

The process of creating value from resources is based on the interaction and combination of resources. The role of organizational capabilities is to perfect the integration of resources in the firm. The quality and strength of the linkages between resources (e.g., interconnections between technologies, relationships between the production process and distribution network) depend on the level and kind of organizational capabilities developed by the firm (Schoemaker, 1990). This horizontal dimension of linkages and interactions between assets and capabilities need to be recognized and further developed in the systemic approach suggested by Sanchez and Heene (1996).

Establishing relationships between resources and competences is essential to the creation of specificity within an organization and the process of creating value from the firm's resources, assets and competences which have been accumulated over time. The value creation process depends on the development of such capabilities (Aaker, 1989; Leonard-Barton, 1992; Amit and Schoemaker, 1993) and on the organizational routines which give these relationships a combinatory and interactive character.

INTEGRATIVE CAPABILITIES AND THEIR ORGANIZATIONAL DIMENSION

We have previously emphasized the dual character of the processes of integration that lead to competences: they may be based on formal, explicit procedures as well as on organizational routines which are less codified and tacit. Integration may take the form of team organization, modes of communication (meetings, team projects), intra-divisional relations, and those between subsidiaries. It does not merely involve the creation of a pool of resources but also the development of specific capabilities in connecting and coordinating resources (Sanchez, Heene, and Thomas 1996). The capabilities to integrate different resources of the firm aim to ensure coherence within the firm: coherence of its different activities, and coherence of its choices for development with its existing growth policy (Dosi, Teece and Winter, 1991; Teece, Rumelt, Dosi and Winter, 1994).

Capabilities for integrating the resources of the firm can take on several dimensions. Examples include the integration of various technologies (e.g., the case of Canon, as developed by Prahalad and Hamel, 1990), the coordination of production know-how (e.g., project groups) and the implementation of a quality control system. The integration of resources and capabilities that exists in a firm adapts to specialization of certain resources; consequently, it reinforces the interdependencies between specific resources as it creates routine work methods. Such capabilities are developed either formally (procedures) or via informal organizational routines. In short, integrative capabilities structure and organize the firm in a particular form that is unique to the firm.[2]

---

[2] The capabilities that create interdependencies can, during the development of the firm, become rigidities (Leonard Barton, 1992) and an obstacle in the search for new flexibility (Sanchez, 1995).

THE ORGANIZATIONAL STRUCTURE OF CAPABILITIES

To extend the resource-based view, it is necessary to explore more fully the firm as an entity in itself, not defined merely by an incomplete and imprecise notion of "frontier of the firm" (Richardson, 1972). The approach that we develop here presents a conception of the firm that is less vertical than suggested in Sanchez and Heene (1996).[3] It attempts to highlight the types of capabilities that can exist at different levels of the firm's structure.

To understand the role of organizational capabilities, it is necessary to accept the notion of an organizational structure. This structure is not defined in terms of the authority to control as one traditionally finds in literature on administrative hierarchy. Rather, we use this term in the sense of hierarchy of integration in order to assume an organizational structure of capabilities. We could use the term "architecture of capabilities" as Henderson and Clark (1990) used "architectural innovation" to point to the integration of specialized knowledge across functional boundaries in industries characterized by rapid innovation (e.g. biotechnologies, multimedia industry) (cf. Sanchez 1995).

This organizational structure of capabilities is superimposed on the formal structure and takes on the form of multi-functional and horizontal mechanisms in order to institute efficient relations between different decision centers in the firm. Globally, the structure fulfills two missions:

- it ensures the sharing and the diffusion of knowledge associated with each of the competences and the profit centers of the firm;
- it ensures the coordination of different competences in order to develop a new activity.

---

[3] In response to this necessity, Sanchez and Heene's (1996) systemic approach is interesting because it attempts to represent the firm in terms of resource flows and current assets, of the role of managerial cognition, and of three properties, namely, causal relationships, perceptions of managers and dynamic response times of the system. This approach seems to us to be vulnerable to several criticisms. On the one hand, it attempts to integrate the environment of the firm, while neglecting the transactional dimension of the relations of the firm with its suppliers and service providers, with its clients, and in more general terms, with its industrial environment. On the other hand, the approach is based on a very strong (but to us, not very supported) hypothesis that the perceptions of leaders and the coordination methods they adopt are more difficult to change than the stock of intangible resources. This point of view of the leader's role in the strategic restructuring of certain large firms is worth further examination. The market for leaders seems to us to be more flexible than that of specific capabilities and coordination abilities.

This organizational structure of capabilities plays a fundamental role in the stability of the firm, the continuity of tasks and performance. It is fundamental to the development of a dominant logic within the firm (Prahalad and Bettis, 1986).

This approach to understanding the structure of the firm differs significantly from the structure traditionally represented by organization charts, especially for both intermediary and higher levels. Although this architecture of capabilities does not precisely correspond to the formal structure of firms, it is nevertheless clear that there exists links and a relationship with structures of authority, communication and of internal decision processes.

In view of the size and variety of activities and the diversity of the organizational levels concerned, three levels of integration of resources and capabilities in the firm can be distinguished:

- an elementary level concerning specialized activities of the firm (product lines) and the capabilities associated with this specialization (technical, commercial). Such specialized knowledge is often owned by members of the organization but can also be accumulated in systems such as databases, specialized equipment or computer programs;
- an intermediary level that brings together the capabilities which integrate specialized capabilities; these integrative capabilities are often functional, such as research and development, manufacturing, marketing;
- higher level, inter-functional, horizontal capabilities of the firm, often mobilized to obtain a more efficient coordination of resources; this level of the capabilities architecture requires management systems which elaborate inter-functional liaisons and which develop organizational routines to guide the accumulation of resources and capabilities and their deployment in the firm. In fact, the coordination of resources and capabilities is particularly vital for the success of the firm's development projects in terms of technology and innovation.

Certainly, cross-functional and organizational capabilities are resources provided by managers. Nevertheless, it seems important to us to emphasize that these capabilities are not exclusive to the team of leaders, but can also be mobilized at SBU or divisional levels, for example through projects. This notion of "level" must be understood as a level of specificity of resources and capabilities and not merely as a hierarchical level.

The absorptive capability of a firm which may involve all of the three levels, also involves the capability to exploit current knowledge

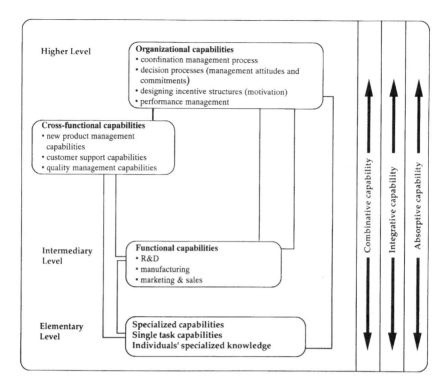

FIGURE 8.1   The Organizational Structure of Capabilities

efficiently by creating new combinations and integrating new ideas. Thus, it is the organizational capability essential to the access of external competences and to the creation of new combinations of knowledge. From one branch of activity to another, from one subsidiary to another, this capability is an essential component in the learning process; at the same time, in the case of the firm's relations with its environment (suppliers, clients or competitors), all levels of the firm's structure may be concerned or involved. For instance, the elementary level would be involved in the acquisition of technical skills of suppliers or competitors; the intermediary level would be involved in the appropriability of technological capabilities; and the higher level would be involved in the learning of organizational skills, of team work management. We are therefore led to consider that each capability possesses an absorptive capability that is more or less distinct. As we will see, absorptive capability plays an important role in the management of strategic alliances.

TRAJECTORY OF THE FIRM AND PATH DEPENDENCE: A TEMPORAL DIMENSION

The firm's organizational competences and capabilities, developed through the accumulation of resources, assets and knowledge, lead to firm specificity (Cohen and Levinthal, 1989). A temporal process based increasingly on the emergence of routines in the organization, the integration of capabilities to achieve competences leads the firm to choose both resources and customs and organizational practices. Organizational routines can also be conceived as interactions or combinations which are efficient at a given moment in time (Nelson and Winter, 1982). This selection creates strong effects by separating certain resources and by privileging a certain manner of operating within the organization.

The capability development trajectory adopted by the firm, then, leads it to develop resources and capabilities that limit its choice of new activities and its participation in new markets. The legacy of past actions results in a path dependence that constrains future actions (David, 1985; Dosi and Nelson, 1994). Furthermore, the adoption within the firm of projects to develop new activities is influenced by existing activities; consequently, the firm typically resorts to using its specific assets. This tendency may limit the firm's ability to create new strategic options (Sanchez and Thomas, 1996) because the firm's choices for the future may be strongly conditioned by this path dependence. There exist, in other words, constraints to the flexibility of the firm and its possible options in the technological and organizational trajectories previously adopted. In its development, then, the firm has a tendency to privilege the coherence of its current fund of accumulated resources and capabilities (Teece, 1982; Teece, Rumelt, Dosi and Winter, 1994). Hence, the growth of the firm along the path of an existing trajectory biases the firm towards resources that can be reproduced and duplicated because the firm already controls or understands them and they are based on well-leveraged organizational routines.

The cumulative nature of competences and resources also leads to the institutionalization of routines that leads to a certain continuity of strategic choices within the firm. The reinforcement of the coherence of the firm obtained through this pattern of development of organizational capabilities is also a factor in the selection of strategic orientations and the emergence of organizational inertia. Selection mechanisms lead to the limiting of options, to the foregoing of opportunities to develop some new resources capabilities, and (ultimately) competences. Generally, the renewal of competences necessarily entails a discontinuity in the methods and the organization of the firm. At the same time, the building of new resources is needed to access external resources in order to create new capabilities and competenc   . Building new resources thus becomes a key step in developing a new competence trajectory.

Building new resources is doubly restricted by the specificity of the firm's current competences and by the inefficiency of markets for accessing highly specific resources. Yet, at the same time, new resources are necessary to the renewal of competences. Therefore, a firm must resort to organizational mechanisms, such as cooperation with other firms, to overcome this double constraint. Inter-firm cooperations can be understood as an external oriented activity for challenging rigidities and path dependencies which limit the building of new firm competences.

INTEGRATION OF EXTERNAL KNOWLEDGE AND CAPABILITIES

A firm is faced with this paradox: the competences developed are sources of competitive advantage, but the value of a competence is susceptible to decline over time (cf. Dierickx and Cool, 1989). Furthermore, although the firm's maintenance and the enhancement of its competences is a condition to success in the short term, their continuation may be a threat to success in the long term.

The architecture of capabilities (Figure 8.1) aims to accelerate the reduction of costs and, associated with technological development, the launch of new products. It plays a significant role in the behavior of firms' innovation and entry into new markets. In order to evaluate its own capabilities and in order to gain access to other knowledge, the firm must develop some integrative capabilities that are oriented towards the external environment.

The external part of this integrative capability concerns the management of technologies and relationships with suppliers, commercial networks and partners involved in cooperations. The existence of capabilities in managing these linkages is essential for the firm both to succeed in obtaining a more efficient combination of resources and assets and to strengthen its idiosyncratic nature. Each firm needs to gain access to the most recent knowledge incorporated in the best equipment and in the best performing organizations. This requires a capability to identify and to transfer knowledge and know-how of clients, suppliers, competitors and even firms with dissimilar businesses. The challenge when a firm tries to create additional knowledge and capabilities with other firms is to be able to absorb them. The firm must also continue both to invest in developing directly its internal expertise and to integrate knowledge acquired externally.

Alliances are an organizational form that may facilitate the process of gaining access to resources and competences that the firm does not currently possess. The strategic intent in forming alliances, which should not be the objective solely of the top managerial team, is to gain access to new assets and to develop new competences. This requires that the firm be involved in a cooperation that links its own competences and resources to those of its partners. These interconnections and groupings of existing competences are necessary in order to succeed in building new competences.[4] They are key means of establishing the combinations and complementarity of resources, of creating synergies and of establishing new interdependencies between the assets of firms.

By emphasizing the importance of the integration of resources and competences, we are able to better define the resource-based approach to the firm (Quélin, 1996), which can be considered as an organization capable of integrating specialized knowledge of individuals and of coordinating them with physical, technical and commercial resources at an organizational level. This calls attention to the specificity of the firm: it is an organization which is more efficient than the market (understood as an alternative to the firm) in coordinating and integrating knowledge, specialized know-how, and tangible and intangible assets (Kogut and Zander, 1992).

This capability to integrate resources and capabilities in building new competences is an essential function of the firm, since it is the process that reinforces the specificity of the firm. This integration influences the firm's culture as well as organizational customs that in turn affect its behavior in terms of irreversibility of choices and of path dependence.

CREATION OF NEW CAPABILITIES AND ORGANIZATIONAL FORMS

The capability to integrate resources, capabilities and competences plays a fundamental role in the transformation of the specificity of the firm into a competitive advantage. However, this integrative capability must also play a role in the re-combination and re-orientation of resources for the firm in a changing environment by improving the firm's access to resources and external competences which it does not possess or control but which are vital for the development and growth of the firm.

In view of this necessity, the firm's organizational choices for growth are internal growth, external growth, and strategic alliances. Strategic

---

[4] Sanchez, Heene and Thomas (1996) distinguish between competence leveraging and building. The former is considered as a quantitative development of flows to the inventory of existing assets, whereas the latter corresponds to qualitative changes in asset flows needed to develop new competences.

alliances are an important organizational mechanism to gain access to assets, capabilities and competences.

LEVERAGING AND BUILDING COMPETENCES THROUGH INTERNAL AND EXTERNAL GROWTH

Internal growth raises the question of the capacity of the firm to develop internally new competences and activities, given the irreversibility of its previous choices, of the path dependence and of the rigidity of the firm (Leonard-Barton, 1992). Internal growth responds to the need for renewal of the firm's competences and knowledge in numerous domains such as the organizational mode of production, or of marketing (Mowery, 1989). This renewal of competences requires different learning processes than those required for the enhancement of existing competences. It requires an internal flexibility to mobilize and to combine assets and specific capabilities (e.g. core technologies) in a different manner. Different units must be mobilized in order both to access the competences that they each possess (elementary and intermediary levels in Figure 8.1) and contribute to the creation of assets, capabilities and of competences. This is all the more difficult if the units are strongly decentralized in strategic units or in autonomous product lines. The managers must thus encourage and organize the mobility and the sharing of these competences, an activity that is organizational at a higher level in Figure 8.1.

Certainly, this mechanism can allow the firm to invest in the development of a firm-specific competence which it does not possess or which was previously inaccessible. Internal development is an organizational mechanism that cannot be easily imitated because it is usually based on the most intangible internal capabilities. This type of development leads firms to focus on their internal innovation capabilities. In this case, then, that which is essential to the development of the firm is based on in-house firm-specific capabilities which are not easily imitated or duplicated (Figure 8.2).

The substitutability of a resource which the firm does not possess remains limited (Barney, 1991; Amit and Schoemaker, 1993). Development time may therefore be long, and internal growth an expensive strategic choice for development in terms of capital and time.

External growth through acquisitions is another way to obtain the knowledge or capabilities that a firm does not possess or would have difficulty accessing or obtaining from another organization. This strategic move can, of course, be justified if the knowledge and capabilities are critical and are sources of a competitive advantage.

However, an acquisition does pose a certain number of problems. First, it often forces firms to take control of activities which are not linked to the firm's current activities and thus not part of the firm's current competences. Second, the financial risk may be high, particularly for diversification operations. Third, despite the takeover of control, the integration of the involved parties and of resources and competences may be challenging. A substitution of practices and organizational routines from one firm to another may be required for the convergence and combination of resources and competences of the two firms take place. It is thus interesting to note that a takeover still requires the consecration of time to organizational learning, a factor necessary to the success of the integration of resources and competences of the acquiring and acquired firms (Fiol and Lyles, 1985). Fourth, acquisitions are frequently judged, in retrospect, to be financially expensive in terms of restructuring processes and, therefore costs of integration may be underestimated at the time of purchase. Thus, in an acquisition, an acquirer needs to dedicate significant time and effort to learning and assimilation.

THE ROLE OF STRATEGIC ALLIANCES AS ORGANIZATIONAL MECHANISMS

On the basis of the preceding analysis of the firm's organizational dimension, the cooperation between partners possesses three important

	Creating internal resources	Accessing external resources through mergers and acquisitions
Characteristics	• Internal growth • Relying on the internal capabilities of the firm	• Acquiring another firm which owns a desired knowledge
Implications	• New knowledge must be available, learned and understood to various levels in the organization	• To bring together existing competences and develop products
Limitations	• Path-dependence trajectory • Limited by the firm's capabilities • Limited by the learning process	• Difficulties to integrate specific knowledge and organizational capabilities

FIGURE 8.2 Creating Internal Resource and Competence Acquisition

characteristics. First, the organizational form (joint venture, contract, consortium) and the orientation of the cooperation (research, development, manufacturing, marketing, distribution) depends on the strategic intentions of the managers of the firm, but also depends on the knowledge and competence accumulated (impact of the adopted trajectory). Second, the cooperation depends on the accumulation of experience in this domain (Ring and Van de Ven, 1992). Third, it is based on an absorptive capability that is developed by the firm and that translates into a learning and assimilation of new competences and knowledge.

Cooperation between firms is an organizational mechanism which facilitates the firm's gaining access to competences and to specific capabilities for which a market does not exist or which are not truly substitutable. The cooperation facilitates the targeting of resources and competences desired. Nonetheless, specific resources and competences of a firm remain difficult to access. On the one hand, due to their often tacit, intangible, and organizational aspects, a true market for these resources may not exist, even if certain components do succeed in circulating, as in the case of the market for high-level managerial capabilities where mobility could be significant in certain industries or economic zones. On the other hand, in light of their temporal dimension, the resources and capabilities that the firm has accumulated are linked to its history, and their development cannot be temporally disconnected. Furthermore, strong disparities in the combination of resources contribute to the existence of significant asymmetries between firms (Rumelt, 1984; Hamel and Heene, 1994; Brousseau and Quélin, 1996).

The organization of cooperation and the distribution of responsibilities among the partners are significant dimensions that need to be managed (Kogut, 1988; Hennart, 1988; Garrette and Quélin, 1994). There exist numerous motivations for inter-firm cooperations. Besides reasons such as transaction cost economics or market power, the acquisition of technologies, know-how or capabilities is a very important motivation (Kogut, 1988; Hagedoorn, 1993). To differentiate important categories of objectives of the firms involved, we distinguish three types of strategic alliances in terms of the type of assets and competences at issue.

The first type corresponds to an enlargement of the range of application of competences held. This competence leveraging process is a way of obtaining new applications (e.g. on the geographic level) that are nevertheless similar enough to the firm's original activities.

The second type corresponds to the need to combine existing competences and to enrich them with others which are highly complementary and which one of the firms does not already possess. This objective often centers on the need to access complementary assets possessed by the other firm (Teece, 1986) in response to new needs or new problems, or to generate innovation processes. This is in fact largely confirmed by the examination of the motivations in high technology sectors (Hagedoorn, 1993; Garrette and Quélin, 1994).

The third type corresponds to objectives to create new competences and new assets needed to respond to unsatisfied demands, to create new market segments or to seize opportunities. This type of alliance is often founded on a cumulative investment strategy which is transactional and which is based on a reciprocity system (Williamson, 1985).

In literature devoted to the subject, works on inter-firm cooperations for the most part do not sufficiently distinguish access to existing resources from the creation of new resources. Three types of cooperations can thus be identified by the following criteria: access to specific resources for which a true market does not exist; co-specialization and unilateral dependence; the development of new resources and bilateral dependence.[5]

Access to Existing Assets and Competence Building

Concerning the first type of strategic alliance, for one of the partners, the assets developed are available but are not systematically transferable (e.g. the case of physical or commercial networks). For the other partner, the cooperation is an efficient means of creating value from resources and competences where this process cannot be realized by the market (Balakrishnan and Koza, 1993). This operation presupposes that each partner contributes and divides up tasks and that a rule for division of expenses and profit is established (Figure 8.3).

The second type of alliance concerns innovation which requires knowledge, know-how, and specific complementary assets (Teece, 1986; Von Hippel, 1988) in terms of deployment (new activities, new markets) and of application (technology, equipment). This translates to a strong specificity of certain assets or competences since their substitutability, or ability to be imitated, may be very limited over time (Barney, 1991). The complementarity of assets significantly affects certain innovations, and it manifests itself as a unilateral dependence, an asymmetry between firms (Brousseau and Quélin, 1992). One can treat the question in terms of

---

[5] This conception elaborates on the notion of competence building developed by Sanchez and Thomas (1996) in our third category of alliances, which is characterized by a bilateral dependence, a strong uncertainty and a strategic choice to create new resources.

appropriability of profit and innovation (Teece, 1986; Von Hippel, 1988; Hamel, 1991). This type of cooperation is a mechanism that tends to be characterized by unilateral dependence and the co-specialization of the assets.

Creation of New Capabilities and the Appropriability Dimension

The third type of alliance differs from the other two in that a large part of the potential costs cannot be revealed and doubt exists about the genuine nature of the involvement of each party concerned. In exchange for know-how and competences in the short term, profits in the long term are anticipated; however, significant uncertainty exists concerning the selection of partners for the development of a cooperation. In fact, there exists a strong doubt, even a causal ambiguity, not only about the genuine intentions of the partner, but also about its mastery of the competences and capabilities necessary to the building of new resources. How to evaluate a potential partner's resources becomes a central concern of firms engaged in an alliance aiming to create resources. This type of cooperation is characterized by a high level of uncertainty about the success of the project and the length of time of development of new resources. As this cooperation aims to build specific common resources, it creates a bilateral dependence between the partners without concretely clarifying the modes of profit sharing prior to the success of the project.

In this type of alliance, the development of the relationship between the partners is subject to certain conditions, among which three are dominant:

- the creation of communal knowledge (e.g. in R&D, the exchange of technical data, the confrontation of calculation methods, the comparison of projects undertaken);
- the establishment of functional rules (regularity of meetings, decision structure, sharing of responsibilities);
- the development of organizational routines that stabilize the process of creation of new capabilities and knowledge.

These three conditions are stabilizing effects of the cooperation and condition its development. This type of cooperation favors the progressive establishment of a new and distinct organizational structure in units and coordination to progressively reduce uncertainty. Furthermore, certain behaviors become routines, such as the shared interpretation of technical problems and the use of common means to resolve them. However, these structuring elements and this convergence may tend, but should not be allowed, to reduce the benefits of the diversity of competences or the capability to innovate.

The question of internalization of resources and competences originating from the external environment must, then, be posed in terms of linkages with the know-how and knowledge developed internally; the existence of an integrative capability in the organization; and a capability which is equivalent to the "absorptive capability" analyzed for the R&D by Cohen and Levinthal (1989). This latter capability can be defined as a capability to evaluate the external knowledge and competences, to absorb them and to appropriate them by creating new links to the existing knowledge of the firm and its internal learning. The absorptive capability is crucial to the success of the alliance since new competences must be created.

This absorptive capability may follow the decomposition of the architecture of capabilities presented above (Figure 8.1). This capacity does not concern solely the elementary level of this architecture, that is, the capacity of the human resources function in the firm to obtain and incorporate, individually, new knowledge and know-how acquired externally. Collectively obtaining this knowledge and know-how via a learning process is also characteristic of the intermediary level of the organization (such as a Research and Development laboratory or the marketing department). Finally, in firms which have created a complex of routines and horizontal management systems, the higher level of this architecture of capabilities is also involved.

The notion of the building of new capabilities encompasses different types of assets. For tangible assets, it is possible to mention new kinds of production, new delivery systems, or even more flexible equipment. As for intangible assets, they are composed of new skills, new knowledge or new cognitive frameworks based on interaction processes between the partners' resources and reciprocal learning processes. Such processes depend on the learning between partners, on their integrative and absorptive capabilities and on the new combinations of resources of each partner.

This type of cooperation should adopt an organizational form which facilitates access to resources and the development of a collective learning (Argyris and Schön, 1978). It is thus the origin of an organizational dependence between the partners since it requires adapted cooperative structures, an organization of collective work and coordination of the activities of the partners. Thus, this type of cooperation removes from the market a part of the coordination of activities and resources. Finally, the competitive dynamics result in the strategic choices of firms to create new assets, capabilities, and perhaps even joint competences, all the

	Cooperation to access existing competences	Cooperation to combine existing complementary assets	Creating new capabilities through cooperation
Characteristics	• Cooperation with other firms to access (or enhance) competences	• Co-specialization • Unilateral dependence	• Cooperation with other firms to build new competences and internalize them • Bilateral dependence
Implications	• To access non-transferable assets (e.g. commercial networks)	• Effectively combining existing complementary assets needed to innovate (skills, capabilities)	• Competences which neither firm would have been able to develop alone may be built • Ability to apply new competences and capabilities developed through cooperation
Limitations	• Opportunism	• Opportunism • Capacity to transfer skills and intangible assets	• Opportunism • Capacity to gain leverage over partner in relationship • Learning process and appropriability

FIGURE 8.3   Accessing Resources and Creating New Capabilities Through Alliances

while searching to coordinate and to integrate these new resources with existing capabilities.

PERSPECTIVES

We have developed the analysis that inter-firm cooperations are organizational mechanisms that firms adopt in order to gain access to capabilities that they do not possess internally, but which are useful for their development. Indeed, then, these cooperations are an organizational form which attempts to respond to market and hierarchical failures.

The market cannot ensure the mobility of capabilities that are tacit and collective in nature. In fact, the integration and creation process cannot be ensured by markets due to the bilateral individual/collective nature of many capabilities and due to the tacit nature of certain knowledge and capabilities. For internal growth, this hierarchy of capabilities does not allow the firm to search for an organizational mechanism that is flexible enough to limit associated lock-in risks. In terms of external growth, a takeover does not reduce financial risks and frequently leads the acquiring firm to buy competences attached to activities and products in which it is not interested.

Inter-firm cooperation plays, then, an important role in the extension of the firm's knowledge base. All the same, its success requires that an efficient organization be adopted so as to allow the partners to learn. This acquisition of new knowledge and capabilities implies that the internal organization must also be adapted to the learning directed towards the external environment. It necessitates, therefore, an efficient management of the two higher levels of the architecture of capabilities.

Firms exist to produce goods and services from resources using knowledge and capabilities. The firm is indeed an institution whose existence can be justified in two ways. On the one hand, the firm has a capacity to integrate specialized knowledge that numerous individuals have. On the other hand, it also creates collective knowledge and capabilities that are organizational in nature.

Our analysis of the forms of cooperation emphasizes the problem with which the management of a firm is confronted. Information useful to the cooperation must be revealed to the partner, all the while preserving one's own specific competences. It is necessary to develop together with the partner knowledge and know-how, all the while establishing internal learning processes to appropriate developed competences.

Finally, the analysis also stresses the complexity of the learning phenomenon. Indeed, each of these three types of cooperations, but to differing degrees, is an organizational learning process. Knowledge and competences which the firm wants to control are mobilized. Three factors condition the success of such a process: the intention to internalize the competences of the partner; the more or less transparent nature of the organization and of its intangible capabilities; the learning capabilities of partner firms.

In general, the first factor may be known by the different partners since it is one of the central motivations for strategic alliances. The second factor emphasizes the difficulty of learning and internalizing organizational capabilities that firms protect and that are not necessarily totally implicated in the alliance, particularly because the alliance is often limited to an activity or to a part of the organization. Furthermore, a good number of firms look to protect their organizational capabilities or their intangible assets. The third factor concerns the internal capability of each of the firms not only to internalize new knowledge, but also to combine it with its own knowledge and to reorganize its poles of competence.

One can also distinguish between different learning forms that improve the knowledge of the partner: learning that improves the realization of tasks and engagements; learning that enriches the management of the negotiation process (choice of partner, relationships with partners, conflict management). These learning forms will contribute to the improvement of capabilities in the management of alliances.

This analysis provides a framework for better understanding of the role of building of new capabilities in competitive dynamics. It explains the variety of the core of resources that we analyze as strategic within firms, which are constrained by path dependence, past choices and strategic vision. This final notion certainly deserves further development in order to explain, in particular, the role of managerial perceptions, strategic behavior, and deviations in terms of mastery of competences.

References

Aaker, D. A. (1989). "Managing assets and skills: The key to competitive advantage", *California Management Review*, winter, pp. 88–101.

Amit, R. and P. J. Schoemaker (1993). "Strategic assets and organizational rent", *Strategic Management Journal*, **14**(1), pp. 33–46.

Argyris, C. and D. A. Schön (1978). *Organizational Learning: A Theory of Action Perspective*, London: Addison-Wesley.

Balakrishnan, S. and M. P. Koza (1993). "Information asymmetry, adverse selection and joint-ventures", *Journal of Economic Behavior and Organization*, **20**, pp. 99–117.

Barney, J. B. (1986). "Strategic factor markets: Expectations, luck and business strategy," *Management Science*, **42**, pp. 1231–1241.

Barney, J. B. (1989). "Assets, stocks and sustained competitive advantage", *Management Science*, **35**, pp. 1511–1513.

Barney, J. B. (1991). "Firm resources and sustained competitive advantage", *Journal of Management*, **17**, pp. 99–120.

Brousseau, E. and B. Quélin (1992). "User's knowledge as a specific asset: The case of added-value services", *Journal of Information Technology*, **7**, pp. 233–243.

Brousseau, E. and B. Quélin (1996). "Asset specificity and organizational arrangements: The case of new telecommunications services market", *Industrial and Corporate Change*, (forthcoming).

Cohen, W. M. and D. A. Levinthal (1989). "Innovation and learning: The two faces of R&D", *Economic Journal*, **99**(397), pp. 569–596.

David, P. (1985). "Clio and the economics of QWERTY", *American Economic Review*, Papers and Proceedings, **75**, pp. 332–337.

Dierickx, I. and K. Cool (1989). "Asset stock accumulation and sustainability of competitive avantage", *Management Science*, **35**, pp. 1504–1511.

Dosi, G., D. Teece and S. Winter (1991). "Les frontières de la firme: Vers une théorie de la cohérence de la grande entreprise", *Revue d'Economie Industrielle*, **51**, pp. 238–253.

Dosi, G. and R. Nelson (1994). "An introduction to evolutionary theories in economics", *Journal of Evolutionary Economics*, **4**, pp. 153–172.

Fiol, M. and M. Lyles (1985). "Organizational learning", *Academy of Management Review*, **10**(4), pp. 803–813.

Garrette, B. and B. Quélin (1994). "An empirical study of hybrid forms of governance structure: The case of telecommunication equipment industry", *Research Policy*, **23**(4), pp. 395–412.

Ghemawat, P. (1991). *Commitment*, New York: Free Press.

Grant, R. (1991). "The resource-based theory of competitive advantage: Implications for strategy formulation", *California Management Review*, **33**(3), pp. 114–135.

Hagedoorn, J. (1993). "Understanding the rationale of strategic technology partnering: Interorganizational modes of cooperation and sectoral differences", *Strategic Management Journal*, **14**(5), pp. 371–385.

Hall, R. (1992). "The strategic analysis of intangible resources", *Strategic Management Journal*, **13**(2), pp. 135–144.

Hamel, G. (1991). "Competition for competence and interpartner learning within international strategic alliances", *Strategic Management Journal*, **12**, pp. 83–103.

Hamel, G. and A. Heene (eds) (1994). *Competence-based Competition*, London: Wiley.

Henderson, R. and K. Clark (1990). "Architectural innovation: The reconfiguration of existing product technologies and the failure of established firms", *Administrative Science Quarterly*, **35**, pp. 9–31.

Hennart, J.-F. (1988). "A transaction cost theory of equity joint-ventures", *Strategic Management Journal*, **9**, pp. 361–374.

Itami, H. (1987). *Mobilizing Invisible Assets*, Cambridge, MA: Harvard University Press.

Kogut, B. (1988). "Joint-ventures: Theoretical and empirical perspectives", *Strategic Management Journal*, **9**, pp. 319–332.

Kogut, B. and U. Zander (1992). "Knowledge of the firm, combinative capabilities, and the replication of technology", *Organizational Science*, **3**, pp. 383–397.

Leonard-Barton, D. (1992). "Core capabilities and core rigidities: A paradox in managing new product development", *Strategic Management Journal*, **13** (Special Issue), pp. 111–125.

Lippman, S. and R. Rumelt (1982). "Uncertain imitability: An analysis of interfirm differences in efficiency under competition", *Bell Journal of Economics*, **13**, pp. 418–443.

Mahoney, J. T. and J. R. Pandian (1992). "The resource-based view within the conversation of strategic management", *Strategic Management Journal*, **13**(5), pp. 363–380.

Mowery, D. C. (ed.) (1989). *International Collaborative Ventures in U.S. Manufacturing*, Cambridge, MA: Ballinger.

Nelson, R. R. and S. Winter (1982). *An Evolutionary Theory of Economic Change*, Boston, MA: Harvard University Press.

Penrose, E. (1959). *The Theory of the Growth of the Firm*, Oxford: Basil Blackwell.

Prahalad, C. K. and R. Bettis (1986). "The dominant logic: A new linkage between diversity and performance", *Strategic Management Journal*, 7, pp. 485–501.

Prahalad, C. K. and G. Hamel (1990). "The core competence of the corporation", *Harvard Business Review*, 68(3), pp. 79–91.

Quélin, B. (1996). "Coopération inter-entreprises et création de ressources", in J. L. Ravix, editor, *Coopération entre les entreprises et organisation industrielle*, Paris: Editions CNRS (forthcoming).

Richardson, R. (1972). "The organization of industry", *Economic Journal*, 82(327), pp. 883–896.

Ring, P. S. and A. H. Van de Ven (1992). "Structuring cooperative relationships between organizations", *Strategic Management Journal*, 13(7), pp. 483–498.

Rumelt, R. P. (1984). "Toward a strategic theory of the firm", pp. 556–570, in R. Lamb, editor, *Competitive Strategic Management*, Englewood Cliffs, NJ: Prentice-Hall.

Sanchez, R. (1995). "Strategic flexibility in product competition", *Strategic Management Journal*, 16 (Special Issue), pp. 135–159.

Sanchez, R. and A. Heene (1996). "A system view of the firm in competence-based competition", in R. Sanchez, A. Heene and H. Thomas, editors, *Dynamics of Competence-Based Competition: Theory and Practice in the New Strategic Management*, London: Elsevier Pergamon Press.

Sanchez, R., A. Heene and H. Thomas (1996). "Towards the theory and practice of competence-based competition", in R. Sanchez, A. Heene and H. Thomas, editors, *Dynamics of Competence-Based Competition: Theory and Practice in the New Strategic Management*, London: Elsevier Pergamon Press.

Sanchez, R. and H. Thomas (1996). "Strategic goals", in R. Sanchez, A. Heene and H. Thomas, editors, *Dynamics of Competence-Based Competition: Theory and Practice in the New Strategic Management*, London: Elsevier Pergamon Press.

Schoemaker, P. (1990). "Strategy, complexity and economic rent", *Management Science*, 36, pp. 1178–1192.

Selznick, P. (1957). *Leadership in Administration: A Sociological Interpretation*, New York: Harper & Row.

Teece, D. J. (1982). "Towards an economic theory of the multiproduct firm", *Journal of Economic Behavior and Organization*, 3, pp. 39–63.

Teece, D. J. (1986). "Profiting from technological innovation: Implications for integration, collaboration, licensing and public policy", *Research Policy*, 15, pp. 285–305.

Teece, D., R. Rumelt, G. Dosi and S. Winter (1994). "Understanding corporate coherence", *Journal of Economic Behavior and Organization*, 23(1), pp. 1–30.

Teece, D., G. P. Pisano and A. Shuen (1994). "Dynamic capabilities and strategic management", *CCC Working Paper*, 94-9: University of California, pp. 4–9.

Von Hippel, E. (1988). *The Sources of Innovation*, New York: Oxford University Press.

Wernerfelt, B. (1984). "A resource-based view of the firm", *Strategic Management Journal*, 5(1), pp. 171–180.

Williamson, O. E. (1985). *The Economic Institutions of Capitalism: Firms, Markets, Relational Contracting*, New York: Free Press.

Winter, S. (1987). "Knowledge and competence as strategic assets", pp. 159–184 in D. J. Teece, editor, *The Competitive Challenge*, Cambridge, MA: Ballinger.

Section IV

Strategic Knowledge Management

Effective strategic management of a firm's knowledge assets requires recognition of the potential strategic value of a firm's different stocks of knowledge. Sanchez proposes a framework for analyzing a firm's knowledge assets that suggests several approaches to leveraging and controlling a firm's strategic knowledge assets. After a critical appraisal of the strategic value of "tacit" knowledge within organizations, he suggests that knowledge within firms has different *contents*—which are characterized as *know-how, know-why*, and *know-what*—that are used in different strategic *contexts*. He proposes a framework for developing knowledge management strategies based on analysis of the contents of a firm's knowledge and the context in which knowledge will be used.

Modularity in product design may create an important framework for managing knowledge within a firm and within networks of firms. Post explains the use of modularity by Baan Company, a rapidly growing Dutch software firm, as an architecture for creating software applications programs for business. Explaining how the concept of modularity was developed through the strategic logic and management processes of Baan Company, Post shows how modular product architectures create knowledge structures that enable flexible reconfigurations of the firm's software products. The flexibility derived from its modular knowledge architecture becomes a strategic means for improving the competence leveraging and building of Baan Company.

Modularity in product design as a knowledge management strategy may enable the adoption of modular organization designs. Lang investigates the relationship between modular product design and modular organization structures through a study of ARM Ltd, a developer of RISC-chip technology that has managed to use modular product design to improve its flexibility and adaptability in a highly dynamic product market. Using a modular product architecture to structure a network of licensing relationships, ARM Ltd has developed complementary capabilities in alliance management and control and technology transfer that give it considerable ability to build and leverage new competences.

9

Managing Articulated Knowledge in Competence-based Competition

RON SANCHEZ

This chapter proposes a framework for analyzing a firm's knowledge assets and for devising effective strategies for leveraging and controlling different kinds of knowledge in competence-based competition. "Tacit knowledge" is critiqued for its limited ability to be leveraged and controlled. A framework for identifying categories of articulated knowledge is developed by examining differences in the *contexts* and the *contents* of articulated knowledge and the processes by which articulated knowledge is transferred or diffused between contexts. In managing processes of *knowledge articulation, codification, and apprehension* strategically, it is useful to recognize three distinct kinds of knowledge—*know-how, know-why*, and *know-what*—that will be of different relative strategic importance in various competitive contexts. This framework is applied in an analysis of three different competitive contexts to illustrate strategies for managing knowledge that appear to be effective in leveraging less critical kinds of articulated knowledge while controlling more critical kinds of knowledge. Concluding comments suggest issues for further research of interest to both researchers and managers.

Strategic Learning and Knowledge Management.
Edited by Ron Sanchez and Aimé Heene.
Copyright © 1997 John Wiley & Sons Ltd.

INTRODUCTION

Achieving competence requires both knowledge and effective processes for deploying knowledge within and across an organization's boundaries. This chapter proposes a framework for analyzing a firm's knowledge assets and for evaluating alternative processes for leveraging and controlling different forms of knowledge in competence-based competition. In so doing, it addresses some issues that are critical both to managers trying to develop and manage knowledge assets effectively and to researchers trying to develop a better understanding of organizational knowledge and processes for building and leveraging knowledge.

The first section examines the concept of "tacit knowledge" and some current ideas about the strategic role which it may play in competence-based competition. The section argues that relying on "tacit knowledge" (as currently conceived) as a potential source of strategic advantage imposes severe limitations on an organization's ability to leverage and control its knowledge effectively. The inherently limited strategic usefulness of "tacit knowledge" suggests that inquiry into knowledge management in competence-based competition requires more careful investigation of articulated (non-tacit) knowledge and of ways in which articulated knowledge can be managed strategically within and between organizations.

A framework for identifying categories of articulated knowledge is developed by examining differences in the *contexts* and the *contents* of articulated knowledge. The second section of this chapter addresses three cognitive contexts relevant to articulated knowledge:

(i)   individuals who articulate knowledge,
(ii) organizations which seek to codify and transfer the articulated knowledge of individuals,
(iii) potential competitors and collaborators to whom an organization's articulated knowledge may be transferred or diffused[1] as organizations interact in competence-based competition.

Strategically managing knowledge in these three cognitive contexts requires understanding the processes by which knowledge can be transferred or diffused between these contexts. Essential elements of knowledge transfer and diffusion are therefore considered through a discussion of the processes of *articulation, codification,* and *apprehension.*

---

[1] The convention used here is that knowledge is *transferred* when it is conveyed intentionally, while knowledge is *diffused* when it is conveyed unintentionally.

To use its knowledge to greatest strategic advantage, a firm must be able to leverage its knowledge effectively within and across the boundaries of the firm, while at the same time maintaining control of knowledge whose diffusion would seriously diminish the firm's competitive advantage. The third section of the chapter suggests that in managing this process it is useful to recognize three distinct kinds of knowledge—*know-how*, *know-why*, and *know-what*. Each of these forms of knowing has a distinct *content* of knowledge which has a particular strategic importance for the firm. Examples are used to illustrate common manifestations of each kind of knowledge in firms.

The fourth section combines considerations of the *contexts* and the *contents* of knowledge to propose a framework for strategically managing the tension between leveraging and controlling knowledge in competence-based competition. This framework suggests that in different competitive contexts, know-how, know-why, and know-what will occupy different positions in a *hierarchy* of strategically important knowledge. In some contexts, know-how may be widely leveraged (transferred) within and across organization boundaries without loss of strategic advantage, while know-why and know-what are strategically critical and should be contained and controlled within the firm. In other contexts, the relative importance of know-how, know-why, and know-what may be reversed. This framework is applied to three different competitive contexts to illustrate strategies for managing knowledge that appear to be effective in broadly leveraging less critical kinds of knowledge while controlling more critical kinds of articulated knowledge.

Concluding comments suggest issues for further research of interest to both researchers and managers.

1 BEYOND "TACIT KNOWLEDGE"

Much current discussion of knowledge in competence-based competition advances the proposition that a firm's "tacit knowledge"[2] is more

---

[2] The notion of "tacit knowledge" in general requires further examination, beginning with careful definitions of terms. Using the definition of knowledge as a "set of beliefs held by an individual about causal relationships among phenomena" of interest to the individual or an organization (Sanchez, Heene and Thomas, 1996), it is evident that such beliefs may be "tacit" in the sense that they are *unarticulated*. Indeed, an individual may have to make considerable effort to articulate his or her current "tacit knowledge". Some discussions of "tacit knowledge", however, assume (often implicitly) that "tacit knowledge" may include "knowledge" that is *not capable* of articulation by individuals. A notion of *knowledge that is not capable of being articulated* (as distinct from "knowledge that is articulable only with difficulty") appears to be epistemologically problematic. In this regard, the quotation marks used in this discussion indicate the author's view that "tacit knowledge" that might include some form of *inarticulable* knowledge is a concept that has yet to be satisfactorily explained and substantiated.

likely to be a source of competitive advantage than the firm's articulated or "non-tacit" knowledge. The reasoning in support of this notion often goes something like this: knowledge may be either "tacit" or non-tacit (i.e. articulated). If "tacit knowledge" becomes articulated, it can readily be understood by anyone and as a result can diffuse beyond the boundaries of an organization. Other firms that acquire a firm's non-tacit knowledge once it diffuses can then use that knowledge to replicate any distinctive competence the articulating firm may derive from that knowledge. Thus, non-tacit knowledge cannot be a source of a distinctive competence that leads to strategic advantage. "Tacit knowledge", on the other hand, if it is transferable from one person to another at all, can only be transferred after protracted personal interactions between a learner and teacher, often in the manner of an apprentice patiently trying to imitate the skillful moves of the craftsman (or role model). The difficulty of observing and acquiring "tacit knowledge" limits its diffusion beyond the firm, which serves to preserve the distinctive nature of a firm's "tacit knowledge". Thus, "tacit knowledge" can serve as a basis for distinctive competence and competitive advantage, while non-tacit knowledge cannot.

While this argument appears plausible at first, careful analysis raises questions about some key assumptions and inferences in this line of reasoning. Some of the most salient problems in this reasoning are considered next.

Problems of comprehension. If an individual's knowledge is articulated within an organization, the ability of individuals outside that organization to apprehend the full meaning of that articulated knowledge cannot be presumed. The idiosyncrasies of the sense-making processes that go on within an organization may create problems of both *comprehension* and *valuation* for individuals outside the organization who try to understand and appraise the significance of some articulated knowledge they may happen to discover. Individuals within organizations often engage in an organizational "languaging" process (von Krogh, Roos and Slocum, 1994), for example, that creates words whose idiosyncratic meanings within the context of a firm may not be fully (or even basically) comprehended by individuals outside the firm. Even when knowledge is articulated in a non-idiosyncratic language—for example, in the form of an engineering formula, a technically specified product design, or a detailed description of a procedure—the full meaning of such statements may not be comprehended by other firms whose analytic and technical capabilities differ in some respects from those of the articulating firm.

Education theory suggests that comprehension of knowledge may occur at four levels of "mastery": reproduction, explanation, application, and integration (Heene, 1993). *Reproduction* is like recall; an acquirer of articulated knowledge can only write it down, but is not able to impute a meaning to the articulated knowledge. *Explanation* indicates an understanding of the articulated knowledge in the sense that the acquirer can explain the knowledge in terms of some imputed meaning. *Application* implies an ability to apply some articulated knowledge correctly when asked to do so. *Integration* indicates attainment of mastery of some knowledge in the sense that the acquirer understands the uses to which the knowledge can be applied and can selectively choose to apply that knowledge in situations where it is beneficial to do so. These recognized levels of knowledge mastery suggest that it would not be warranted simply to assume the ability of a competitor acquiring some articulated knowledge to fully comprehend the meaning of that knowledge and to apply that knowledge correctly in situations where it might be used most effectively. Thus, problems which other organizations may have in fully comprehending one firm's articulated knowledge may act to limit the diffusion and use of that knowledge beyond the articulating firm.

Differences of valuation and value. Even when one firm's articulated knowledge can be understood technically by another firm, *causal ambiguity* (Lippman and Rumelt, 1982) about the importance of that knowledge to the competence of the articulating firm may obscure the strategic value of that knowledge to outside observers. Indeed, the existence of *internal causal ambiguities* (Sanchez, Heene and Thomas, 1996) may prevent the value of a firm's knowledge from being well understood even within the firm articulating the knowledge. Thus, the cognitive limitations of managers and others may lead to reduced incentives for firms to adopt and apply articulated knowledge which may diffuse beyond the boundaries of an articulating firm.

Moreover, the value of applying some articulated knowledge *in the context of another organization* may not be of the same magnitude as the value of that knowledge applied in the context of the articulating firm. In essence, using some knowledge to create a competence requires other knowledge and capabilities that must become systemically interrelated (Sanchez and Heene, 1996). Articulated knowledge which may serve as a basis for distinctive competence in combination with other knowledge and capabilities in one firm may not be as well suited as a basis for creating distinctive competence in combination with the knowledge and capabilities of another firm, even if the articulated knowledge of the first firm is fully understood by the other firm. A well-articulated, technically comprehensible statement of Sony's engineering design principles for miniaturizing electronic components, for example, would have a reduced value to competitors that lack Sony's complementary knowledge of precision machining that is also required to produce miniaturized components.

Thus, the diffusion of articulated knowledge beyond a firm may be limited by differences in both the *perceived value-in-use* of knowledge to different firms and by differences in the *actual value-in-use* of knowledge applied in the specific contexts of different firms.

Time dependency of the value of knowledge. The actual value of articulated knowledge to a firm may also depend on when the firm acquires some knowledge. When articulated knowledge is comprehended by another firm, the value of the acquired knowledge to the acquiring firm may depend greatly on how effective the articulating firm has been in leveraging that knowledge up to that time. In the extreme case, an articulating firm may have already leveraged its articulated knowledge in ways that give it an entrenched position of advantage in an industry. A competitor who might today acquire McDonald's Corporation's articulated knowledge about systems and techniques for managing a fast food business, for example, may be in large measure preempted from applying that knowledge to comparable strategic effect by McDonald's prior establishment of thousands of fast food restaurants in prime locations.

Problems of knowledge migration. The notion that the "tacit knowledge" of individuals is more secure as a source of distinctive competence than articulated knowledge overlooks the fact that people with "tacit knowledge"—sometimes referred to as "competence carriers"—have the right to leave the employment of one firm and may even go to work for competitors.[3] When a "competence carrier" whose knowledge has not been articulated and diffused within the firm leaves the firm, that firm simply loses that person's "tacit knowledge", which essentially migrates to another firm. By contrast, if employees articulate knowledge of strategic importance to the firm and if the firm codifies and transfers that knowledge to other employees, the exit of one or even a few "competence carriers" may allow knowledge to diffuse to other firms, but it will not deprive the firm of a strategically critical knowledge asset. Thus,

---

[3] One might argue that a firm may be able to take legal action to prevent a "competence carrier" from using his or her "tacit knowledge" on behalf of a competitor. However, such arguments first have to explain how a firm, as a precondition to asserting a property right to such knowledge, could *identify* with sufficient specificity some knowledge that has never been articulated by an individual within the firm. How a firm might try to identify—and assert a property right to—"tacit knowledge" which is "unarticulable" is, of course, an even greater imponderable.

from the strategic perspective of the firm, maintaining the knowledge assets of the firm in the form of "tacit knowledge" contained in the heads of employees may be much less secure than articulating, transferring, and widely embedding critical knowledge within the organization.[4]

Problems of limited leveragability. Relying on "tacit knowledge" as a source of strategic advantage limits the ability of a firm to leverage its knowledge when transfer of that knowledge can only be accomplished by physically relocating human "competence carriers". When knowledge can be articulated and codified by the firm, it may become possible to disseminate new knowledge much more quickly and widely than would be possible simply by moving humans. AT&T, for example, has begun a program to create a global information system linking all its manufacturing facilities (Sykes, 1994). A key objective of this system is to gather, codify, and disseminate the knowledge created through learning-by-doing in the operation of its plants worldwide. To the extent that AT&T is successful in electronically gathering and transferring the lessons learned in one plant to its other plants, it will be able to leverage its knowledge much more widely and quickly than if it simply tried to send employees from one plant to other plants in its system. Although there are certainly challenges in identifying and abstracting generally useful lessons from the complex knowledge structures of the different units of a large organization, the potential for leveraging such knowledge is much greater when that knowledge can be articulated, codified, and disseminated (electronically or through other media) than when the knowledge remains "tacit" in the minds of a few employees.

Reconsidering the importance of articulated knowledge. Because non-tacit knowledge may not in fact diffuse quickly to other firms, and because "tacit knowledge" may be relatively difficult to leverage effectively within a firm, the presumption that "tacit knowledge" is likely to be the

---

[4] The practice of physically relocating people to move "tacit knowledge" has been noted within Japanese firms (Hamel and Heene, 1994; Nonaka and Takeuchi, 1995). Relying on movements of individuals with "tacit knowledge" may be a feasible approach to managing knowledge in Japan, where skilled and knowledgeable workers often have no desire—and perhaps very limited opportunities—to change jobs. However, in societies with higher levels of labor mobility, processes for articulating, codifying, and transferring the knowledge of individuals who may eventually leave the firm become essential to managing knowledge strategically. Learning how to capture and leverage the knowledge of employees in countries with mobile workers is now a major challenge to Japanese firms. Many of these firms now need to develop a global competence base, but are in effect handicapped in more mobile societies by knowledge management methods that are premised on retaining the lifetime services of employees with "tacit knowledge".

only viable source of distinctive competence and competitive advantage appears unwarranted. To understand how *articulated knowledge* can become a source of advantage in competence-based competition, we have to understand both *forms* of articulated knowledge and *processes* for leveraging and controlling articulated knowledge. The next sections examine the *contexts* and the *contents* of strategically significant knowledge to develop a framework for analyzing the transfer and control of articulated knowledge.

2 The Contexts of Knowledge: Individuals, Within Organizations, and Between Organizations

Knowledge begins with the understanding of an individual, but creating and leveraging organizational competences requires that an individual's knowledge be linked to and coordinated with the knowledge and capabilities of other individuals within an organization and, potentially, within other organizations. To leverage the knowledge of individuals in this manner, organizations must first be able to *identify* the strategically useful knowledge of its own members and of other organizations that are firm-addressable resources. After identifying the subject of the knowledge available to the firm, to create competence managers must understand how to *transfer* specific aspects of the knowledge of certain individuals to other individuals or groups within the organization (Nonaka and Takeuchi, 1995) or, in many cases, to other organizations. Managers must also understand how to *control diffusion* of certain knowledge when diffusion could diminish the distinctiveness of the firm's competences. Controlling knowledge diffusion thus becomes a critical issue in knowledge management, because some of the firm's knowledge must be transferred to outsiders whenever the firm seeks to leverage its knowledge beyond its own boundaries.

This section discusses the *contexts* in which knowledge may reside, the mechanisms by which transfers of knowledge from one context to another may take place, and some of the factors which affect both the intentional transfers and unintended diffusion of strategically important knowledge between organizations. Figure 9.1 summarizes the basic knowledge contexts and processes which managing knowledge must address: articulation by individuals, codification by an organization, and apprehension within and between organizations.

Knowledge articulation by individuals. For an organization to identify its knowledge resources, individuals must articulate what they know.

Individuals	Within Organizations	Between Organizations
Articulated	Codified	Apprehended
vs.	vs.	vs.
Unarticulated	Uncodified	Not-apprehended

FIGURE 9.1   Contexts of Knowledge

Knowledge articulation is the explanation of an individual's knowledge (which may be at varying degrees of specificity) in a way which can be comprehended by at least one other person in the organization.[5] Since articulating knowledge requires time and effort by individuals within an organization—and therefore happens only at some cost to a firm—a central issue in managing knowledge is assessing the degree to which the potential benefits of articulating some knowledge may exceed the costs of articulation. Although it may be important to identify all the basic kinds of useful knowledge held by individuals within an organization, some knowledge that is not strategically critical may not be worth the cost of being extensively articulated within an organization. Knowledge of central importance to a firm's competences, however, may justify substantial efforts by the organization to elicit explanations of an individual's beliefs about some phenomena of strategic importance to the firm. Thus, it may be sufficient for a firm simply to identify that John knows how to drive a truck to deliver packages without knowing in detail how John drives the truck, while the same firm may need to know not just that Mary knows how to organize effective advertising campaigns, but also what it is that Mary actually does—and why—when she organizes effective campaigns.

Knowledge transfer from one individual to another requires articulation of an individual's knowledge in words, drawings, symbols, or some other representations to which other people attribute meanings that are basically similar to the meaning intended by the speaker. In addition, since "knowledge" is a set of beliefs, and since the manner of explanation is often important in the formation of beliefs, the rhetorical style and

---

[5] Basing the concept of articulation on a condition of comprehension by some group of other people (rather than defining articulation by some concept of knowledge as an absolute) allows for the cognitive limitations and differences of both individuals and organizations and leads to recognition that the comprehension and credibility of articulated knowledge may be constrained by contextual factors specific to individuals and organizations.

mode of reasoning employed by an articulating person may greatly affect whether the set of beliefs the person articulates is effectively transferred to others.[6] The organizational context in which knowledge articulation takes place may significantly affect the choice of words used, the meanings which both articulator and listeners attribute to specific words, and the rhetorical style and logic used to frame statements of beliefs. Thus, knowledge articulation is likely to be context dependent to at least some—and perhaps a considerable—degree. A group of individuals in a specific organizational context may therefore develop a mode of communication (vocabulary, rhetorical style, mode of reasoning, etc.) that results in a shared *knowledge set* expressed in terms that have explicit meanings to those individuals, but that may nevertheless be difficult for people in other organizations to understand fully.

Knowledge codification within organizations. To transfer the knowledge of individuals and groups within an organization, the knowledge sets shared by individuals in a specific context within the organization must be made comprehensible and available to other individuals in other contexts in the organization. *Knowledge codification* is a term used here to refer to several knowledge management processes within organizations, beginning with processes that seek to identify the subject matter of the knowledge of individuals and the knowledge sets of groups in terms which other individuals and groups within the organization can comprehend. Codification may also require helping individuals and groups articulate their knowledge in language whose meanings can be understood (in a manner intended by the articulators) by other concerned individuals in the organization. Articulated knowledge and knowledge sets must also be made accessible to others in the organization by establishing a schema for categorizing and locating identified knowledge within the organization (Boisot, 1995; Boisot, Griffiths and Moles, 1996).

The need to categorize knowledge to make it accessible creates an opportunity to clarify the relationships among the various knowledge sets within the organization—for example, by identifying the interactions (actual and potential) of knowledge sets with others in a knowledge process map of the organization. When knowledge is codified within an organization in this manner, culminating in the mapping of interrelated knowledge sets, knowledge codification processes may uncover and make explicit what may be thought of as the *knowledge architecture* of an organization.

---

[6] These issues are addressed by reader-response theory in the education literature (see, for example, Rosenblatt, 1978, 1993; Veach, 1993), which addresses ways in which the meaning attributed to some transferred knowledge depends on the nature of the transaction between the writer/speaker and the reader/listener.

Clarification of the knowledge architecture of an organization may facilitate the linking and coordination of knowledge within an organization, as well as the transfer of knowledge generated in one part of an organization to other interested groups.

Knowledge apprehension by other organizations. For one organization to *apprehend* the knowledge of another organization, it must be able to observe (in some sense), to comprehend (at a useful level), and to reasonably appraise the value of the knowledge that may be transferred or diffused from another organization.

"Observation" of another firm's knowledge may occur in a variety of ways. A firm may send another firm (for example, a subcontractor) a set of engineering drawings that enables the second firm to observe directly how to make a product; competitors, however, may also be able to use inferential analysis of a physical product ("reverse engineering") to observe how to make a firm's products.[7] Different kinds of knowledge within a firm may be articulated and codified in different forms and thus have different degrees and modes of observability. Boeing's aircraft design algorithms and procedures for simulating the performance of aircraft designs on computers are highly articulated and codified knowledge that could no doubt be understood if studied at length by other aeronautical engineers. However, strict security that controls access to Boeing's computer design software has thus far prevented the complex knowledge codified in that software from being observed by other firms. Analogously, Michelin has traditionally decomposed its closely guarded tire making operations into several physically separated steps to prevent all but a top group of managers from observing the company's overall tire making process.

As suggested earlier in the discussion of "tacit knowledge", moreover, the apprehension of articulated knowledge by other organizations may also be limited by problems which other organizations may have in fully

---

[7] In this regard, it is worth noting a common misconception that "tacit knowledge" is always difficult to imitate. While it may be the case that "tacit knowledge" cannot be imitated as long as it remains tacit *and* unapplied, the application of "tacit knowledge" may result in artifacts which can be analyzed to infer and articulate the "tacit knowledge" embodied in the artifact. Thus, to learn techniques for capturing light, color, and form in painting, art students routinely copy the paintings of great masters who saw no reason to articulate their "tacit knowledge" about light, color, and form. Similarly, the "tacit knowledge" of early microprocessor designers, as expressed in their microprocessor designs, was analyzed by Professor Carver Mead to discover the "tacit" design principles being followed by those designers (Gilder, 1989). Mead's articulation of those design principles enabled the development of the first software programs for designing microprocessors, current generations of which now make possible the design of microprocessors of a complexity well beyond the capabilities of any human mind to process "tacitly".

comprehending and correctly valuing any knowledge which they may observe. The comprehensibility of articulated knowledge by outsiders may be limited by the use of an organizational language (von Krogh, Roos and Slocum, 1994) whose essential meanings are idiosyncratic to a given firm, or by other contextual factors. Even knowledge that is articulated in a non-idiosyncratic or technical lanugage may not be fully comprehended by other firms with different technical capabilities. In addition, other firms may have different perceptions of the value-in-use of a firm's articulated knowledge, and indeed the actual value-in-use of that knowledge may be different in the contexts of other firms.

To manage knowledge effectively within an organization, managers need to understand not just the stocks of knowledge within the firm (Dierickx and Cool, 1989), but also how to manage the actual or potential transfers and diffusions (flows) of knowledge within and across the boundaries of the firm. Managing knowledge strategically essentially requires facilitating the articulation and codification of the firm's knowledge resources, apprehension of some of the firm's knowledge by groups within the firm and in other firms that can help the firm leverage its knowledge most widely, and (at the same time) controlling the apprehension of any knowledge by competing firms which might be able to use that knowledge to enhance their own competences to the detriment of the firm.

3   THE CONTENTS OF KNOWLEDGE: KNOW-HOW, KNOW-WHY, AND KNOW-WHAT

Strategically controlling flows of knowledge requires recognition of some basic differences in the *contents* of an organization's stocks of knowledge. Taking the view that in dynamic competitive environments a fundamental process of the firm as a system (Sanchez and Heene, 1996) is knowledge creation and leveraging, this section suggests that there are three "levels" of understanding which a firm may develop about its processes for competing: *state, process,* and *purpose* forms of knowledge. These three levels of understanding suggest that there are three different contents of knowledge within an organization: *know-how, know-why,* and *know-what.* In different competitive contexts, these different kinds of knowledge may be more or less critical as a source of distinctive competence and strategic advantage for a firm. Transfers of each kind of knowledge within and across organizational boundaries will therefore have different strategic implications in different competitive contexts. Thus, each of the three kinds of knowledge within a firm must be managed in a distinct manner in a given competitive context.

Knowledge processes within the firm-as-a-system. In dynamic environments, a firm's assets and capabilities, processes for coordinating assets and capabilities, and strategic logic for directing coordinated deployments of assets and capabilities (Sanchez, Heene and Thomas, 1996) are likely to be in a constant state of change (i.e. learning) if the firm is to survive and succeed. Central challenges to the cognitive abilities of strategic managers are (i) making sense of a complex and changing environment, and (ii) imagining new assets and capabilities, new coordination processes, and new strategic logics for competing that provide rationales for how the firm might achieve an acceptable level of goal attainment in a future subject to significant uncertainties. This process of strategic sense making and imagining may be thought of as a process of theory building at the firm level (Mahoney and Sanchez, 1996) in which strategic managers try to develop theories of how to compete successfully in the context of their perceived environments.

Of course, a firm must also "test" its theories about how it might attain its goals in a given environmental context—i.e. its *strategic logic* (Sanchez, Heene and Thomas, 1996)—by applying its strategic logic through competitive and cooperative interactions with other entities: customers, suppliers, competitors, employees, governments, etc. Thus, in competitive environments, the strategy theories of managers are conceived and tested in the crucible of the market place. Superior strategy theories[8] that meet the test of the marketplace are rewarded with commercial success, while inferior theories lead to poor performance, financial and organizational distress, or extinction.

Fundamentally, then, the processes for creating knowledge within a firm are processes of theory building and testing carried on within the specific context of a firm's environment. For this reason, insights into theory building from the philosophy of science may have direct relevance to both managers and researchers interested in understanding knowledge creation processes within firms.

State, process, and purpose knowledge. In an effort to understand causal relationships between phenomena, people may articulate theories addressing different "levels" of causality. In building theory about the behavior of physical or social systems, theory may be developed at either the *state* or *process* level (Simon, 1962).

---

[8] The concept of strategic logic proposed by Sanchez, Heene and Thomas (1996) includes both a *rationale* or plan for competing in a product market or industry context and an organizational *process design* for acquiring and coordinating the assets and capabilities of a firm in pursuing that plan. Strategic logic thus provides for the joining of content and process concerns (Mahoney and Sanchez, 1996) in the theory of competence-based competition.

A *state theory* is essentially a proposition about how elements of a system are interrelated in the current state of a system. For example, in terms of knowledge about products, an understanding of the way in which the parts of a given product design fit and function together constitutes a state theory about *how* that specific product design works. Similarly, in terms of production knowledge, an understanding of the way in which the machines of a production system fit and function together is a state theory about *how* a specific production system works. Firms may use knowledge based on state theories about products and processes to produce existing product designs by operating existing production systems. Over time, a firm may advance its state-theory level of knowledge through learning-by-doing, which is essentially a process of testing state theory by initiating or reacting to limited changes in a product or production system, observing the consequences, and inferring ways in which the state theory about the product or production system could be further refined in light of those consequences.[9] Knowledge developed at the state-theory level may be used to *maintain control of current product designs and production systems* over a limited range of variations in internal or external conditions.

A *process theory* is a proposition about the underlying principles which govern the relationships between the elements of a system. In terms of product knowledge, process theory is the understanding of *why* the parts of a given product design function together to produce the overall function of a product. Process theory in production knowledge is an understanding of *why* the machines in a production system function together to provide the capabilities of a production system. Knowledge based on process theories about products and processes may enable a firm to *adapt existing products and processes or to develop new product designs and production systems* in response to perceived change in the competitive environment. A firm may try to advance its process-theory level of knowledge in two ways: (i) by trying to infer underlying principles governing a system through incremental learning-by-doing, and (ii) by importing and testing process theories developed about other systems that appear to be analogous in some basic respects to the system the firm needs to understand and manage.[10]

---

[9] Firms that lack process-theory level understanding may be cognitively bounded in the range of experimentation they perceive to be useful in increasing know-how. Organizations with process-theory knowledge, however, may be able to use their theoretical understanding of the principles underlying a process to develop superior designs for experiments and to better infer new know-how knowledge through *theoretically directed* learning-by-doing.

[10] For example, the process theory stating the principles governing the diffusion of heat was "borrowed" by financial economists Fischer Black and Myron Scholes to serve as a process theory for the principles governing movements in asset prices (Black and Scholes, 1972). This imported process theory was used to develop the "Black–Scholes options pricing model" that has passed the test of acceptance by financial markets, becoming the prevailing process theory for pricing options in financial markets.

The firm as a system is more complex than most physical systems. The atoms, molecules, or physical bodies that compose one physical system will behave in the same way in another physical system, and as a result a state or process theory developed in the context of one physical system can therefore be expected to be applicable in other comparable systems. The firm as a system, however is made up of humans. Although humans may share some characteristics at universal, cultural, national, and local social levels, they also have significant differences in cognitive capabilities, work and consumption preferences, and other characteristics that affect the actual and potential competences and goals of a given firm. Individual firms will therefore be characterized by different sets of beliefs about what it is possible and desirable *for that firm* as an organization of individuals to achieve.[11]

Managers' beliefs about what actions a firm might take and about the causal relationships between those actions and the expected impacts on the firm of pursuing those actions represents a distinct kind of knowledge within a firm. It is not knowledge simply about the current states of the firm's product designs and production systems or about the processes by which a firm might change those states. It is knowledge of—i.e. a set of beliefs about—alternative feasible *purposes* to which the firm's state and process levels of knowledge may usefully be applied in an ongoing effort to achieve the goals of the firm (Sanchez, 1995). This knowledge will differ across firms, because managers and other people in one firm may have different cognitions and aspirations from those of people who populate other firms. Thus, in describing different kinds of knowledge within a firm, it is important to recognize a third category of knowledge based on a theory of purpose(s) that is likely to be idiosyncratic to each firm in at least some important respects.

A *purpose theory* is therefore a proposition about what courses of action are available to a firm and what the likely outcomes of specific courses of action might be. In essence, purpose theory is the understanding of *what* the firm might reasonably try to do with its available competences or

---

[11] In an effort to create a purely positivist science, many economists try to suppress individual differences among people and firms by stipulating that people can be viewed simply as utility maximizers and firms as profit maximizers. The premise that individual preferences fundamentally distinguish people is *not* inconsistent with the assumption of utility maximization. Only when utility is construed narrowly to include only those preferences which can be readily represented by a financial value to which all individuals attach equal value does utility maximization conflict with a theoretical representation of people in which individual differences matter. Likewise, stipulating profit maximization as the objective of the firm imposes a narrow conception of firms as economic entities that exist only to generate financial gains for their legal owners—a stipulation that ignores differences in the (non-financial) utilities of owners, as well as the complex utilities of managers, employees, and other stakeholders.

competences it conceivably could develop; purpose theory enables the firm to *identify and define new goals* for applying its state and process understanding in the creation of products and processes. Purpose theory addresses the potential future uses of current or new state and process understanding of the firm—i.e. in effect, the "possible worlds" (Bruner, 1986; Bowman, 1990) in which the firm may be able to survive or prosper in the future.

Knowledge based on purpose theories enables a firm to *imagine new kinds of products and processes*. Changing a firm's purpose-theory level of knowledge is akin to changing a firm's strategic logic: change may be driven from the "bottom-up" or from the "top down" (Sanchez and Heene, 1996). "Bottom up" changes are changes in a firm's state- and process-theory levels of knowledge that may lead to inferences of new purposes to which new state and process knowledge can be applied. For example, importation or internal development of a new manufacturing technique may make possible the creation of new kinds of products; if managers actually infer some possibilities for the firm to offer new products based on the new process or state knowledge, the act of imagining those new possibilities will constitute a change in the purpose-theory level of knowledge in the firm. "Top down" changes in purpose knowledge, on the other hand, may occur when managers consider emulating new kinds of activities undertaken by other firms, when they apply analogies or metaphors drawn from other industries to their own business, or when managers otherwise manage to perceive a potential market opportunity that can be served by an existing technology, a new technology, or a potential technology that could be created to serve an existing or potential market demand.

Know-how, know-why, and know-what. State, process, and purpose theories lead to different kinds of knowledge within the firm as a system that, for simplicity, may be thought of as *know-how, know-why,* and *know-what* (Sanchez, 1996).[12] These different kinds of knowledge represent different *contents* of knowledge within a firm.

Know-how is "practical understanding" that enables a firm to perform various operations like running a production line, processing documents, or servicing existing customers. Analogously, in terms of product knowledge, know-how is the ability to *produce* and (within some limited range) *refine* an existing product design.

---

[12] The term *know-how* has been used by other writers in a much broader sense that often includes elements of know-why and perhaps even know-what as defined in this discussion.

Know-why is "theoretical understanding" of the principles governing the functioning of a process that enables a firm to change the state of a system in response to significant environmental changes. In terms of product knowledge, know-why enables a firm to *adapt* a product design or to *develop* a new product design to produce significant new variations.

Know-what is "strategic understanding" of the purposes to which available or potential know-why and know-how can usefully be applied. Know-what enables the firm to *imagine* new kinds of products and processes.

Some examples of the management of each kind of knowledge are discussed in Section 3.

Figure 9.2 summarizes these kinds of knowledge; their relation to state, process, and purpose theory; their associated learning processes; and the kind of competence which may result from each kind of knowledge.

A (variable) strategic hierarchy of knowledge. Know-how, know-why, and know-what are very likely to have different degrees of strategic significance in different competitive contexts. In competitive environments with stable technologies and market preferences, there may be little actual competitive pressure for significant change. In this event, the most important kind of knowledge may be know-how that enables a firm to control its current production, distribution, and marketing processes effectively within the modest range of variations in environmental conditions. In dynamic competitive environments, however, know-how

Kind of Knowledge	Theory Base	Learning Process	Derived Competence
Know-how	State theory	Learning-by-doing	Maintain control of existing processes for making current products
Know-why	Process theory	Theoretically directed learning-by-doing; Importing new theory	Adapt existing products and processes; develop new products or processes
Know-what	Purpose theory	"Bottom up" learning from changes in state and process theory; "Top down" learning by emulation, metaphor, or imagination	Identify and define new kinds of products and processes

FIGURE 9.2   Contents of Knowledge

about the current state of products and activities in the firm may be less important than know-why that enables a firm to change those states (while holding to a constant purpose) or know-what that enables a firm's managers to imagine new purposes for existing or potential firm capabilities. A firm's strategies for managing knowledge must therefore recognize the nature of competitive conditions in its environment. In general, stable environments may favor an emphasis on internal development of deeper know-how level knowledge (about existing products and production systems), while dynamic environments may call for an emphasis on imaginative, flexible thinking that expands perceived possibilities at the know-what level (possible products and systems).

In different competitive contexts, therefore, each of the three kinds of knowledge may take a different position in a hierarchy that represents the relative strategic significance of each kind of knowledge to the competences of an organization. In competence-based competition, recognizing this hierarchy of strategically valuable knowledge is essential to developing a strategy for effectively leveraging *and* controlling a firm's strategically important knowledge.

4 ACHIEVING STRATEGIC LEVERAGE AND CONTROL OF KNOWLEDGE

A basic objective in the strategic management of knowledge in competence-based competition is to achieve the most advantageous leveraging of the firm's knowledge in the coordinated deployment of firm-specific and firm-addressable resources. Implicit in this objective is a tension between the benefits of leveraging knowledge and the hazards of losing control of critical knowledge. On the one hand, a firm would benefit by leveraging its knowledge quickly and widely both within and across its boundaries, while on the other hand the firm has an interest in maintaining control over strategically important knowledge whose diffusion to other firms would erode the distinctiveness of the firm's competences based on its knowledge. This section applies the preceding analysis of knowledge contexts and contents to suggest an approach to strategically managing this tension. Evidence that some firms appear to be following this approach to managing knowledge is also presented through examples.

The discussion in Section 2 of the individual, organizational, and inter-organizational contexts of knowledge and its transfer between contexts suggests that to achieve the greatest leverage of its knowledge a firm should encourage individuals to articulate their strategically important knowledge and should codify that knowledge so that it can be transferred to wherever it can be applied within the organization. In addition, the firm's ability to leverage its knowledge widely will be enhanced if some of its knowledge can also be used by other firms on behalf of the firm.

In order to leverage articulated knowledge beyond the boundaries of the firm *and* prevent the loss of control of strategically valuable knowledge, a firm must understand what kinds of knowledge are the primary sources of its strategic advantages and thus are critical contributors to its distinctive competence(s) in its competitive context. In effect, managers must try to determine the relative importance of the firm's know-how, know-why, and know-what in maintaining or creating its distinctive competences. A basic approach to managing the firm's knowledge to greatest advantage is to try to *leverage* as broadly as possible (i.e. to firm-addressable resources in other firms) the least strategically critical kind of knowledge of the firm, while maintaining close control within the firm of the kind of articulated knowledge that is most critical to the firm's distinctive competence. The following discussion examines three different examples of knowledge leveraging that appear to reflect this approach to managing knowledge in competence-based competition. Several aspects of knowledge management in each case are summarized in *Figure 9.3*.

Case A represents a competitive environment with stable market needs and technologies. In this context, the most critical form of knowledge is know-how in producing existing products and know-how in servicing existing market requirements. Know-what is not likely to be strategically important as long as existing products effectively satisfy existing market demands. Know-why that improves the ability of a firm to improve its current stock of know-how through theoretically informed learning-by-doing (see Note 8) will be important; know-why that would enable a firm to develop new kinds of products, on the other hand, would be relatively less important. In this case, a firm may manage its knowledge to control its critical production know-how and related know-why knowledge, while widely leveraging its know-what knowledge.

This strategy for managing knowledge, which may result in a pattern of contracting for complementary specialized know-how, may be observed during periods of technological and market stability. In the home appliances product market (refrigerators, stoves, washers, dryers, etc.), for example, some firms develop and control know-how in the low-cost production of high-quality standard home appliances, others use know-how in marketing and servicing customers to sell home appliances made by others (e.g. Sears), while a few companies try to control both forms of know-how (e.g. Whirlpool and Maytag). Firms with production know-how may cooperate with firms with marketing know-how to leverage

Competitive Context	Knowledge Hierarchy	Management of Kinds of Knowledge		
		Know-how	Know-why	Know-what
Case A: Contracting for complementary know-how				
Stable markets and technologies	Know-how Know-why Know-what	Controlled within firm	Controlled within firm	Shared with firms with complementary know-how
Case B: Subcontracting for know-how-based services				
Evolving markets and technologies	Know-why Know-what Know-how	Product know-how shared with firms with component know-how/why	Product-level know-why controlled within firm	Controlled within firm
Case C: Modular product and organization design				
Dynamic markets and technologies	Know-what Know-why Know-how	Contract for production know-how	Contract for component know-why; Control product know-why	Controlled within firm

FIGURE 9.3   Three Examples of Knowledge Management in Competitive Contexts

know-what knowledge—i.e. to produce existing product designs for appealing, reliable appliances. In some cases, firms with both forms of know-how may share know-what knowledge by contracting for production or marketing services with firms that have only one form of know-how.

Case B represents a competitive environment with evolving market needs and product technologies. In this environment, the most critical kinds of knowledge are likely to be know-what that identifies viable new product concepts and product know-why that enables development of new product designs. When product know-what and know-why can be combined with subcontractors' component-level production know-how to redirect their knowledge to new purposes, controlling production know-how is less likely to be strategically critical than controlling the know-what and product know-why that redirects component production know-how to better product ideas.

This strategy for knowledge management leads to a pattern of *subcontracting for component know-how services* by firms that control critical know-what and product know-why knowledge. These firms develop new product know-how knowledge (specifications) that can be readily apprehended by subcontractors, while keeping secret the product know-why and know-what knowledge which generated the specific form of product know-how knowledge shared with subcontractors. The airframe industry reflects this pattern of transferring know-how knowledge about a product design, while "hiding" know-why and know-what knowledge about how to define and design new products. Boeing's engineering specifications and drawings for the fabrications of a fuselage section for the 777, for example, convey the know-how needed to make the desired 777 fuselage section in a form which can be readily apprehended by a subcontractor. However, the product know-how provided in component design drawings and specifications reveal little or nothing of the design theory (know-why) that enabled Boeing to develop that new fuselage design, nor does it reveal the know-what knowledge which led Boeing to identify and define the 777 product concept as a viable application of available know-why and know-how.

Articulating, codifying, and leveraging readily apprehensible knowledge at the product know-how level allows Boeing to access a global network of firms with addressable skills and capabilities in component manufacture and (in some cases component design), e.g. jet engines and avionics. Transferring codified know-how does not compromise Boeing's ability to maintain control of its product know-how, know-why, and know-what essential to maintaining its distinctive competence in defining and designing new generations of passenger aircraft.

Case C represents an advanced form of Case B that is increasingly evident in highly dynamic competitive environments with rapidly evolving technologies and new product opportunities. In some such product markets, know-why that enables development of specific new kinds of components and know-how for producing and assembling new components may be widely available and thus are less strategically critical kinds of knowledge. In such markets, the most critical kind of knowledge may be know-what that identifies viable new production concepts by imagining new applications of existing or potential technologies to existing or new product opportunities, plus know-why that enables the definition of new product architectures (Henderson and Clark, 1990; Lang, 1996; Sanchez, 1995) in ways that allow development and production of components for new product concepts to proceed quickly.

This environmental context may lead some firms to adopt a *modular product and organization design* in which a firm uses a modular product architecture to define the outputs of development and production processes that will be carried out by other firms (Sanchez and Mahoney, 1995). By defining the desired outputs (in functional terms) of the development and production activities of component suppliers, a modular product architecture allows the firm to draw on the component development know-why and component production know-how of subcontractors. The modular product architecture which defines the desired

outputs of supplier development and product processes reveals little, if
any, of the know-what which enabled the firm to identify the new product opportunity or the product know-why which enabled the firm to
develop the modular product architecture that serves the new product
opportunity. Nike in the specialized shoe market, Ikea in the furniture
business, and Sun Microsystems in the workstation market are firms that
use modular product designs to access the component-level know-why
and know-how of a global network of component suppliers, while maintaining control of the critical know-what and product design know-why
that are the sources of their competences in imagining and developing
new product concepts in rapidly changing competitive environments
(Sanchez, 1995).

5   Conclusions

This chapter has proposed a framework for analyzing the sources and
kinds of knowledge within an organization. That framework has then
been applied to suggest an approach to strategically managing the tension arising from the possible benefits and hazards of leveraging a firm's
articulated knowledge. This discussion has suggested several areas important to strategy researchers and managers interested in effective
knowledge management.

Better understanding of the *cognitive processes* by which individuals
form, structure, and articulate their knowledge may suggest processes for
assisting firm members in articulating their strategically critical knowledge. Also, it is important for firms to be able to elicit not just the state-
level knowledge of individuals, but also their problem framing and solving process-level knowledge. This objective has been the central concern
of researchers building knowledge-based expert systems (KBES) and the
artificial intelligence field in general for almost a decade (see, for example,
Winston and Prendergast, 1984 and Haugeland, 1985), yet the strategy
field has thus far paid little attention to this work. Similarly, to improve
the ability of firms to *codify knowledge*, it may be beneficial to explore
concepts for characterizing and relating knowledge sets within an organization to facilitate the mapping of organizational knowledge structures
and processes in ways that will be readily comprehensible and accessible
to firm members. Perhaps some models for mapping firm processes (i.e.
activities based on state-level knowledge) "borrowed" from the business
process reengineering literature would be useful in this regard.

An interpretation of ideas from education theory (see Note 5) about
the *transaction dependency of processes for conveying knowledge* could suggest ways both to improve processes for transferring articulated

knowledge to cooperating firms and, conversely, for obscuring articulated knowledge that may inadvertently reach competing firms.

The interrelationships of state, process, and purpose knowledge offer a rich and relatively unexplored area. How does process-level understanding (know-why) facilitate and/or constrain changes in the state-level understanding (know-how) of an organization, and *vice versa*? A similar question can be asked about the interdependency between process-level knowledge (know-why) and purpose-level knowledge (know-what). Better insights into the *systemic interdependencies within this hierarchy of knowledge* (see, for example, van der Vorst, 1996) could suggest approaches to managing what may be the most difficult challenge faced by strategic managers—managing their own cognitions (Sanchez and Heene, 1996).

In the strategically critical processes for changing a firm's know-what knowledge, strategy researchers and managers could benefit greatly from developing better understanding of both *analytic and narrative processes* for making meaning (Bruner, 1986). It would be useful to understand, for example, the ways in which managers' "strategic imagination" can be fueled by the "logico-deductive" reasoning of science versus the contextual-inferential reasoning processes characteristically used in the arts. Since the academic branch of strategy aspires to base strategic management on scientific principles and methods, while successful strategic managers often speak of the "art" of managing, it is worth considering what strategy research might be missing by being generally unwilling (thus far) to explore the strategy-making process using the concepts and methods of inferential logic and creative processes.[13]

REFERENCES

Black, Fischer and Myron Scholes (1972). "The pricing of options and corporate liabilities", *Journal of Political Economy*, **81**(3), pp. 637–654.

Boisot, M. H. (1995). *Information Space*. London: Routledge.

Boisot, M. H., Dorothy Griffiths and Veronica Moles (1996). "The dilemma of competence: Differentiation *versus* integration in the pursuit of learning", in *Strategic Learning and Knowledge Management*. Ron Sanchez and Aimé Heene, editors, Chichester: John Wiley & Sons.

Bowman, Edward H. (1990). "Strategy changes: Possible worlds, actual minds", pp. 19–37, in *Perspectives on Strategic Management*. James Frederickson, editor, New York: Harper Business Press.

---

[13] Mahoney and Sanchez (1996) suggest that development of competence theory may require an expansion of strategy research to include more grounded theory building (Glaser and Strauss, 1967) in which inferential reasoning plays a leading role. They suggest a much greater degree of collaboration between academics and managers in research to develop a theory of competence-based competition.

Bruner, Jerome (1986). *Actual Minds, Possible Worlds*, Cambridge, MA: Harvard University Press.

Dierickx, Ingmar and Karel Cool (1989). "Asset stock accumulation and sustainability of competitive advantage", *Management Science*, **35**, pp. 1504–1511.

Gilder, George (1989). *Microcosm: The Quantum Revolution in Economics and Technology*, New York: Simon & Schuster.

Glaser, Barney G. and Anselm L. Strauss (1967). *The Discovery of Grounded Theory: Strategies for Qualitative Research*. New York: Aldine De Gruyter.

Hamel, Gary and Aimé Heene (eds) (1994). *Competence-Based Competition*, Chichester: John Wiley & Sons.

Haugeland, John (1985). *Artificial Intelligence: The Very Idea*, Cambridge, MA: MIT Press.

Heene, Aimé (1993). "Classifications of competence and their impact on defining, measuring, and developing 'core competence' ", paper presented at Second International Workshop on Competence-Based Competition, EIASM, Brussels, Belgium, November 1993.

Henderson, Rebecca and Kim B. Clark (1990). "Architectural innovation: The reconfiguration of existing product technologies and the failure of established firms", *Administrative Science Quarterly*, **35**, pp. 9–30.

Lang, John W. (1996). "Leveraging knowledge across firm boundaries: Achieving strategic flexibility through modularisation and alliances", in *Strategic Learning and Knowledge Management*, Ron Sanchez and Aimé Heene, editors, Chichester: John Wiley & Sons.

Lippman, S. A. and R. P. Rumelt (1982). "Uncertain imitability: An analysis of interfirm differences in efficiency under competition", *Bell Journal of Economics*, **13**, pp. 418–438.

Mahoney, Joseph T. and Ron Sanchez (1996). "Competence theory building: Reconnecting management research and management practice", in *Competence-Based Strategic Management*, Aimé Heene and Ron Sanchez, editors, Chichester: John Wiley & Sons.

Nonaka, Ikujiro and Hirotaka Takeuchi (1995). *The Knowledge-Creating Company*, Oxford: Oxford University Press.

Rosenblatt, Louise (1978). *The Reader, The Text, The Poem: A Transactional Theory of The Literary Work*, Carbondale, IL: Southern Illinois Press.

Rosenblatt, Louise (1993). "The transactional theory against dualisms", *College English*, **55**(4), pp. 377–386.

Sanchez, Ron (1995). "Strategic flexibility in product competition", *Strategic Management Journal*, **16** (summer Special Issue), pp. 135–159.

Sanchez, Ron (1996). "Strategic product creation: Managing new interactions of technology, markets, and organizations," *European Management Journal*, **14**(2), 121–138.

Sanchez, Ron and Joseph, T. Mahoney (1995). "Modularity, flexibility, and knowledge management in product and organization design", BEBR Working Paper No. 95-0121, Champaign, IL: University of Illinois.

Sanchez, Ron and Aimé Heene (1996). "A systems view of the firm in competence-based competition", in *Dynamics of Competence-Based Competition*, Ron Sanchez, Aimé Heene and Howard Thomas, editors, Oxford: Elsevier.

Sanchez, Ron, Aimé Heene and Howard Thomas (1996). "Towards the theory and practice of competence-based competition", in *Dynamics of Competence-Based Competition*, Ron Sanchez, Aimé Heene and Howard Thomas, editors, Oxford: Elsevier.

Simon, Herbert (1962). *The Sciences of the Artificial*, Cambridge, MA: MIT Press.

Sykes, Charles (1994). "AT&T adopts a global manufacturing architecture", *Manufacturing Systems*, January, pp. 34–39.

Veach, Richard (1993). *A Teacher's Introduction to Reader-Response Theories*, National Council of Teachers of English, Urbana, IL.

van der Vorst, Roland (1996). "The blind spots of competence identification: A systems theoretic perspective", in *Competence-Based Strategic Management*, Aimé Heene and Ron Sanchez, editors, Chichester: John Wiley & Sons.

von Krogh, Georg, Johan Roos and Ken Slocum (1994). "An essay on corporate epistemology", *Strategic Management Journal*, **15** (Special Issue), pp. 53–71.

Winston, Patrick H. and Karen A. Prendergast (1984). *The AI Business: Commercial Uses of Artificial Intelligence*, Cambridge, MA: MIT Press.

10

Modularity in Product Design, Development, and Organization: A Case Study of Baan Company

HENK A. POST

This chapter addresses the development of Baan Company's competence-based strategy. This Dutch developer of package software for enterprise resource planning and business process reengineering started in 1978 as a one-man consultancy firm. From its inception, the company made several important decisions which were departures from the normal way of building a software firm. These decisions led the firm to distinctive strategic logic, management processes, and approaches to building up and acquiring tangible and intangible assets, which gives the firm notable strategic flexibilities in its resources and its coordination capabilities. The company is now a global player distributing its product in 60 countries. The evolution of Baan Company is discussed in the light of several theoretical strands developed in the emerging literature on competence-based competition.

INTRODUCTION

Baan is a global provider of open-system, client-server-based Enterprise Resource Planning (ERP) software. ERP systems facilitate the enterprise-

Strategic Learning and Knowledge Management.
Edited by Ron Sanchez and Aimé Heene.
Copyright © 1997 John Wiley & Sons Ltd.

wide management of resources, and the integration of sales forecasting, component procurement, inventory management, manufacturing control, project management, distribution, transportation, finance, and other functions across an organization. Baan's product line is designed to permit rapid implementation of new applications and to provide companies with information technology flexibilities required to support continuous organizational change and Business Process Reengineering (BPR). Baan Company offers its software products in the UNIX and Windows NT market of open systems. This market is growing very fast, currently over 50% a year, largely because industries are moving away from inflexible, proprietary information systems—"legacy" systems—"that have caused frustration in the past, in favor of open systems that support rather than hamper the flexibility required by modern manufacturing" (*Financial Times*, 6 September, 1995).

Baan's product family consists of Software and Orgware. Baan's Software is designed on the principle of modularity (Sanchez, 1995; Sanchez and Mahoney, 1995) to allow the creation of a great variety of customized information systems for clients that are interconnectable, upgradable, and scalable. Orgware is a set of standardized methodologies, services, and software tools developed by Baan for configuration, reconfiguration and rapid implementation of applications customized to the end user's unique requirements. It also includes project management tools to assist in planning and monitoring the implementation process. Baan Orgware supports the multiple approaches to creating information systems and implementation of customized software packages used by its service partners. To date, Baan has sold over 1500 systems to more than 1300 customers worldwide, with the result that in recent years the company's revenues have grown rapidly, increasing from $35.2 million in 1991 to $122.9 million in 1994 and to $216 million in 1995.

This discussion explains the use of modularity in developing and managing the knowledge which becomes incorporated into Baan's Software and Orgware products and services. We first discuss the concepts of modularity and knowledge management. We then survey the evolution of Baan Company and the use of modularity in the company's product, service, and organization strategies. To conclude, we assess the implications of Baan's modularity strategy for theory and practice in strategic management.

MODULARITY: DISCUSSION OF THEORETICAL CONCEPTS

Modularity is a concept which can apply at both the organizational and the product level. Daft and Lewin (1993) have suggested that the "modular organization" is a new paradigm that meets "the need for flexible, learning organizations that continuously change and solve problems through interconnected coordinated self-organizing processes". Sanchez and Mahoney (1995: 9) define modular design as a special form of product design which intentionally seeks a high degree of independence or "loose coupling" between components. They argue that creating modularity in product designs is the first step to be taken in achieving the modular organization design described by Daft and Lewin (1993).

> Decomposition of a product into component parts is central to the process of creating new products. After defining the overall functionality desired from a new product, designers create a new product design by decomposing the overall product functionality into an interrelated set of functional components. The functional decomposition of a product into components and the specifications of the interfaces that define the relationships between those components constitute the product architecture. (Sanchez, 1995: 10)

A modular product design is one in which the input and output relationships between subsystems or components—i.e. the interfaces—have been fully specified and standardized to allow for a range of variations in subsystems or components (Sanchez and Mahoney, 1995: 1, 14). Fully specifying standardized subsystem or component interfaces in a modular product architecture "creates an information structure that coordinates component development processes. However, creating modular product designs requires advanced knowledge about how components will interact within a product" (Sanchez and Mahoney, 1995: 1). However, Sanchez and Mahoney argue that a firm may achieve important coordination and strategic flexibility benefits when its advanced state of technological knowledge about component interactions can be used to create modular product designs.

Sanchez and Mahoney propose that modularity decomposes a product design into a nearly independent system of components that makes possible the concurrent development of components by processes carried out autonomously by loosely coupled organization structures (Orton and Weick, 1990). Hence, creating modularity in product design is essential to achieving modularity in organization design, which Sanchez and Mahoney characterize as a form of organization in which autonomous organizational structures can execute concurrent, effectively coordinated processes. Establishing standardized component interfaces results in "embedded coordination" in the sense that the work of product development organizations is coordinated and governed to a significant degree by these interfaces. "Using fully specified component interfaces to govern the outputs of development processes may greatly reduce the need for overt exercise of managerial authority to achieve coordination of development processes carried out by component development organizations" (1995: 1–2).

The interest of Sanchez and Mahoney (1995) is in understanding hierarchical systems for the creation of products in which there is little or no need for overt exercise of managerial authority to achieve subordination—or coordination—among subsystems. Hierarchy refers to a structured ordering of a complex system, decomposable into successive sets of subsystems (Simon, 1962). In this structural sense, it is a feature of designs both for products and organizations. Within structural hierarchies, interactions *between* subsystems will be lower in intensity and frequency than interactions *within* subsystems (interactions between the component parts of those subsystems). Sanchez and Mahoney (1995) suggest that such decomposition of designs into modular components creates information structures that can reduce the cost and difficulty of adaptive coordination, thereby enhancing the strategic flexibility of firms to respond rapidly and efficiently to technological or market change and to adapt to new opportunities or threats.

Sanchez and Mahoney (1995: 9) suggest that the nature and degree of decomposition of a product design fundamentally determine the content—and thus the feasible designs—of organizational processes for creating that product.

> A component in a product design performs one or more functions within a functional subsystem of interrelated components whose collective functioning provides the overall functionality of a product. The degree to which a given component is loosely coupled to (relatively independent of) or tightly coupled to (relatively dependent on) other components in a product design is determined by the degree to which the design of that component affects the design of other components, and vice versa. Relationships between components in a product design are defined by the specifications of input and output relationships between all components in that design. (Sanchez and Mahoney, 1995: 10)

The complete set of component interface specifications which determine the input and output relationships between components defines a product architecture (e.g. Morris and Ferguson, 1993). A product design composed of tightly coupled components will therefore require tightly coupled development processes, which as Sanchez and Mahoney (1995: 11) stipulate, "in turn are likely to require the continual exercise of overt managerial authority to coordinate and adjudicate highly interdependent development processes. The exercise of overt managerial authority, however, requires a tightly coupled organization structure based on an operative authority hierarchy." Further, "There is growing evidence that an alternative product design methodology is being pursued by some firms in dynamic product markets" (Sanchez and Mahoney, 1995: 12). This methodology intentionally creates standardized component interfaces such that functional and other relationships between subsystems or components within a product design, once specified, are not permitted to change during a product development process. Each development organization must then assume that the subsystem or component it is responsible for developing conforms to the relevant standardized input and output interfaces.[1]

A modular product design creates considerable flexibility in the sense that:

- different versions of modular components can be substituted so that the product can be renewed or improved easily;
- different components can be left out or included so that different product assemblages are deliverable on short term;
- some components may be re-usable in new product versions.

(See also Sanchez and Mahoney, 1995; Sanchez, 1996a; Garud and Kumaraswamy, 1993.)

This means that a product architecture with a modular design facilitates generating a variety of component packages giving each package— or each product—distinctive functionalities, features and/or performance levels (Langlois and Robertson, 1992). Product innovation may occur by creating new modular components that incorporate new technology or functionality. The new product provides better or extended performance while still conforming to the existing product architecture (Sanderson and Uzumeri, 1990; Sanchez, 1995, 1996a). Product development based on "mixing and matching" modular components can be observed in markets as diverse as jet aircraft, cars, consumer

---

[1] Sanchez and Mahoney pay attention to the fact that specifying standardized interfaces to create loosely coupled (subsystems or) components allows each component within a product design to be treated as a black box (Clark and Fujimoto, 1991; Wheelwright and Clark, 1992) by the product developing firm. "In developing new car models, many car makers now provide their suppliers with only a black box specification of the (standardized) functional, spatial, and other interfaces of the required component, leaving the actual design and development of the component to the supplier. The only information a component developer needs to have about other component development processes is the standardized specifications that define how one component relates to others in the product design. Compatibility between black box components can be achieved *ex ante* by specifying standardized interfaces, or may be accomplished *ex post*—usually at greater cost or loss of efficiency—by using converters or adapters between components" (Sanchez and Mahoney, 1995: 13; see also Clark and Fujimoto, 1991; Sanchez and Sudharshan, 1993; Farrell and Saloner, 1989).

electronics, personal computers, and power tools (Sanchez and Mahoney, 1995; Morris and Ferguson, 1993; Sanderson and Uzumeri, 1990; Sanchez and Sudharshan, 1993).

Modular product design facilitates use of a network approach (Kogut and Kulatilaka, 1994) or "constellation" (Norman and Ramirez, 1993) of component developers and software vendors to source new functionalities for product package(s) and a broad range of product variety. A modular product design leads to flexibility in sourcing components (Sanchez and Mahoney, 1995) through the network approach and thus enables greater strategic flexibility (Sanchez, 1995). To coordinate dispersed activities within global manufacturing and assembly networks, computer systems may be developed providing electronic links to coordinate distributed organizations (Sanchez and Mahoney, 1995; Sanchez, 1996b; Adler, 1989; Boyton, 1993).

An important aspect of a modular product design is embedded coordination (Sanchez, 1995). Modularity permits partitioning of the component development processes into specific tasks (Von Hippel, 1990) that can be performed autonomously and concurrently. Moreover, "the product developing firm does not need to monitor or overtly manage individual component developers' processes in order to assure the effective coordination of developmental processes" (Sanchez and Mahoney, 1995: 17). The coordination of organizational processes is achieved by specifying their required output in the form of standardized interfaces to which developed components must conform.

The "network organization" is a modular type of organization. The modular organization is an organization form that uses "interconnected coordinated self-organizing processes" to support continuous learning and flexible responses to problems posed by a changing environment (Daft and Lewin, 1993: I). Sanchez and Mahoney (1995: 20) define a modular organization as one in which embedded coordination permits organizational processes to be carried out within a loosely coupled organization structure in which each participating organizational unit can function autonomously and concurrently. A modular organization may therefore allow superior flexibility by linking together the resources and abilities of several organizations to develop, manufacture, and deliver a product or service. This implies substantially less direct coordination effort and little exercise of authority managing the overall product or service creation process compared to an organization providing non-modular product designs. As the rate of change and associated degree of uncertainty in the firm's environment increases, management faces an increasing need to create the organizational flexibility to quickly assemble and coordinate resource chains for developing, producing, marketing, distributing and supporting new products or services before competitors can do so. Therefore, standardized interfaces of a modular product design and a shared information system are increasingly important to improving organizational competence in dynamic environments (Sanchez, 1995c). The information needed to coordinate product development processes within a modular organization structure must include:

1. adequate technical description of the components and the product or service to be created;
2. clear assignments of specific development tasks to participating organizations;
3. a schedule for carrying out and completing development and delivery tasks.

(See Sanchez and Mahoney, 1995: 26).

A high level of explicit knowledge (Boisot, Griffiths and Moles, 1996; Wright, 1996) about the functions of the components to be developed and the way these components will interact in a product design is required to create an unambiguous information structure before an efficient development process can start (Sanchez and Mahoney, 1995: 26). A knowledge-building process takes place when a firm chooses to develop new knowledge about components and component interactions during a product development process. Learning appears to be managed efficiently when processes for building knowledge are intentionally separated from processes for applying—or "leveraging"—knowledge (Sanchez and Mahoney, 1995: 27).

The product development process generally consists of product concept development, feasibility testing, product design, development processes, pilot production, and final production (Takeuchi and Nonaka, 1986: 138–139). Sanchez and Mahoney (1995) distinguish two prior models of knowledge management in this process (sequential development processes and overlapping problem solving) and they propose that

> Modular product design implies a new model for managing information flows and knowledge creating and leveraging processes in product development. In contrast to the evolving information structures characteristic of the sequential and overlapping problem-solving models for managing product development, a modular product design creates a complete information structure—the fully specified component interfaces of a modular product architecture—that defines the desired outputs of development tasks before beginning processes for development and detailed design of components. (1995: 35)

Thus, building knowledge to create a modular product architecture upgrades the ability of a firm in leveraging knowledge—i.e. using its

knowledge to develop new products efficiently. The information structure resulting from fully specifying the component interfaces allows
component development processes to be carried out concurrently by
development teams. Sanchez and Mahoney formulate the modularity
principle:

> Modular product architectures provide complete information structures which
> can effectively coordinate concurrent, autonomous organizational processes
> carried out by loosely coupled organization structures. Modular product de-
> signs must be based on technical knowledge which is at an advanced level of
> development and therefore requires the intentional separation of processes for
> creating new knowledge and for applying existing knowledge in product de-
> sign and development. The carefully managed loose coupling of knowledge
> creating and leveraging processes is therefore a necessary (but not sufficient)
> condition for creating modular product designs and modular organization
> structures. (1995: 37)

Decoupling knowledge creation and leveraging processes also may help
a firm to be effective in exploiting its current stock of knowledge (March,
1991), while it also has the freedom to explore new technology learning
opportunities by not focusing only on the short-term use of current
knowledge but also on the future by building new competencies (see
also Sanchez and Mahoney, 1995: 38–39). Further, in developing the new
Boeing 777 aircraft (Woolsey, 1994), the modular product architecture of
the Boeing 777 created a positive environment for efficient "localized"
learning in developing specific components. The localized learning environment that ensues when development of components can be carried
out through autonomous processes facilitated the involvement of
Boeing's lead customers for the 777 in developing improved designs for
key components. Thus, Sanchez and Mahoney (1995) argue that a modular product architecture creates a knowledge-building framework in
which it is easier to involve key users in product development (see also
Von Hippel, 1988).

Sanchez (1996c) identifies three types of strategic product markets, one
being the dynamic product market. This type of market results when
high rates of technological change make possible a fast evolution of
product concepts. A firm operating in this type of market will need
strategic flexibility to cope with the high rate and uncertainties of
change. When the technological and market environment is in constant
flux, the focus of strategic management ought to be redesigning the firm
as a system for rapidly configuring and redeploying a changing array of
assets and capabilities, partly existent within the firm, partly residing in
other firms. Emphasis should therefore be put on building flexible intellectual assets—capabilities and knowledge—that can be leveraged in a

variety of ways as market conditions change. Moreover, "driving the new product strategies and creation processes are concepts of modularity in the design of products and organizations" (Sanchez, 1995: 9). One area of application of the modularity principle is software, where modularity is usually referred to as "object technology". "Object-oriented programming is a modular design process for software that creates application software composed of modules of routines and data that can be mixed and matched to create new program variations to suit the needs of different users" (Sanchez, 1995: 13).

As Sanchez (1995) recognizes, leveraging new product variations by introducing another combination of components costs much less and takes much less time than creating another *de novo* product model by the conventional design process. The ability to leverage product variations from a modular product architecture reduces product development cost, improves the responsiveness of a firm, and/or heightens profitability.

MODULARITY IN PRODUCT DESIGN AT BAAN COMPANY

Baan Company was founded in 1978 to provide financial and administrative consulting services. In 1979, Baan developed its first financial software package. Two years later, it undertook the task of developing broadly applicable, enterprise-wide information systems based on modularity to be readily adaptable to changing technologies and end user needs. Baan sold its first information system in the Netherlands in 1982. Since then it has introduced several new generations of products and expanded its operations to encompass most major markets around the world. Today, the company sells and supports its products through two corporate headquarters in Ede, The Netherlands, and Menlo Park, California, through three International Service Centers in The Netherlands, the United States and India, and through direct and indirect distribution channels in 58 countries.

Baan Software is the application packages component of the modular product and service architecture indicated in Figure 10.1. The company's software consists of a comprehensive set of standard packages to enable Business Process Reengineering. Each package—such as Manufacturing or Distribution—is a modular subsystem consisting of a number of business objects. A total of 450 business objects has been assembled from 6000 different modular programs or "sessions" which can all be grouped together (or "mixed and matched") in various ways. The interface relationships between the business objects have been standardized. The information system required for a specific customer is assembled from the 450 available business objects. The functioning of a specific information

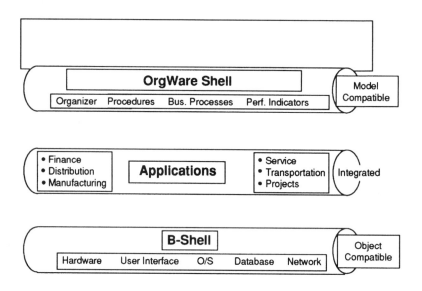

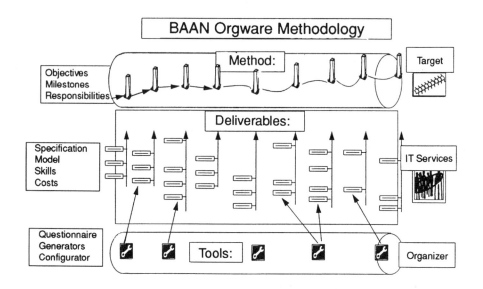

FIGURE 10.1   Baan's Product Architecture

system depends on the assembly of the selected business objects and on the setting of the parameters which determine the inner working of the programs or modules. Every parameter reflects a variable that contributes to the customization of the information system. The complexity of assembling and implementing the information system is managed and strongly reduced by the modular Orgware methodology, services, and tools. Baan Orgware facilitates relatively easy adaptation of functionalities and reassembling—reconfiguration—of the information system. This is called "Dynamic Enterprise Modeling".

The Baan software product is characterized by a generic form of modularity. Software re-use is realized by developing libraries that provide a maximum of standard—or "generic"—functionality. Today, a module such as purchase or inventory is a compilation of functionally grouped modular components called "sessions"; this is the lowest level of modularity created within Baan. On the higher levels Baan applies generic thinking in combining these and other levels of modules to create standard process capabilities, such as purchasing or inventory management systems. Baan's current modular product architecture allows ready integration of modules into customized information systems for specific end users. The company intends to create even more loosely coupled "plug & play" application components called "BOCSs" which can be developed and implemented completely independently from each other, while maintaining the advantages of smooth integration. Modularity in software architecture is also achieved by developing abstraction layers or shells. Developing and maintaining the abstraction or generality levels of modularity contributes to the flexibility of the software packages and the information systems. The function of the abstraction layers is isolating the consequences primarily of changes in the environment and also of idiosyncracies of specific customers.

Standard software has three main dimensions: modularity, parameterization, and flexibility. Flexibility has been improved by writing the Baan software in a 4GL[2] environment, so that the user can make subsequent adaptations in an easy way. A balance has to be struck, however, between developing specific modules and developing parameters for generic modules. For a small piece of functionality it makes sense to develop a specific parameter. But if the adaptation of the module would have far-reaching consequences, it is preferable to write a new module for a specific purpose.

Nucleus is the internal code name for Baan's next generation of modular software including the development of Corba, a platform for the

---

[2] 4GL stands for "4th generation language". 4GLs allow the user to modify or create programs by using simple language and/or graphics, rather than by writing complex code.

exchange of information between objects. First, new product interfaces will be built, then new modules created to work within these interfaces. When an interface has been defined, also third-party suppliers can provide the modules to be developed. The role of Baan Research in this next generation product will be to design Baan's new technology environment:

- it will create the kernel of the next generation product—the complete technology environment, i.e. the software to build, distribute, and run the applications—after which other organizational entities such as Baan Development will build application components based on this technology;
- the next generation technology will be based on an open architecture that enables grouping around and integration of third-party technology and application components;
- around the next generation product Baan will build an organization that will differ considerably from the current organization, with respect to the way the product will be sold, distributed, implemented and supported.

Thus, Baan's evolving modularity strategy reflects the intentional separation of knowledge building—by Baan Research—and knowledge leveraging—by Baan Development—suggested by Sanchez and Mahoney (1995) for greater efficiency and effectiveness in managing knowledge. Baan will also adopt a kind of "modular" or "virtual" form of organization (Sanchez, 1996c). The firm will play the key role of coordinator, drawing together expertise and capabilities of a potentially large number of network collaborators. This means that modularity in the product architecture facilitates organizational modularity in writing the programs, and in the next phase of implementing information systems for end users.

Building its own modular development has helped Baan in a number of ways:

- improving the firm's strategic flexibility and independence in a rapidly changing market;
- helping to adopt new technologies earlier than competitors;
- improving productivity in the development organization;
- providing a complete environment for the design, development, distribution and implementation of complex standard enterprise applications.

With the launch of Baan Research at the beginning of 1995, Baan began a new process for creating the new product architecture that will determine the company strategy for the next ten years or even longer. Today, Baan's technology strategy is to be "open to . . . but independent of . . .". Developing its modular product architecture, the company has learned to support its applications in heterogeneous hardware environments with many different UNIX flavors. Maintaining the flexibility and independence of Baan's current solution offering for Enterprise Resource Planning (ERP) and Business Process Reengineering (BPR) depends on consistent use of abstraction layers. In Baan's layered product architecture, shells represent layers of abstraction and modularization that decouple a functional component from the idiosyncracies of other components, such as a specific database, operating system, user interface, or customer's organization and business.

As Baan starts to define its next generation technology environment (TE), it is useful to consider the notion of abstraction layers in a modular architecture more closely to gain a better understanding of some of their advantages and disadvantages:

Advantages

- By being free of specific information technology component or end-user idiosyncracies, abstraction layers help to increase flexibility, openness, and portability;
- Therefore abstraction layers improve independence, for instance when new products, platforms, or standards emerge;
- Abstraction layers sometimes give the opportunity to implement more advanced functionality, for instance by anticipating expected technology changes;
- Abstraction layers may make it easier to adopt technology changes by implementing them at the abstraction layer level, rather than in specific software applications.

Disadvantages

- Developing an abstraction layer takes time. When development starts too late, there may not be enough time to create a true abstraction layer in the software and to present it to the market in time. An example is Baan's MS-Windows port. The company was late bringing this product to market, partially because Baan first wanted to complete development of an abstraction layer for X-Windows. On the other hand, if development starts too early, the abstraction layer may not be necessary after all, because the market may converge in another way. Again, MS-Windows can be used as an example. The need to provide the customer with anything other than an MS-Windows platform has disappeared almost completely from Baan's market. Thus, the X-Windows abstraction layer became redundant;

- Second, abstraction layers often mean that not all the functionality of a given technology component—such as a database management system or a library—can always be utilized. An example of this is that access to the stored procedures within an RDBMS (relational database management system) may not be possible without making application code RDBMS specific, which is something to be avoided in creating a true abstraction layer.

The abstraction layers in Baan's current product technology environment are essential in making Baan's software flexible and independent. However, the relative benefits and limitations of abstraction when creating software for specific purposes may change as markets evolve, and these trade-offs must be considered in defining each new generation of product architecture (Sanchez, 1996a). For example, abstraction to maintain database independence will definitely be a requirement in the next generation; however, whether the same holds true on the user interface side is an open question, since many users are converging to Windows platforms.

Another important aspect of modularity beyond increased flexibility and maintainability is its greater connectivity and upgradability. As it becomes common for organizations to use third-party software components, new standards such as Corba—a platform for software developers for worldwide standardization—and COM—a standard for communication and integration of application software—will allow the smooth integration of software components developed in different languages by different providers. This movement to a truly open-system environment will clearly change the software business. Today, software choices are clear cut: either a company uses standard software, or it builds its own. In the near future, mixtures of these approaches will become very common. Baan's modular product strategy builds products that can "live" in this new world in which the ability to "mix and match" software components will increasingly be a source of competitive advantage. To achieve this goal, a very visible characteristic of Baan's current architecture is that the company has chosen to implement an abstraction layer—the B-Shell—to make its software platform independent.

For Baan, it is clear that the modularity of object technology is becoming a "dominant logic" (Prahalad and Bettis, 1986; Sanchez, 1995) for creating software and is not "just another fashion". It is currently influencing all software levels, including operating systems, databases, programming languages, and applications, bringing advantages of increased re-usability, flexibility and maintainability. As Baan begins to define its next generation product architecture, it is committed to leading the paradigm shift to object technology and modular software.

The current generation of Baan's application software has been largely designed as a modular product. That means that the overall functionality has been decomposed into interrelated but "loosely coupled" groups of functional components such as Financials and into modules within a given application group. The next generation of Baan's product architecture will fully apply the modularity principle by building modularity from the basic level of the individual objects. However, an issue the firm is currently studying is, to what level should modularity be extended? In other words, how far down the hierarchy of Baan's software architecture should modularity be pushed?

MODULARITY IN THE ORGANIZATION DESIGN OF BAAN COMPANY

In Baan Company, modularity also exists at the level of the organization as well as in software applications. Modularity in the design of Baan's product architecture makes possible a modular division of responsibilities and work in developing and implementing the firm's product at the organizational levels of Research, Development, Distribution, Implementation, and Consultancy.

The loose coupling of components within Baan's product and service architecture is the foundation for Baan's strategic alliances program. Independence of components in the modular product and service design make possible the loose coupling of Baan and its partners in a network organization as suggested by Sanchez and Mahoney (1995). This results in a superior ability to link together the resources and abilities of various partners to develop and deliver Baan's package of products and services. In effect, a substantial amount of coordination has been embedded in the architecture of the modular design.

Sanchez and Mahoney (1995) are also right in stating that creating a modular product design requires advanced knowledge about how components will interact within a product. The current generation of modular software at Baan is composed of well-understood objects. However, developing the next generation product architecture with full implementation of the modularity principle will again require building up knowledge. Because modularity is not followed completely in its current generation software, Baan cannot really apply concurrent engineering as a development principle. Relationships between and within the applications require a high degree of coordination between software developers. Baan overcomes this difficulty by maintaining a high level of open communication.

One very important step Baan was able to take in the past, however, was the decoupling of R&D and implementation of the product: R&D focused on building up new knowledge, and the implementation division focused on leveraging this knowledge, thereby improving the ability to prioritize on product development. A further step has been the recent decoupling of Research and Development, enabling Research to focus on long-term knowledge building, and Development to focus on more specific short-term building up of knowledge. This organizational decoupling will strengthen the ability of the firm to develop its next generation of ERP software.

The modular design of Baan's software and service products has enabled the firm to "quick-connect" (Sanchez, 1996b) with a global network of providers of consultancy, implementation, and customization services for its customers. A global information system solution is guaranteed by a worldwide network of uniformly operating local subsidiaries, local distributors, and global strategic partnerships with service companies. All participants use Baan's Orgware service package to provide and coordinate services. Baan has developed relationships with leading global providers of implementation, customization, and consulting services, including systems integrators such as Cap Gemini and Origin and consulting groups of major accounting firms such as KPMG and Ernst & Young.

As early as 1981, Baan initiated its modular approach to software development. At a time when developing custom software by assigning software engineers to specific projects was very lucrative, the firm started to "manufacture" software as a product composed of "generic" or modular components. Knowledge within Baan is thus leveraged widely by being incorporated into re-usable products that can benefit from a process of continuous improvement. The results of this effort are greater flexibility in providing customized software, a reduction of software delivery time, more reliable solutions, and greater economies of scale than with the traditional approach.

In 1989, Baan made a further strategic organizational decision to separate the distribution of the software from the Research & Development activities. This decision had a major positive influence on the evolution of the company. By separating distribution and development, the application of the factory concept was facilitated because R&D staff were no longer directly involved in customer projects—i.e. implementation and customization. In 1992, Baan also decided to outsource its customization services—i.e. the customization of the standard software to the needs of specific end users—to BSO (Origin, worldwide). On this occasion, Baan and BSO/Origin also made a worldwide cooperation agreement in which Origin became a provider of customization and implementation services for Baan. At the same time, Origin set up a corporate competence center specializing in customizing Baan's software package.

In 1993, Baan introduced Orgware as a package of services that are complementary to and integrated with its software to achieve a global, uniform approach in providing high-quality professional services for implementing and customizing Baan's software. Using Orgware, implementation becomes less person and provider dependent and more predictable in its conformity with standards. In order to maintain the quality of the services provided by these providers, as well as to provide internationally uniform implementation services, Baan also selects and trains these organizations and evaluates their performance on a regular basis. The methods and tasks necessary to use Orgware successfully in an implementation project are communicated through training courses, reference models, materials, and tools.

Orgware further extends Baan Company's ability to offer both software and associated services to end users around the world. Through Orgware, modular software components are configured into unique customer-oriented information systems. The ability of implementers around the world to use Orgware to implement and customize Baan's modular software allows the separability of production and consumption of software and greatly reduces its heterogeneity. There, Orgware becomes a ready basis for coordinating a global network of firms in Baan's internationalization. While a traditional software service firm is not able to obtain economies of scale, Baan has this opportunity through Orgware. The ability to leverage Baan's software globally through use of Orgware justifies a higher level of investments in R&D and finances ongoing innovation. By standardizing procedures and methods, Orgware also reduces transaction costs and thus facilitates collaborative non-equity arrangements. In 1996, Baan's objective is to continue expanding its global infrastructure in order to provide sales and support services throughout the major markets of the world. This global presence not only allows the company to capture a share of local markets, but also to support its multinational customers.

Essential to the success of strategic partnerships is the selection of partners. Changing industry conditions are a key factor in selecting the partners. Baan's global partnership network is characterized by a three-dimensional capability fit: a strategic fit, an operational fit, and a chemistry fit. To achieve strategic fit, partners must share Baan's long-term objectives. Operational fit is evidenced by compatibility of experiences, business ethics, and future prospects. This assures that on the operational level, Baan and its partners are complementary and can work in a uniform and standardized way. Chemistry is a measure of the quality of the relationships between the people involved in operating the partnership. It is about compatibility of mind, attitude, and feelings.

Baan has divided its strategic partners into four categories:

• Technology Partners—hardware and database vendors
• Development Partners—software manufacturers
• Consultancy Partners—business consultancy firms
• Services Partners—information technology service companies.

With its Technology Partners, Baan has established R&D programs. The partnerships create an understanding of the development strategy of Baan and promote collaborations on local, regional, and global levels. Together with the Development Partners, Baan has set up its Enterprise Application Group. A number of key global suppliers of complementary applications have recognized the value of linking their products with Baan's products and of using the "Modular Software Factory" concept, and as a result have joined Baan in this group. This cooperation enables Baan and its partners to achieve standardization with the help of Baan Tools architecture that facilitates a high degree of integration between their respective products. The Enterprise Application Group works with standard interfaces, a common data model, a common architecture, and a common GUI (graphical user interface). It creates linked packages based on Baan's product family in the areas of human resource management, payroll management, shop floor control engineering, office management, automotive/JIT, product data management, work flow, and other types of applications. Together with its Consultancy and Services Partners, Baan undertakes programs to develop and implement products which are consistent with Baan's tools, products and services. Implementation products are developed to model and simulate each customer's business situation. Baan's consultancy partners help the client to optimize its business design using Baan's software. Baan's Service Partners are specialized in systems integration and the development of tailor-made solutions using Baan's modular software. Uniformity and standardization are thus achieved through common use of Orgware.

CONCLUSIONS

Modularity is a concept which the experience of Baan Company suggests can be central to developing and implementing a successful competence-based strategy. As is clear from Baan Company, modularity can be the basis for strategic flexibility (Sanchez, 1995) and has played a key role in helping to make the firm successful in the emerging global market of ERP systems. Modularity has been applied by the firm in several stages, each one progressively increasing the range of modularity used in its product designs and organization designs. Modularity is the source of the firm's flexibility to offer many customers the customized products they want.

Baan follows the example of the automobile and other industries that use modular product designs to achieve flexibility and simplicity in assembling and delivering products. This trend is reflected not only in Baan's product strategy, but also in the software preferences of all of its major customers. The software industry is becoming an industry based on the general principles of modularity. Baan was among the first firms to anticipate this power of modularity.

From Baan's perspective, modularity is essential to strategic management. Of course, modularity is not the only cornerstone of Baan's success. Also relevant are a commitment to ongoing innovation and the willingness to break away from current practice. And of course, the firm has always paid much attention to developing the capabilities and well-being of its staff.

REFERENCES

Adler, P. S. (1989). "CAD/CAM: Managerial challenges and research issues", *IEEE Transactions on Engineering Management*, **36**, pp. 202–215.

Boisot, Max, Dorothy Griffiths and Veronica Moles (1996). "The dilemma of competence: Differentiation versus integration in the pursuit of learning", in *Strategic Learning and Knowledge Management*, Ron Sanchez and Aimé Heene, editors, Chichester, UK: John Wiley & Sons.

Boyton, Andrew C. (1993). "Achieving dynamic stability through information technology", *California Management Review*, **35** (winter), pp. 58–77.

Beer, Stafford (1966). *Decision and Control*, New York: John Wiley & Sons.

Clark, Kim B. and Takahiro Fujimoto (1991). *Product Development Performance: Strategy, Organization, and Management in the World Auto Industry*, Boston MA: Harvard University Press.

Daft, Richard L. and Arie Y. Lewin (1993). "Where are the theories of 'new' organizational forms? An editorial essay", *Organizational Science*, **4**(4), pp. i–vi.

Farrell, Joseph and Garth Saloner (1989). "Converters, compatability, and the control of interfaces", Working Paper, number 3106-90 (December), University of California at Berkeley.

Garud, Raghu and Arun Kumaraswamy (1993). "Changing competitive dynamics in network industries: An exploration of Sun Microsystems' open systems strategy", *Strategic Management Journal*, **14**(5), pp. 351–369.

Kogut, Bruce and Nalin Kulatilaka (1994). "Operating flexibility, global manufacturing, and the option value of a multinational network", *Management Science*, **40**(1), pp. 123–139.

Langlois, Richard N. and Paul L. Robertson (1992). "Networks and innovation in a modular system: Lessons from the microcomputer and stereo component industries", *Research Policy*, **21**(4), pp. 297–313.

March, James G. (1991). "Exploration and exploitation in organizational learning", *Organization Science*, **2**(1), 71–87.

Morris, Charles R. and Charles H. Ferguson (1993). "How architecture wins technology wars", *Harvard Business Review*, **71** (March–April), pp. 86–96.

Norman, Richard and Rafael Ramirez (1993). "From value chain to value constellation: Designing interactive strategy", *Harvard Business Review*, **71** (July–August), pp. 65–77.

Orton, J. Douglas and Karl E. Weick (1990). "Loosely coupled systems: A reconceptualization", *Acadamy of Management Review*, **15**(2), pp. 203–223.

Prahalad, C. K. and R. A. Bettis (1986). "The dominant logic: A new linkage between diversity and performance", *Strategic Management Journal*, **7**(6), pp. 485–501.

Sanchez, Ron (1995). "Strategic flexibility in product competition", *Strategic Management Journal*, **16**, pp. 135–159.

Sanchez, Ron (1996a). "Integrating technology strategy and marketing strategy", in Don O'Neal and Howard Thomas, editors, *Integrating Strategy*, Chichester: John Wiley & Sons (forthcoming).

Sanchez, Ron (1996b). "Quick connect technologies for product creation: Implications for Competence-Based Competition" in *Dynamics of Competence-Based Competition*, Ron Sanchez, Aimé Heene and Howard Thomas, editors, Oxford: Elsevier.

Sanchez, Ron (1996c). "Strategic product creation: Managing new interactions of technology, markets, and organizations", *European Management Journal*, **14**(2), pp. 121–138.

Sanchez, R., A. Heene and H. Thomas (1996) "Towards the theory and practice of competence-based competition," in *Dynamics of Competence-based Competition*, R. Sanchez, A. Heene and H. Thomas, editors, Oxford: Elsevier.

Sanchez, Ron and Joseph T. Mahoney (1995). *Modularity, Flexibility, and Knowledge Management in Product and Organization Design*, University of Illinois Working Paper No. 95–0121.

Sanchez, Ron and Devanathan Sudharshan (1993). "Real-time market research: Learning-by-doing in the development of new products", *Marketing Intelligence and Planning*, **11**(7), pp. 29–38.

Sanderson, Susan Walsh and Vic Uzumeri (1990). "Strategies for new product development and renewal: Design-based incrementalism", Working Paper, Center for eScience and Technology Policy, Rensselaer Polytechnic Institute, Troy, New York.

Simon, Herbert A. (1962). "The architecture of complexity", *Proceedings of the American Philosophical Society*, **106** (December), pp. 467–482.

Takeuchi, Hirotaka and Ikujiro Nonaka (1986). "The new new product development game", *Harvard Business Review*, (January–February), 137–146.

Von Hippel, Eric (1988). *The Sources of Innovation*, New York: Oxford University Press.

Von Hippel, Eric (1990). "Task partitioning: An innovation process variable", *Research Policy*, 1995, 4070418.

Wheelwright, Steven, C. and Kim B. Clark (1992). *Revolutionizing Product Development: Quantum Leaps in Speed, Efficiency, and Quality*, New York: Free Press.

Williamson, Oliver E. (1975). *Markets and Hierarchies: Analysis and Antitrust Implications*, New York: Free Press.

Wright, Russell W. (1996). "Tangible integration versus intellectual codification skills: A comparison of learning processes in developing logic and memory semiconductors", in Ron Sanchez and Aimé Heene, editors, *Strategic Learning and Knowledge Management*, Chichester, UK: John Wiley & Sons.

Woolsey, James P. (1994). "777", *Air Transport World*, (April), pp. 22–31.

11

Leveraging Knowledge Across Firm Boundaries: Achieving Strategic Flexibility Through Modularization and Alliances

JOHN W. LANG

This chapter investigates the relationship between modularity in product design, organizational design, technology transfer and strategic alliancing. The tapping into, and creation of, standard product/process interfaces can help facilitate inter-firm coordination while helping to minimize the transaction costs at those firm interfaces.

A case study is used to illustrate how one small Cambridge-based supplier of RISC chip technology, ARM Ltd, has retained strategic flexibility within its markets through International Strategic Alliances and the modular approach to its products and its own internal organization. This approach has helped protect the small firm from unwelcome advances of larger suitors and ensured its adaptation to emergent markets.

The "umbrella of licensing as a strategic alliance option" has enabled the firm to trade successfully within its environment without ceding

Strategic Learning and Knowledge Management.
Edited by Ron Sanchez and Aimé Heene.
Copyright © 1997 John Wiley & Sons Ltd.

control to its larger partners. The crucial competence areas developed by the firm are: alliance management and control, and technology transfer.

ARM Ltd (Company Background)

ARM Ltd emerged in 1990 as a business spin-out from Acorn Computers in Cambridge, UK. As far back as 1983, Acorn was involved in RISC[1] chip design, but saw its core business as mass produced, low cost computers for the education market, and the production of the RISC (Reduced Instruction Set Computing) device as a secondary objective. ARM Ltd was set up as a joint venture between Acorn and its partners as shown in Figure 11.1.

ARM Ltd sits at the confluence of a number of simultaneous developments in the computing and telecommuncations industries, mainly:

1. the need by those industries for faster, lower cost core processor technologies
2. the need for low power consumption processors
3. the need for smaller, simpler, "reduced instruction set" processors.

Cost, size and power consumption are the key benchmarks of the microprocessor industry and ARM was conceived as a company to address the emerging needs of these emerging markets. It rapidly acquired and developed the competences necessary, for the design and production of its core processor, from its parent organizations, from its alliance partners and from the acquisition of key personnel.

In many emerging industries—RISC processors, biotechnology, multimedia—firms are forming extensive networks of alliances to develop and promote their products. Often, the competition in these industries pits small start-up companies against large established firms, the small firms typically resorting to alliances to consolidate their positions and enhance their capabilities.

From the outset, ARM realized that a partnering (alliance) strategy was the key to market exploitation, growth and survival and so it set up links with the key semiconductor industry partners given in Figure 11.2. Mass produced, low cost microprocessors need large fabrication plants

---

[1] RISC = Reduced Instruction Set Computing is essentially a streamlined approach to microprocessor design. Traditional microprocessor design, called CISC (Complex Instruction Set Computing) was based on the theory that the more complex the instruction set embedded in the chip's design, the more efficiently the computer operated. RISC challenges this premise, claiming that, in practice, only 20% of the conventional instructions were called upon to perform 80% of the computer's functions.

to realize economies[2] and with short openings in the strategic windows for their products, there was a need to manufacture and market early in the product/industry life cycle. D'Aveni (1994) characterizes the type of competition faced by ARM as "hypercompetition", that is, a fast pace of change occurring within the industry, small strategic windows of opportunity, and new and changing forms of competitive conditions.

Partnering, strategic alliances (elaborated in the next section) and competence alliances, via licensing agreements in the case of ARM, provide them with the tangible and intangible assets to realize the missing competences of the full manufacture/market cycle. These competence alliances are instrumental in two areas: (1) competence building—where the firm incorporates newly acquired competences from partners; and (2) competence leveraging—where the firm uses its assets in newly opened product/market arenas (Sanchez, Heene, and Thomas, 1996b). The competence alliances also give ARM access to firm addressable assets (i.e. those critical assets to which ARM may have access without ownership) such as software tools, methodologies, technical expertise and knowledge, which are held within the partner firms. There is an implicit view of the firm here as embodying specific competences to coordinate certain activities and to structure, adopt, adapt, absorb, integrate, and diffuse newly acquired competences as in the cycle given in Figure 11.4.

STRATEGIC PARTNERSHIPS AS ENABLERS

The strategic partnerships of ARM may be viewed as "enablers", giving the firm access to complementary or co-specialised assets (Teece, 1986), enabling the firm to leverage its competences into new markets, giving rise to:

- World-wide market acceptance
- Global manufacturing capabilities
- Shorter development times
- Broader product offering
- Reduced development, manufacturing and marketing costs
- Setting of common architecture, software, and bus standards

ARM'S PARTNERING STRATEGY

The number of strategic alliances between large (usually well-established) firms and small start-up new technology-based firms

---

[2] Current estimated cost of establishing a fabrication plant for a full range of microprocessor production is $500 million.

("small firms with a higher inherent innovative potential than large and small firms in general", Oakey *et al.*, 1988) has increased in the 1980s and 1990s. The rationale for these alliances can often be attributed to synergies arising from small firm competences which may be leveraged into emergent markets and the large firm (firm-specific) competences, and value adding capabilities, which help realize their potential within those markets (Niederkofler, 1991). The main perceived benefits are often cited as: access to new technologies and expertise that complements existing firm competences; sharing of costs and risks; reduced time to market; and marketing benefits (Lorange and Roos, 1993; Dodgson, 1993; Littler *et al.*, 1995). It can therefore be said that the small firms are stretching their capabilities to acquire new competences.

Strategic alliance networks have been useful for "small firms" such as ARM Ltd, particularly in the area of reducing their resource constraints, assisting them to utilize existing competences while simultaneously sharing partner competences and then internalizing (and / or reconfiguring, redefining) these to overcome resource constraints. (The co-evolutionary development of this is the auditing–unframing–reframing of the systemic elements and higher and lower order cognitions of the firm's management: see Sanchez and Heene, 1996.) This also highlights two properties of competences: first, their inertial and cumulative features, and, second, the varying degrees of tacitness of the knowledge on which they are based (Dosi and Teece, 1993). Firms must recognize that the organizational (functional) requirements for leveraging competences into markets and building competences organically will put different stresses and strains on the organization's systems.

The design and management of networks of alliances, such as those shown in Figure 11.1, can often be critical to success of the small company in particular and highlight a number of important competences that the small firm management must display, namely, the management of the governance relations (higher and lower order control loops: Sanchez and Heene, 1996), the mix of firms' personnels, and the technology mix and technology transfer.

As can be seen in Figures 11.1 and 11.2, ARM Ltd is an integral part of a network of alliances that includes sources of capital and technological expertise (Figure 11.1, "Owners") and product users and value adding firms (Figure 11.2, "Licensees").

Strategic alliances are taken to be collaborations between firms and other organizations, both short and long term, which can involve partial or contractual ownership, developed for strategic reasons. The equity investment alliance partners of Figure 11.1 and the licensing partners of ARM Ltd (Figure 11.2) are therefore included in their immediate strategic alliance network.

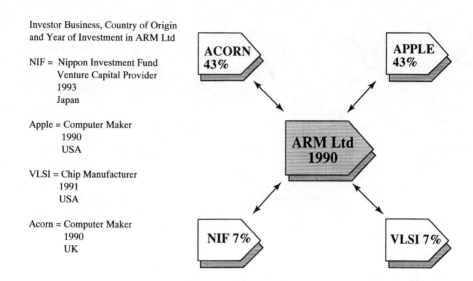

FIGURE 11.1   Equity Investment Partners of ARM's Strategic Alliance Network
(% denotes amount of equity ownership)

In summary, ARM's partnering strategy is as follows:

- ARM licenses to leading semiconductor partners who manufacture and market ARM chips world-wide;
- Partners manufacture and sell ARM standard products;
- Partners design, manufacture and sell their own products using the ARM core architecture combined with their technologies (this "group" is the focus of this chapter and is shown in Figure 11.2);
- ARM also licenses leading software, systems and design companies its software tools and models to enable rapid acceptance of the ARM architecture;
- ARM's focus is on core technology in systems, architecture, silicon circuits, software and hardware development tools;
- ARM provides design consultancy and training for its partners, large electronics companies and independent design houses to expand the total ARM market;
- ARM also coordinates partner activity.

The firm-specific assets and competences of ARM are mostly of an intangible nature, however wide ranging, and include (after Hall in Hamel & Heene, 1994):

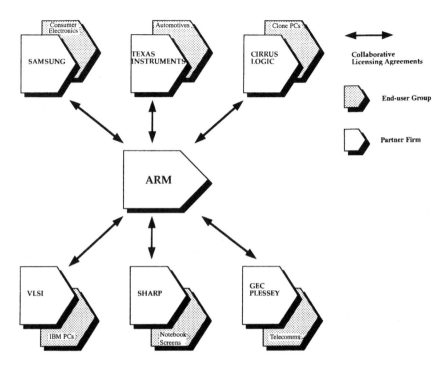

FIGURE 11.2   The Licensing Agreement of ARM (each value chain represents a different geographical market and end-user group)

Firm-specific Assets:

- The licence contracts possessed by ARM;
- The image and reputation of all of its alliance partners, owners and licensees;
- Personal and organizational networks;
- Software tools and methodologies, libraries of code;
- The intellectual property rights on products and processes.

Firm-specific Competences:

- The ability of their employees, owners and alliance partners (their individual and collective ability) to transform resources through the application of firm-specific or firm-addressable knowledge. The group founders came to ARM with knowledge acquired while working at Acorn in their R&D laboratories and in large computer system designers. This gave the personnel a good knowledge of large system integrators, their internal workings and potential problem areas with regard to procedures and decision-making unit composition. The ability to adapt, absorb and integrate a number of knowledge bases gives ARM their flexibility in dealing with a variety of licensees.

● The organizational culture/structure (flat and flexible in the case of ARM).

The partners of ARM all operate in mutually exclusive end-user markets and geographical areas and so reduce any conflict of interest that may occur. At the same time, this diversity increases the potential for "problems associated with customization of products/designs". This is ameliorated to a great extent by the "modularization" of product/processes employed by ARM (see later discussion). The licences between ARM and its partners will contain varying degrees of tangible and non-tangible assets. The modularization (expanded later) of technologies and product elements reduces the assets specificity to each contract and opens potentially new applications environments with partners, allowing some of the elements (modules) of the products to be transported across environments.

As can be seen from the above two lists, alliances and networks figure very heavily in the overall strategy of the firm. The logic of which will now be discussed.

THE LOGIC OF ALLIANCES (LICENSING)

The licensing agreements signed by ARM have allowed the company to develop a more or less standard set of responses (governance structures) to their partners.

The licensing agreements, the sole governance structures used by ARM with its network partners, show a commitment to present relationships between ARM and those partners (the contract itself is the legal expression of this), while keeping future options open for ARM. The current licensing contracts imbue those relationships with trust, commitment, rationale and logic, while the designed-in obsolescence of those contracts (the contracts are signed typically on three-year cycles) keep open the future options for technological development within the relationships (Sanchez 1993, 1995). This allows lead time to develop next version/generation products.

The setting up and management of the licensing contracts is important for the "perceived success" of the relationships established, and this often comes down to the "structure and culture" of the organizations' teams involved at the boundary of the firms.

These licensing agreements (i.e. the small firm "licensing out") have the benefit of leveraging the competences of the firm into a number of markets simultaneously and building new competences through technology transfer at the boundary between the partner firms. The leveragibility of ARM's competences is intrinsically bound up with its ability to coordinate and deploy its own firm-specific and firm-addressable resources of its partners.

In this sense, whether purposively or by accident, the

> managers [are] seeking to maximize the firm value [by a] continual recursive process of leveraging a firm's existing competences to exercise some of the firm's existing strategic options, generating cash flows, directing some cash flows to competence building to create new strategic options, leveraging some of the firm's new and previous competences to exercise new strategic options, generating new cash flows, directing some cash flows to creating new competences that bring new strategic options, and so on. (Sanchez and Thomas, 1996)

The risk/reward profile of its alliances is optimal for the small firm, giving it the "balance" of both competence leveraging and building with limited resources. The degree of risk and cost (mainly resource commitment) of competence-building activities may be shared between the partners in the alliance relationships. Competence building and leveraging will often be most evident in the exchanges occurring at the firm boundaries, where "actions" structure the socio-technical exchange relations, and these exchanges stimulate and legitimate actions, in a recursive fashion, as discussed below.

FIRM BOUNDARY; ACTION AND STRUCTURE

The recognition that competence gaps exist on both sides of a dyadic alliance is easy to comprehend; what is more difficult, however, is understanding what is causing these competence gaps to open and close and what is happening at that interface. Useful concepts to give an insight here are now briefly discussed.

Organizational processes and norms that exist between firms in alliances may be viewed as manifestations of action, based upon the existent and emergent cognitions of managers (of firm strategy) who perceive and attempt to close competence gaps. A product of this will be qualitative changes (learning in one of its guises) in "higher order system elements" (Sanchez and Heene, 1996). The primary conduit for these cognitive changes is the boundary spanner (in this case ARM's project-specific personnel and their partner's corresponding teams) who have interlocking procedures of action within a specific structure. This action–structure–action loop (*ad infinitum*) adds a dynamism to the overall competence framework analysis and links actions—structured relations—the opening and closing of competence gaps. Organizations such as ARM may be seen "adapting their internal structures" and "absorbing interdependencies" of their alliances with each partner interaction.

Structuration theory offers a bridge between the qualitative and quantitative frameworks which often examine strategic resources and resource dependencies as if they were "inert" entities. This is due to the de-contextualized manner in which the resources are examined. (The purpose of this chapter is not to fully argue the merits and demerits of one mode of research over another, nor to explain structuration theory in depth. But, I am pointing to a tool of analysis which has great explanatory and exploratory potential for alliance and network analyses.) Structuration theory relates resources to rules (of signification and legitimation) and focuses on the interplay of those rules and resources.

The very simplified picture looks like that below (for further development of this see Lang, 1996).

Firms possess certain competences which may be used and augmented by the actions of the personnel, who may upload and download knowledge (individual and organizational, codified and uncodified: Boisot, 1995) within a structured set of relations (between the organizations) determining who is responsible, what is exchanged in terms of resources and what control measures are necessary to facilitate this process. This is seen as a recursive process as illustrated by the interconnectivity of the elements in the diagram above.

There is a permeability at the firm boundary facilitated by the constant interaction of the personnel (boundary spanners) between the firms.

These exchanges constantly reshape a firm's members' perceptions of their own competences, update their knowledge of useful assets and capabilities, and suggest new ways of organizing and coordinating, all of which contribute to a process of continuous (alliance-) based competence building and leveraging. (Easton and Araujo, 1996)

Alliances become important vehicles for freeing the cognitive limits of managers and are used by firms as important sources of innovation. This supports the hypothesis that qualitative changes in managerial cognitions (at "higher order system elements", see Sanchez and Heene, 1996 for full explanation) will lead to potential innovations. Related to the above will be the culture of the organization as inhibitor and/or facilitator of exchanges between those at the firm boundaries. I now turn to this in the next section.

TEAM ORGANIZATION AND CULTURE (OPERATIONAL COMPETENCES)

The teams used by ARM in the projects with their partners are based on the capabilities of the members rather than the hierarchical authority relationships of manager–managed. Although there is a "named person" responsible for the overall reporting of the progress of the alliance relationship, this is more for the development of "trust" with the partner, than for the team management *per se*. Each licensee is assigned a "project manager" (named individual contact point within ARM) who coordinates the team that will contribute to the licence relationship.

The organizational "structure and culture" that pervades ARM reflects the need for the alliance relations to be based on mutual trust and the need for greater degrees of freedom (flexibility) of the personnel within the teams working on specific projects. I have termed the culture of ARM an "achievement culture" after Pheysey (1993). Flexibility and responsiveness are the key attributes possessed by the smaller firm. The organizational flexibility, that goes hand in hand with the achievement culture, aids the competence building and leveraging within the firm.

Organizations possessing an achievement-oriented culture make high demands on the energy and time of their personnel with the assumption that the personnel enjoy working at the tasks which are intrinsically satisfying. The project work itself can then be seen to be performed out of the satisfaction in the excellence of the work and the achievement and/or personal commitment to the goal or task at hand. The power/control base of the relationship between ARM and its partners then becomes "expertise" (Pheysey, 1993). This works in the small firm's favour, in that in almost every other manner the small firm is at a potential disadvantage due to its size. It is this very expertise that helps to ensure that ARM, the smaller partner in all of its alliance relationships, does not cede control to the larger partners. This is likened to the example of "microbargains" given in Hamel (1991).

The operational competences, that is, the "set of managerial policies and practices, conventions about how things are done, organization structure and culture, systems for managing innovation, motivating and rewarding employees" (Lorange and Roos, 1993), can be seen in the "achievement culture" (Pheysey, 1992) created by ARM's management in their project teams. The "operational competences allow the firm to adapt to moderate changes in the environment over time" (Lorange and Roos). These operational competences are also "maintaining competences" possessed by the organization that allow adaptation and flexibility to environmental change.

The operational competences are supported and enhanced by standardized interfaces of the design systems (CADD/CAM) used by ARM and their partners. These standardized interfaces enable "quick connect/disconnect" to the alliance partners (Sanchez, 1996) and help further to embed the routines of the exchange relationships (technological and social) that are taking place at the firm boundaries. Transmission of information is less open to misinterpretation with the software/systems engineering methodologies and tools that are used by ARM and its partners. The operational competences come with experience gained in the alliance network and facilitate learning which can be used in successive alliance partnerships.

The use of these software engineering tools also helps create libraries or databases of core codes that may be transferred from one generation (one version) of products to another. In other words, there is an added benefit of "stored re-usability" in components of the product.

For firms like ARM, this is very important as it reduces the cost of adaptation of its core processors from one alliance partner to another. This allows for version and/or product proliferation (see Figure 11.3). The competence that is practised in this situation is that of adaptation of core designs to different end-user application environments. The achievement culture (see above) based on open, flexible communications and expertise coupled with the "modular component (product)" design structure of the ARM processors enhance the degree of adaptability of the small firm.

MODULAR PRODUCT/COMPONENT DESIGN

According to Sanchez and Mahoney (1994), modular product design is:

> . . . a special form of "loosely coupled" product design capable of using standardized interfaces between components to create well-decomposed flexible product designs . . .

220

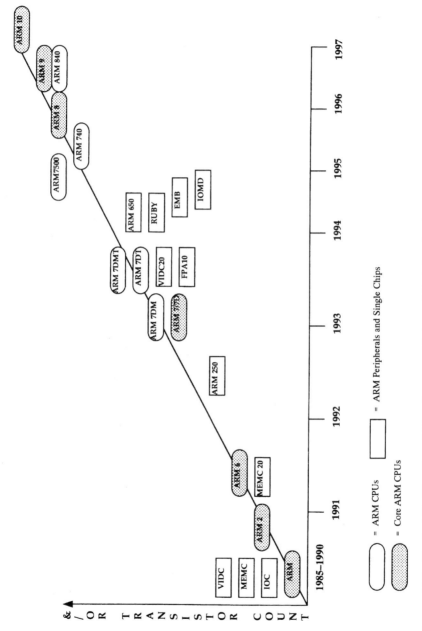

FIGURE 11.3   Product Proliferation of Core Processor Units and Peripherals of ARM

Modular Product Design:
A product design with standardized interfaces between components and/or subsystems of components, at least some of which are specified to allow for a range of variations in components or subsystems.

Modular Component:
A component whose functional, spatial, and other characteristics fall within the range of variations allowed by the specified standardized interfaces of a modular product design. (Sanchez and Mahoney, 1994)

For a small firm, operating in several alliance partnerships simultaneously, with limited resources, the logic of the above becomes clear. Core microprocessor components may be combined in such a way as to reduce redundancy of components to a minimum, leading to efficiency gains; share component architectures across projects; reduce inherent costs of necessary product adaptation and changes from one alliance partner's architecture to another.

In their company promotional literature, ARM recognize the above as a necessary competence (core) and refer to it as *"ARM Quick Design"*.

Thus for ARM, adapting (moving through the cycle shown in Figure 11.4) to varying functionality requirements of, say, Texas Instruments in the automotive markets, to Sharp in the notebook computer markets can be performed more easily (or at least less traumatically, within resource limits) due to the principles of modular product and component design.

In addition, the alliance partners of ARM are also able to couple components from other source firms, due to the standard nature of the interfaces with which they may connect the ARM core processor to the additional components making up the finished product.

The modularization of the products and the standard interfaces created and facilitated by the use of software engineering and design tools (VLSI tools, software design tools from HP, Compass, VLSI), and the licensing of those tools and models to licensees, allows rapid acceptance of the ARM architecture into partner firms. This is analogous to speeding up the cycle shown in Figure 11.4 from the partner firm viewpoint.

This is precisely the argument of Sanchez and Mahoney (1994) when they say:

> . . . a firm may use its CADD and other information systems to leverage its available management and organizational resources by quick connecting with a constellation of networked firms whose diverse resources and capabilities can be readily assembled and coordinated in a large number of quickly enacted value chains . . .

In the case of ARM, the "constellation of networked firms" includes the joint venture partners who are the parent firms of ARM (Apple, VLSI,

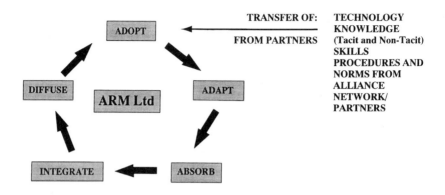

FIGURE 11.4   Cycle of Adoption and Diffusion of Resource Base in Alliances

Acorn, firms in Figure 11.1); the alliance partners with whom ARM has licensing agreements (Sharp, GEC, TI, Cirrus, Logic, etc., firms in Figure 11.2); and other support organizations which supply ARM with software tools and resources, for example Hewlett Packard, VLSI. In addition, ARM becomes a node organization in an extended network which includes, to a greater or lesser degree, suppliers, clients and partners of its partner organizations. In other words the "net-" of the network includes organizations outside the immediate relationships mentioned in this chapter so far.

The potential for greater chaos and/or turbulence may increase with every licensing agreement signed by ARM (Ashby, 1981). However, that possibility is dampened by the modular product form and standardized interfaces installed between ARM and its partners. Furthermore, the standard interfaces embed coordination and control within the technology, and the exchange relationships between the firms enhance operational competences and permit "loosely coupled organization structures", (Sanchez and Mahoney, 1994) which do not require "overt managerial authority" to be exercised over the technology transfer process between ARM and alliance partners.

MODULAR ORGANIZATIONS AS "LOOSELY COUPLED ORGANIZATION STRUCTURES"

The standardized interfaces and modular product designs discussed in the previous section assist in embedding coordination and control between organizations such as ARM and its alliance partners. This in turn can result in "little or no need for the exercise of overt managerial authority over developer processes, and hence little or no need for an organizational structure incorporating an authority hierarchy" (Sanchez, 1995). The standards imbued in the relationships by the design tools, supplied with the technology by ARM, are instrumental in ensuring that the small firm does not cede control to the larger partners in its alliances, but instead instills the routines, protocols and procedural logic that ARM is familiar with.

The "quick-connect" interfaces created as a result of the standards allow the partner firms to "hit the ground running" (Saxby, 1994) which gives them a potential first mover advantage. Speed of coordination in the relationship is enhanced as the partner firm technologies and technological architectures use common methods and procedures at their interface.

As mentioned in the previous section, the benefit to the partners is that they may draw in components from other suppliers, in their own wider networks, and be assured that the ARM component will have compatibility with the bought-in components from their other suppliers. Thus ensuring overall product integrity. This is the practical outcome of what is meant by Sanchez and Mahoney (1994) when they say:

> ... we propose that modular organization is greatly facilitated by, and may even depend on, the realization of a significant degree of embedded coordination achieved through standardized interfaces in product and organization designs that permit loosely coupled organization structures to carry out tightly coupled processes.

Using Sharp (briefly) as an example in the case of ARM's partners in the alliance network, the following occurs:

1. Sharp licenses the core RISC processor from ARM;
2. Teams from Sharp and ARM work out the necessary adaptations to ensure true compatibility;
3. Sharp incorporates the ARM core into the circuit architecture used in its notebook;
4. Motherboard components are sourced from other suppliers, as are other major notebook parts, e.g. screen, drives, etc.

Outsourcing and assembly, by Sharp, of this "loosely coupled organizational" nature can only be achieved when there is a common logic (through modularization) behind the overall product architecture. As a consequence, the need for "overt managerial authority", as would be evidenced by a hierarchy (Williamson, 1985), is considerably reduced.

The added benefits for ARM are that it can manage several (currently six in core processors licensing, and more in software licensing) very large partners (in size and revenue terms) simultaneously. This increases its chances of becoming a *de-facto* industry standard and it is exposed to a wide array of competences, technology and practices which adds to its knowledge base through those collaborations.

CONCLUSION

Because of the nature of its chosen route to market, the licensing agreement/alliance form, ARM needs time to "connect into" the partner firms' technology and organizational structure. The main, or most important, elements (generic) of the alliance relationships are:

- Competence fit between the component organizational and technological architectures of ARM and its partners' competences (technological/organizational competences);
- The social exchange relationships that take place between the project teams at the firm boundaries (operational competences).

This combination of technological/organizational competences has been summed up in Figure 11.5. Three generic competences can be identified in firms such as ARM.

1. Background competences are the minimum set of combined organization/technology/knowledge competences to be a potential market entrant. These will be the existing stock of competences already contained within the organization before new alliances are formed and will also have been more or less diffused organization-wide.

   These exist at the *Meta-level within the firm as part of its codified dictionary of knowledge.*
2. Enabling competences will be the reconfigured (customized) technologies/knowledge/recombined component organizational and individual skills which may be developed during the contract with partner organizations, but which will have applications on other contracts.

   These are at the *Mezzanine level between firms.*
3. Project-specific competences are those unique, internally generated or externally acquired competences which may be licensed exclusively to the sponsor but which will also become part of the future Meta- and/or Mezzanine competences of the licensor.

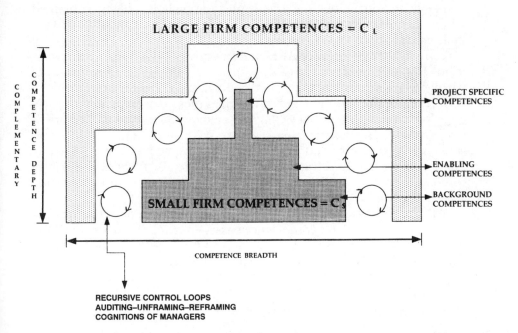

FIGURE 11.5 Background, Enabling, and Project Specific Competence in Alliances

The "recursive loops" at the organizational boundaries in Figure 11.5 represent the "audit-unframe-reframe" (of action and structure) of cognitions of those involved, initially at the project interface, but eventually being diffused throughout the organization. This "structuration" highlights to the recursive character of relations within and between alliance network members. (A future development of this will be discussed in Lang, forthcoming, 1996.)

Studies on the success and failure of strategic alliances have pointed to the "formation of lasting relationships based on trust" as one of, if not the key element to, success (Harrigan, 1986; Contractor and Lorange, 1988; Lorange and Roos, 1993; Bleeke and Ernst, 1993; Dodgson, 1993; Pucik *et al.*, 1992, to name a few).

The social relations at the point of exchange and production (boundary function) must be managed by the participating members of the relationships. The embedded coordination resulting from the standardized interfaces and modular product designs enables the parties involved in the alliance relationships to have more time and latitude to manage the relationship (point 2 above) thereby freeing resources (time, personnel, capital) to concentrate on the coordination of the relationship and the assimilation of non-tacit knowledge inherently present in those exchange relationships (the non-explicit knowledge being contained within the products and procedures laid down in the standard software tools used).

From the point of view of ARM and its partners, this allows the project teams to speed up the cycle of the process of adoption and diffusion of partner technologies into their own organization (Figure 11.4). The speed of the cycle of the adoption and diffusion of those technologies into one's own "technology set" is a key competence required in the hypercompetitive markets discussed in this chapter. The use of common interface standards, procedures and protocols can help speed up that cycle time, thereby increasing the strategic flexibility (Sanchez, 1995) of the firm to respond to, refine and incorporate the technological nuances that may arise in the licensing of technologies.

With each successive licensing agreement signed by ARM, the firm has built upon its assets and competence bases, enabling it to leverage these into new and diverse markets. The adaptability of ARM to each alliance and market is testimony to its strategic flexibility.

REFERENCES

Ashby, W. R. (1981). *An Introduction to Cybernetics*, Chichester: John Wiley & Sons.
Bleeke, J. and D. Ernst (1993). *Collaborating to Compete*, John Wiley & Sons.
Boisot, M. (1995). *Information Space*, London: Routledge.
Contractor, F. and P. Lorange (1988). *Cooperative Strategies in International Business*, Lexington Books.
D'Aveni, R. (1994). *Hypercompetition: Managing the Dynamics of Strategic Manoeuvring*, Free Press.
Dodgson, M. (1993). *Technological Collaboration in Industry*, London: Routledge.
Dodgson, M. and R. Rothwell (eds) (1994). *The Handbook of Industrial Innovation*, Edward Elgar.
Dosi, G. and D. J. Teece (1993). "Organizational competencies and the boundaries of the firm", CCC Working Paper, number 93-11, University of California at Berkeley.
Easton, G. and L. Araujo (1996). "Characterising organisational competences: Combining resource base and industrial networks approaches", in R. Sanchez, A. Heene and H. Thomas, editors, *Dynamics of Competence-Based Competition*, Oxford: Elsevier.
Evans, J. S. (1991). "Strategic flexibility for high technology manoeuvres: A conceptual framework", *Journal of Management Studies*, No. 28, January, pp. 69–89.
Forrest, J. (1992). "Management aspects of strategic partnering", *Journal of General Management*, 17(4) (Summer), pp. 25–40.
Garud, R. *et al.* (1993). "Changing competitive dynamics in network industries: An exploration of Sun Microsystems' open systems strategy", *Strategic Management Journal*, 14, pp. 351–369.
Hamel, G. (1991). "Competition for competence and inter-partner learning within international strategic alliances", *Strategic Management Journal*, 12, pp. 83–103.
Hamel, G. and A. Heene (1994). *Competence Based Competition*, Chichester: John Wiley & Sons.

Harrigan, K. (1986). *Managing for Joint Venture Success*, Lexington Books.

Lang, J. W. (1995). "Strategic alliances between large and small high-tech firms", Paper presented at IAMOT conference, Aston University, July.

Lang, J. W. (1996) "Structuration, alliances and knowledge transfer", (forthcoming paper) MIM 1996 Conference, Leicester University.

Littler, D. *et al.* (1995). "Success factors for collaborative product development: A study of suppliers of information and communication technology", *R&D Management*, **25**, pp. 33–44.

Lorange, P. and J. Roos (1993). *Implementing Strategic Processes*, Oxford: Blackwells.

Niederkofler, M. (1991). "The evolution of strategic alliances: Opportunities for managerial influence", *Journal of Business Venturing*, **6**(4), pp. 237–257.

Oakey *et al.* (1988). *The Management of Innovation in High Technology Small Firms*, Francis Pinter.

Pheysey, D. (1993). *Organisational Cultures*, London: Routledge.

Pucik *et al.* (1992). *Globalizing Management*, Chichester: John Wiley & Sons.

Sanchez, R. (1993). "Strategic flexibility, firm organisation, and managerial work in dynamic markets: A strategic options perspective", *Advances in Strategic Management*, **9**, pp. 251–291.

Sanchez, R. (1995). "Strategic flexibility in product competition", *Strategic Management Journal*, **16**, pp. 135–159.

Sanchez, Ron (1996). "Quick-connect technologies for product creation: Implications for competence-based competition," pp. 299–322 in R. Sanchez, A. Heene and H. Thomas, editors, *Dynamics of Competence-Based Competition*, Oxford: Elsevier.

Sanchez, R. and A. Heene (1996). "A systems view of the firm in competence-based competition", in *Dynamics of Competence-Based Competition*, R. Sanchez, A. Heene and H. Thomas, editors, Oxford: Elsevier.

Sanchez, R., A. Heene and H. Thomas (eds) (1996a). *Dynamics of Competence Based Competition: Theory and Practice in the New Strategic Management*, Oxford: Elsevier.

Sanchez, R., A. Heene and H. Thomas (1996b). "Towards the theory and practice of competence-based competition", in *Dynamics of Competence-Based Competition*, R. Sanchez, A. Heene and H. Thomas, editors, Oxford: Elsevier.

Sanchez, R. and H. Thomas (1996). "Strategic Goals", in *Dynamics of Competence-Based Competition: Theory and Practice in the New Strategic Management*, Oxford: Elsevier.

Sanchez, R. and J. Mahoney (1994). "The modularity principle in product and organizational design", University of Illinois Working Paper Series.

Saxby, R. (1994). "Interview with Robin Saxby, CEO of ARM Ltd.", Cambridge, England.

Teece, D. (1986). "Profiting from technological innovation: Implications for integration, collaboration, licensing and public policy", *Research Policy*, **15**, pp. 285–305.

Williamson, O. (1985). *The Economic Institutions of Capitalism . . . Firms, Markets Relational Contracting*, New York: Free Press.

Index

Logic integrated circuits 93, 94
Long-term surviving companies
 characteristics of 54–7
 stage one survey 55–6
 stage two survey 56–7
Longitudinal problem 55

Management, as part-time role 33
Management styles 52–3
 command and control 10, 39, 54,
  56–7
 evolutionary 56–7
 extraordinary 56–7
 ordinary 53
 revolutionary 56–7
Manufacturing engineering 92
Market value 110–11, 113
Memory devices 92–4
Memory integrated circuits 92, 95
Metal-on-silicon (MOS) 96
Metal-oxide semiconductors (MOS) 92
Modular components 221
Modular organization 191, 222–4
Modular product 183
Modularity 12, 189–209
 dimensions 198
 in organization design 203–6
 in product design 191, 197–203,
  219–22
 theoretical concepts 190–7

Negative feedback 10, 49–51, 53–4
Network knowledge 124
Networks 44
New assets 153
New capabilities 154–7
 creation of 149–50
New competences 153
New process know-how 85
Nike 184
NMB Semiconductor 97–8
Non-linear dynamic systems 49

Objectives 51
Off balance sheet items 41
Operational competences 218–19
Ordinary management 53
Organization design 183

 modularity in 203–6
Organization structures 36
Organizational biases 98
Organizational capabilities
 144–6
Organizational combination 142–3
Organizational competences 87
Organizational culture 57
Organizational forms 149–51
Organizational knowledge 5
 and learning, individual versus
  7–8
Organizational learning 52, 158
Organizational routines 154
Organizational structure and
 culture 218–19

Paradox of value 11, 18, 65–6, 70–4,
 80
Passive determinants of
 receptivity 130
Passive factors 129
Perceived value-in-use of
 knowledge 168
Personal knowledge 47, 49
Personal (or tacit) knowledge 25, 47,
 48, 49, 74, 123, 124, 165–70
Polyani's skater 8
Positional assets 41
Positional capability 48
Positional resource 42, 44
Positive feedback 49, 50–1, 53–4
Problem-solving 69, 76, 77
Process development 91
Process theory 176–7
Product design 89
 modularity in 191, 197–203, 219–22
Product development
 competence 89–92, 98
 competences in 98
 new 84, 87–92
 stages of 88–9
Production know-how 143
Project management 132–3
Project organization 31, 34
Project responsibilities 33
Projects
 connection between 133
 with clients 132–4
PROMs 94

existence inside, between and outside
of the organization   32
framework implications   24–5
in organizations   31
Unit of analysis   23

Value chains   40, 41, 70

Value component   73
Value creation   19–21, 36, 103–4, 109,
116, 117, 142–3
Value of knowledge, time dependency
of   168
Very large scale integrated circuits
(VLSI)   90
Vision   52